A DICTIONARY OF
LEGAL THEORY

A DICTIONARY OF
LEGAL
THEORY

BRIAN H. BIX

OXFORD
UNIVERSITY PRESS

OXFORD
UNIVERSITY PRESS

Great Clarendon Street, Oxford OX2 6DP

Oxford University Press is a department of the University of Oxford.
It furthers the University's objective of excellence in research, scholarship,
and education by publishing worldwide in

Oxford New York

Auckland Bangkok Buenos Aires Cape Town Chennai
Dar es Salaam Delhi Hong Kong Istanbul Karachi Kolkata
Kuala Lumpur Madrid Melbourne Mexico City Mumbai Nairobi
São Paulo Shanghai Singapore Taipei Tokyo Toronto

Oxford is a registered trade mark of Oxford University Press
in the UK and in certain other countries

Published in the United States
by Oxford University Press Inc., New York

British Library Cataloguing in Publication Data
Data available

Library of Congress Cataloging-in-Publication Data
Bix, Brian.
A dictionary of legal theory / Brian Bix.
p. cm.

ISBN-10: 0-19-924462-6 (alk. paper)
ISBN-13: 978-019-924462-1 (alk. paper)

1. Law—Philosophy—Dictionaries. I. Title.
K204.B59 2004
340'.1—dc22   2004012000

3 5 7 9 10 8 6 4

Typeset by Kolam Information Services Pvt. Ltd, Pondicherry, India.
Printed in Great Britain
on acid-free paper by
Biddles Ltd., King's Lynn

PREFACE

ONE inspiration for this work was the mundane experience of intellectual exchange among academic colleagues. Workshops where colleagues present their work to one another can too often have a 'Tower of Babel' feel, because academics working under one tradition do not comprehend the standard terminology of those who come from a different tradition. Those who work in the law and economics tradition rarely understand the terminology of those working within the tradition of analytical jurisprudence, and both sets of scholars may be largely ignorant of the ideas and phrases used by advocates of feminist legal theory or critical race theory. At a minimum, one hopes that this text might work as a translation manual, a Berlitz guide of words and phrases to help scholars understand and exchange ideas with those of other legal-academic cultures. If this book could offer something in the way of mutual understanding (which, one hopes, might be the first step towards mutual appreciation), it will have been more than worth the effort. The text also has more ambitious goals: to present some of the basic ideas from various jurisprudential traditions in a way that is accessible to students and scholars alike.

A few warnings: first, in a work such as this one, there are inevitable difficulties about what to include and what not to include; in determining coverage, I have followed a few principles:

1. There are no entries on authors living (at the time of writing), though living persons are discussed in the context of other entries (evaluations of contemporaries is always difficult, even without taking into account the problem of changing views; also, one is less likely to get angry messages from the deceased regarding their inclusion or exclusion).

2. The topic of legal theory is understood differently by different writers; I have tried to allow a broad scope, but there is always a danger of the project becoming completely unbounded, as legal theory edges into political theory, economics, moral philosophy, metaphysics, social theory, constitutional law, etc. I have allowed for a certain number of forays into these neighbouring categories, but inevitably some readers would have preferred a greater annexation of those other topics, while others might have preferred a more constrained list of topics.

3. When discussing theorists (*e.g.* Immanuel Kant) or topics (*e.g.* affirmative action) whose primary domain and importance is outside legal theory, narrowly understood, the discussion within this text will refer primarily to the relevance of that person or topic to legal theory.

Second, this work does not purport, on the main, to be original. Its main purpose is to present the conventional usage within a field in a way understandable to people outside that field. However, complete objectivity is probably undesirable, even if it were obtainable (which it probably is not). The text inevitably reflects my judgement, and frequently in a way that makes it clear that an editorial judgement is being offered. Another product of this text's purporting to represent the way terms and ideas are generally understood is that while all the entries are my own work, it is possible, perhaps even probable (if not inevitable), that the particular phrases or ways of characterizing ideas may echo those of other texts. Where a particular way of phrasing things is, to my knowledge, distinctive to a certain author, I have endeavoured to state as much in the text.

Third, references to legal practices will inevitably mostly be to those in the United States and England. However, many of the discussions reach a much broader scope, touching on the practices of other common law countries, and, occasionally, civil law countries as well. Similarly, much of the discussion of scholarship is grounded, inevitably, on work that was written in English or has been translated to English.

I am especially indebted to Matthew D. Adler, Sean Coyle, William A. Edmundson, Daniel A. Farber, John Louth, David McGowan, Steven D. Smith, Brian Z. Tamanaha, and two anonymous readers, who read through and commented upon entire drafts of this work; I am also grateful for the comments and suggestions of Martin Golding, Michael Steven Green, Oren Gross, Sarah Holtman, Vladimir Kuznetsov, Stephen R. Latham, Nancy Levit, Miranda O. McGowan, Lukas H. Meyer, Thomas H. Morawetz, and Girardeau A. Spann; and I wish to thank also Christopher Hurd, Galen Lemei, Jasleen Modi, and Erin Steitz for able research assistance.

B.H.B.

Minneapolis
November 2003

A

acceptance (of a rule) The idea of 'acceptance' of a rule plays a key role in H. L. A. Hart's (1907–92) theory of law (elaborated most fully in *The Concept of Law* (1961)). According to Hart, a social rule can be distinguished from a mere habit by the actor's 'accepting' the rule as a standard for behaviour—a basis for justifying the actor's own behaviour, and for criticizing deviations.

Within Hart's practice theory of rules, the existence of a rule was equated with that rule's being accepted by some as a standard for behaviour. This view of rules has been criticized on various grounds (e.g. because there are commonly accepted practices that are the basis of criticism but are not considered rules, and there are rules that are not, or not connected with, common practices).

The idea of 'acceptance' is key within Hart's system at another point. His criteria (in *The Concept of Law*) for the existence of a legal system were obedience to the law by the bulk of the population, combined with the 'effective acceptance . . . as common public standards of . . . behaviour' by the system's officials of the secondary rules (the rule of recognition, the rules of change, and the rules of adjudication). Acceptance of a legal rule, within Hart's system, was something more than mere outward compliance with the rule, but something less than belief that the rule creates a binding moral obligation.

Neil MacCormick (1941–) has argued that acceptance of a rule could be understood as involving either of two attitudes towards the rule: (1) a willing acceptance, involving a wish that others act in accordance with the standard; and (2) a more reluctant acceptance, conforming to the rule and wishing that it be applied generally, or at least consistently, but more because of the rule's current acceptance or enforcement by others, than because of any direct endorsement of the standard.

Some commentators have criticized Hart for not focusing more on the *reasons* for acceptance of a rule, arguing that important issues regarding the normative nature of law (or the proper way to construct a theory of the nature of law) turn on a more careful distinction between kinds of reasons for acceptance.

See gunman situation writ large; Hart, H. L. A.; internal point of view; legal positivism; rule of recognition; rules, practice theory of

adjudication, theories of Theories that purport to describe, interpret, or prescribe how judges decide cases. Some theories are aimed at or based upon a particular legal system, while others purport to make (analytical, conceptual, or prescriptive) claims valid for *all* legal systems.

Theories of adjudication, like all forms of theories regarding social action and social institutions, must consider the criteria for successful theorizing in these areas: are they merely trying to explain outward behaviour (e.g. who wins or loses cases), or should they also be trying to explain the perspective of the participants (a hermeneutic or *Verstehen* approach)? This question is important for theories of adjudication because many such theories argue that judges' actions are explained by political, social, or economic forces of which the judges do not appear to be fully aware.

A large portion of American legal theory centres on theories of adjudication: e.g. the American legal realists' attack on judicial formalism, Ronald Dworkin's interpretive theory of law (which some critics have characterized as more a theory of adjudication than a theory of the nature of law) and all the various theories offered to justify or reform constitutional review of legislation.

See American legal realism; constitutional theory; formalism; hermeneutics; interpretive theory of law; *Verstehen* approach

affirmative action A policy of favouring historically oppressed groups (e.g. women, members of ethnic and racial minority groups, or members of religious minority groups) in admission to schools, hiring and promotion in the private or public sector, the award of government contracts, etc. (the practice is also known as 'reverse discrimination' and 'positive discrimination'). Affirmative action is frequently considered in jurisprudential discussions, either in the context of justice theories (what is the correct response to historical injustice?) or in the context of critical theory (among both feminist legal theorists and critical race theorists there are varying and quite subtle reactions to the place and value of the practice).

Some have argued that in the United States affirmative action practised by government may seem either especially justified, as the government had been instrumental in prior discrimination, or especially problematic, because of constitutional restrictions on government actions based on racial grounds.

See critical race theory; desert; equality

agency costs A term from economic analysis, referring to complications to any discussion of profit maximization in even moderately intricate commercial ventures. As many ventures and transactions involve one person (the agent) acting on behalf of another person (the principal), and as the (short-term) interests of the parties involved could be said to diverge, practical questions frequently arise, e.g. on how principals can be sure that their agents are acting effectively on the principals' behalf, rather than on the agents' own behalf. Other complications arise not so much from a (potential) divergence of interests as from a (potential) asymmetry of information. The 'costs' of agency include those incurred by principals to monitor their agents, and those incurred by agents to give assurances to their principals that the agents are in fact faithfully and reliably serving the principals' interests. Attempts to evaluate, and reduce agency costs, can be seen in the analyses of a wide variety of areas (e.g. employment agreements, executive compensation policies, and franchise agreements). The set of issues is often considered under the label, 'principal–agent problem'.

See **principal–agent problem**

American legal realism The label for a category of legal commentators, primarily from the 1930s and 1940s, but with some significant contributions earlier and later. These commentators were 'realists' in the sense that they wanted citizens, lawyers, and judges to understand what was *really* going on behind the jargon and mystification of the law. The major figures of the movement included Jerome Frank (1889–1957), Karl Llewellyn (1893–1962), Robert L. Hale (1884–1969), Morris R. Cohen (1880–1947), Max Radin (1880–1950), W. Underhill Moore (1879–1949), and Felix S. Cohen (1907–53).

Oliver Wendell Holmes, Jr., (1841–1935) is sometimes included among the realists, though he lived and wrote at an earlier time, because Holmes's work was very influential among the realists, and most of the themes with which the realists are associated are first found in Holmes's work. Similarly, Roscoe Pound (1870–1964) is sometimes counted among the realists, even though Pound wrote work critical of American legal realism, for Pound's early work on 'sociological jurisprudence' influenced and presaged much of the realists' views.

There is a series of overlapping themes that connect the realists. Many raised challenges to the way that judges at the time actually decided cases: that these judges portrayed their work as the deduction from simple premises or basic legal concepts, when in fact the decisions were grounded in policy preferences or the judge's biases. Other realists argued at a more basic and abstract level that legal rules could never determine the outcome of particular cases (or at least not for the more difficult cases), that rules were at best short-hand statements of how judges have decided issues of this sort in the past, or shorthand predictions of how they are likely to decide such issues in the future.

Such beliefs in 'rule scepticism' or 'legal indeterminacy' in turn fed a preference for deciding cases on social science grounds, instead of on the judge's unstated biases. Many legal realists shared a faith that there was a sufficiently objective science of human behaviour, which would eventually lead to objective knowledge of how legal rules could be fashioned better to achieve the common good.

Another aspect of the realist or sceptical view of (many) legal realists was to tie rights to remedies: that is, to emphasize that one's view of a legal protection should be strongly connected to the legal remedies one could obtain for its violation. (This view was to lead some American Contract Law scholars to change the way they taught Contract Law, and the way they wrote textbooks in the area—starting the course with remedies, rather than consideration or offer/acceptance.)

A few among the realists (e.g. Robert Hale) offered analyses that could be taken as critical of the basic foundations of the economic and political system. For most of the realists, however, the criticism of legal, political, and economic life related more to change (though sometimes *substantial* change) *within* the established system. Thus, it was not surprising that many of the realists took up government posts serving President Franklin D. Roosevelt's 'New Deal' economic programmes.

The legacy of American legal realism has also been a point of contention. There are those who assert that the realists have fully prevailed, with their insights and critical views being incorporated into mainstream legal thinking (in some circles, it is a cliché to say, 'we are all realists now'). Some of the more critical modern commentators, such as various adherents of critical legal studies, argued that they were the true inheritors of the realist legacy, taking the critical insights of the realists seriously, while discounting other parts of the realist approach, such as the faith in a neutral and objective social science. A second view of the realists is to see them as the forebears of law and economics—in that they undermined the idea that law was sufficient unto itself, and argued for a 'policy science' to study the implications of alternative legal rules, a role that law and economics has taken up. (In undermining the idea of the autonomy and sufficiency of law, the realists were also in a sense the forerunners of all modern 'law and . . .' interdisciplinary approaches to law.) Yet a third view of the realists was to see them as a kind of intellectual dead end, useful only for their opposition to formalism, but otherwise putting forward no theoretical position or positive programme that has withstood critical scrutiny.

Additionally, the legal process school, which was briefly quite influential in the United States in the late 1950s and early 1960s, was a direct response to legal realism. Responding to the realist argument that legal rules alone cannot resolve many difficult legal disputes, and that judges were not necessarily experts on the kind of moral and policy arguments implicit in many disputes, the legal process movement pointed out that the legal profession could claim some expertise in questions of procedure—in deciding which person or institution decided disputes and according to what process (e.g. adjudication versus arbitration, and legislation versus agency rule-making). Also, legal process scholars argued that while there might not be unique right answers to all legal questions, judges who properly understood their role would be significantly constrained (e.g. by following what one legal process scholar called 'neutral principles').

See adjudication, theories of; autonomy of law; Cardozo, Benjamin N.; conceptualism; critical legal studies; Dewey, John; formalism; Frank, Jerome N.; functionalism; Hale, Robert L.; Holmes, Oliver Wendell, Jr.; Hutcheson, Joseph C., Jr.; indeterminacy; legal process; legal reasoning; Llewellyn, Karl N.; neutral principles; pragmatism; public–private distinction; rule scepticism; Scandinavian legal realism; sociological jurisprudence

analogical reasoning An integral part of legal reasoning, especially, though by no means exclusively, in common law reasoning. The basic structure of analogical reasoning is that if two items or situations are alike in some ways, they are (or should be treated) alike in other ways. In fact, the derivation is at best probabilistic (given some similarities, other similarities are likely, not certain). That analogical reasoning is clearly inferior to deductive reasoning, and arguably inferior also to inductive reasoning, has caused some to be sceptical about legal (or judicial) reasoning generally. However, as some commentators (e.g. Lloyd Weinreb (1936–   )) have pointed out, analogical reasoning plays a central role in day-to-day practical reasoning, and there is no reason to believe that it is any less effective or legitimate in legal (or judicial) reasoning.

Within analogical reasoning generally, and particularly within the analogical reasoning used in judicial decision-making, a key question is which similarities and differences are relevant to the issue at hand, and which are irrelevant. For most purposes, one would not distinguish a prior case because it occurred on a Wednesday rather than a Thursday, or because the defendant had brown hair instead of red hair; but other differences (e.g. the plaintiff's actions helped to increase the risk of accident in one case but not the other; the defendant was a government agency in one case but not the other) *might* be morally and legally significant. How one can distinguish relevant from irrelevant differences, and whether such judgements have an 'objective' basis, remain highly contested.

See common law; legal reasoning

analytical jurisprudence An approach to the philosophy of law which emphasizes the analysis of concepts (e.g. 'law', 'right', 'property'). This approach is connected to the more general 'analytical philosophy'. Analytical jurisprudence can be contrasted both with those forms of legal theory more focused on reforming or criticizing the law (e.g. feminist legal theory, American legal realism, and critical race theory), and with approaches that, while less normative, are strongly informed by particular areas of the social sciences or humanities (e.g. historical jurisprudence, sociological jurisprudence, and law and economics).

In particular, analytical (legal) philosophy is a search for the meanings of terms and concepts. Analytical philosophers tend to believe that conceptual analysis is a tenable approach to understanding parts of our world. Analytical claims are contrasted with claims that are primarily normative (what should be done) and claims that are primarily empirical (how things happen to be, as a contingent matter—they could have been otherwise). As W. V. O. Quine (1908–2000) argued ('Two Dogmas of Empiricism', *Philosophical Review*, 1951), it is highly contentious whether analytical claims and empirical claims can be sharply divided (and the dividing line between descriptive claims and evaluative claims is also sometimes challenged).

Analytical philosophy is commonly contrasted with 'continental philosophy' (though many now think the distinction overstated or unhelpful). In this contrast, analytical philosophy refers to philosophical approaches that emphasize logic, broadly understood, and explorations of the surface or hidden logic of terms and concepts, and is associated primarily with English-language theorists (e.g. Bertrand Russell (1872–1970) and G. E. Moore (1873–1958)). Continental philosophy is usually associated with the broad French and German systematic theories (e.g. G. W. F. Hegel (1770–1831) and Maurice Merleau-Ponty (1908–61)).

See conceptual analysis

analytical legal philosophy *See* analytical jurisprudence

animal rights The relatively abstract question of whether animals (or certain kinds of animals) are capable of having rights is often conflated with the moral question of how human beings ought to act towards animals, while in fact the two questions are relatively independent. As regards the conceptual question, those who believe that only entities with the power of autonomous choice can be said to have rights might deny that animals have rights, but could still maintain (e.g. under a utilitarian moral theory) that human beings should not inflict pain on such creatures without very good reasons. One could similarly argue, under a different conceptual and moral theory, that while animals *are* the type of entity that can have rights, they *in fact* do *not* have any rights, or that any rights they have are overridden in relevant circumstances by stronger rights held by human beings.

See interest theory (of rights); rights; utilitarianism; will theory (of rights)

anthropology of law The application of anthropology to law, whose importance is based in part on what such studies have purportedly shown about the nature and variety of legal (and near-legal) forms of organization, and in part on the reflections on the nature of law that anthropologists have brought to their work, prior to and independent of their subsequent findings in the field. Some of the better-known work, such as E. Adamson Hoebel's *The Law of Primitive Man* (1954), Bronislaw Malinowski, *Crime and Custom in Savage Society* (1926), and Max Gluckman, *Judicial Process Among the Barotse of Northern Rhodesia* (1967), showed the variety of ways in which different communities guided behaviour and settled disputes. (There was also a notable meeting of legal anthropology and American legal realism when Karl Llewellyn and E. Adamson Hoebel co-wrote *Cheyenne Way: Conflict and Case Law in Primitive Jurisprudence* (1941).) Legal anthropology has tended to focus on law as the source of social order. Anthropological studies of law have influenced sociological inquiries: defining 'law' in general ways to allow for more fruitful comparison and analysis. Additionally, anthropological studies have been useful both as support and refutation for various views within the 'historical jurisprudence' school regarding the connection between social development, legal institutions, and legal norms.

See historical jurisprudence; law and society; sociological jurisprudence

Aquinas, Thomas Arguably the most important philosopher and theologian of medieval times, Saint Thomas Aquinas (1224–74) wrote the first detailed and systematic discussion of natural law theory in his most important work, *Summa Theologiae* (unfinished at his death in 1274). Aquinas's work was important for trying to show Church doctrines to be consistent with the teachings of Aristotle, to show Faith as consistent with and supported by Reason (while retaining the idea that some aspects of the true faith will be knowable only through revelation).

Aquinas's writings on law (largely confined to *Summa Theologiae*, I–II, questions 90–7), while not considered central to his theological project, are none the less original and have had lasting significance in theoretical thinking about law, as much of the natural law tradition in jurisprudence can be seen as elaborations on this work.

Aquinas defines law as 'an ordinance of reason for the common good of a community, promulgated by the person or body responsible for looking after that community' (qu. 90, art. 4, corpus). According to Aquinas, human positive law in line with natural law was 'binding in conscience'—a not-quite-equivalent modern translation would be to say that such laws created a prima facie moral obligation. (Natural law in turn is grounded on 'eternal law'—divine providence.)

For Aquinas, the connection between natural law and human positive law (the positive law the lawmaker *should* enact) is sometimes a matter of direct derivation, and sometimes a matter of *determinatio*—a selection among equally legitimate alternatives within a general framework (qu. 95, art. 2).

Unjust laws (laws contrary to the Common Good, exceeding the lawgiver's authority, or imposing disproportionate burdens) do not 'bind in conscience' and may be disobeyed if this can be done 'without scandal or greater harm [*turbationem*—also sometimes translated as "disorder" or "demoralization"]' (qu. 96, art. 4, corpus). This is usually understood as meaning that the decision whether to obey an unjust law, like many moral decisions, may come down to the relative good and harm that might be caused by that action (for example, the public disobedience of an unjust law in an otherwise generally just legal system may work to undermine the legal system, thus causing more harm than good).

Aquinas writes elsewhere that 'every human positive law has the nature of law to the extent that it is derived from the Natural Law. If, however, in some point it conflicts with the law of nature it will no longer be law but rather a perversion of law' (qu. 95, art. 2, corpus).

This is probably as close as Aquinas comes to stating the phrase often associated with him and with natural law theory generally, that 'an unjust law is no law at all' (*lex iniusta non est lex*).

See **determinatio; lex iniusta non est lex; natural law theory**

Aristotle The Greek philosopher (384–322 BC) who, along with his teacher, Plato, is one of the foundational writers of Western philosophy. While his influence is pervasive (if often indirect) in *all* theory, the connection with legal theory is most evident in the following areas: (1) justice—where his analysis of corrective and distributive justice remains central, as well as his distinction between acting strictly according to the rules ('legal justice') and what 'true justice' might require by way of 'equity'; (2) natural law theory—where many of his ideas, translated through Augustine and then Aquinas, particularly about form and teleology, helped to shape the tradition; and (3) the use of rhetoric within law (in making persuasive legal arguments).

See **corrective justice; distributive justice; equity; justice; natural law theory**

Arrow's theorem Also known as 'Arrow's paradox' or the 'impossibility theory', it is a foundational principle of social choice theory, showing that there are often no rational means of aggregating individual preferences into an expression of social choice. More technically, it can be shown that given choice among three or more options, five apparently reasonable and intuitive conditions cannot all be met simultaneously in many situations: (1) minimum rationality (transitivity)—if society prefers outcome A to outcome B, and outcome B to outcome C, then society prefers A over C; (2) Pareto optimality—if at least one person prefers A over B, and everyone else either agrees or is indifferent, then society prefers A over B; (3) non-dictatorship—society's preferences are not simply to be equated with that of any one person; (4) independence of irrelevant alternatives—if option C is not being considered, then whether A is preferred to B should not depend on how either compares to C; and (5) unrestricted domain—there are no restrictions on how the available options can be ranked by individual voters.

While the proof is relatively complicated, examples are common. Consider three voters: Voter 1 prefers A to B, and B to C; Voter 2 prefers B to C, and C to A; and Voter 3 prefers C to A, and A to B. Among these three voters, a majority would prefer A over B, but there is *also* a majority for B over C, *and* C over A. Collectively, transitivity breaks down (that is, though the group collectively prefers A over B *and* B over C, it does *not* prefer A over C), and disparate results can occur depending on the order in which choices are put to the voters.

This theorem can be seen as a generalization or improvement on Condorcet's voting paradox, which had been published two hundred years earlier, though it was not much noticed at that time.

Arrow's theorem has reshaped aspects of political theory and economics, owing to its implications both for predicting what officials will do and for welfare economics—discussing what *should* be done, in terms of maximizing welfare, given people's preferences. The theorem raises questions as to whether one can usefully speak in terms of a social or collective version of, or aggregation of, individual utility curves or preference functions.

See **Condorcet's voting paradox; public choice theory; social choice theory**

Austin, J. L. John Langshaw Austin (1911–60), was an English philosopher of language, whose important works included *Sense and Sensibilia* (1962) and *How to Do Things with Words* (1962). J. L. Austin's work on 'ordinary language philosophy', advocating that distinctions of analytical importance can be found within the resources of ordinary linguistic usage, was influential in H. L. A. Hart's (1907–92) theory of law. Hart's theory of law in *A Concept of Law* (1961) was constructed around ordinary-language distinctions between acting out of habit and acting according to a rule, and between 'being obliged' and 'having an obligation'.

Austin was also known in philosophy of language for his distinction between 'constative' and 'performative' utterances, a 'speech act' theory which recognizes that sometimes language is *part of the performance*, and not merely a report of it. Attempts to build theories of law around this insight can be found in some of the Scandinavian legal realists, and in H. L. A. Hart's earliest writings, though Hart largely dropped this line of analysis by the time of his better-known works.

See **Hart, H. L. A.; Scandinavian legal realism**

Austin, John John Austin (1790–1859) was an English legal and political theorist from whose work modern legal positivism developed, though modern legal positivism has rejected many of his views. Austin was called to the Bar in 1818, but he took on few cases, and quit the practice of law in 1825. Austin shortly thereafter obtained an appointment to the first Chair of Jurisprudence at the recently established

University College London. He prepared for his lectures by study in Bonn, and evidence of the influence of continental legal and political ideas can be found scattered throughout Austin's writings. Lectures from the course he gave were eventually published as *The Province of Jurisprudence Determined* (1832) (a more complete set of Austin's lecture notes were published, posthumously, as a large two-volume set).

While Austin's work was influential in the decades after his death, its impact seemed to subside substantially by the beginning of the twentieth century. A significant portion of Austin's current reputation derives from H. L. A. Hart's (1907–92) use of Austin's theory as a foil for the explanation of Hart's own, more nuanced approach to legal theory.

Analytical Jurisprudence and Legal Positivism

Early in his career, Austin came under the influence of Jeremy Bentham (1748–1832), and Bentham's utilitarianism is evident in the work for which Austin is best known today. However, Austin's particular reading of utilitarianism (at one point equating divine will with utilitarian principles) has had little long-term influence, though it seems to have been the part of his work that received the most attention in his own day.

Austin's importance to legal theory lies elsewhere—his theorizing about law was novel at three different levels of generality. First, he was arguably the first writer to approach the theory of law analytically (as contrasted with approaches to law more grounded in history or sociology, or arguments about law that were secondary to more general moral and political theories). Second, within analytical jurisprudence, Austin was the first systematic exponent of 'legal positivism'—an approach to the study of law centred on the view that law 'as it is' must be separated from any argument about law 'as it ought to be'. Most of the important theoretical work on law prior to Austin had treated jurisprudence as though it were merely a branch of moral or political theory, asking how the state should govern (and what gave governments legitimacy), and under what circumstances citizens have an obligation to obey the law. Austin specifically, and legal positivism generally, offered a quite different approach to law: as an object of 'scientific' study, dominated neither by prescription nor by moral evaluation. Third, Austin's version of legal positivism, a 'command theory of law', was distinctive, though there were broad similarities with the views developed by Jeremy Bentham, whose theory could also be characterized as a 'command theory'. (Austin's work was more influential in this area than Bentham's, largely because Bentham's jurisprudential writings did not appear in a form even roughly systematic until long after Austin's work had already been published.)

Austin's Views

Austin's basic approach was to ascertain what can be said generally about all laws. Austin's analysis is often viewed as either a paradigm or a caricature of analytical philosophy, in that his discussions are dryly full of distinctions, but thin in argument. The texts lack much of the meta-theoretical, justificatory work; where Austin does articulate his methodology and objective, they are fairly traditional: he 'endeavoured to resolve a law (taken with the largest signification which can be given to that term properly) into the necessary and essential elements of which it is composed' (*The Province of Jurisprudence Determined*).

As to what is the core nature of law, Austin's answer is that laws ('properly so called') are commands of a sovereign. He clarifies the concept of positive law (i.e. man-made law) by analysing the constituent concepts of his definition, and by distinguishing law from other concepts that are similar: (1) 'Commands' involve an expressed wish that something be done, and 'an evil' to be imposed if that wish is not complied with. (2) Rules are general commands (applying generally to a class), as contrasted with specific or individual commands ('drink wine today' or 'John Smith must drink wine'). (3) Positive law consists of those commands laid down by a sovereign (or its agents), to be contrasted with those of other lawgivers, such as God's general commands, and the general commands of an employer. (4) The 'sovereign' is defined as a person (or collection of persons) who receives habitual obedience from the bulk of the population, but who does not habitually obey any other (earthly) person or institution (Austin's 'sovereign' is related to, but arguably more precise than the sovereign found in prior theorists, e.g. Thomas Hobbes (1588–1679)); Austin thought that all independent political societies, by their nature, have a sovereign. (5) Positive law should also be contrasted with 'laws by a close analogy' (which includes positive morality, laws of honour, international law, customary law, and constitutional law) and 'laws by remote analogy' (e.g. the laws of physics).

In the criteria set out above, Austin succeeded in delimiting law and legal rules from religion, morality, convention, and custom. However, also excluded from 'the province of jurisprudence' were customary law (except to the extent that the sovereign had, directly or indirectly, adopted such customs as law), public international law, and parts of constitutional law. (These exclusions alone would make Austin's theory problematic for most modern readers.) Within Austin's approach, whether something is or is not 'law' depends on which people have done what: the question turns on an empirical investigation, and it is a matter mostly of power, not of morality. Austin is not arguing that law should not be moral, nor is he implying that it rarely is; neither is Austin taking a nihilistic or sceptical position. He is merely pointing out that there is much that is law that is not moral, and what makes something law does nothing to guarantee its moral value.

In contrast to his mentor Bentham, Austin had no objection to judicial lawmaking, which Austin called 'highly beneficial and even absolutely necessary'. Nor did Austin find any difficulty incorporating judicial lawmaking into his command theory: he characterized that form of lawmaking, along with the occasional legal/judicial recognition of customs by judges, as the 'tacit commands' of the sovereign, the sovereign's affirming those 'orders' by its acquiescence.

Criticisms

As many readers come to Austin's theory mostly through its criticism by other writers (prominently, that of H. L. A. Hart), the weaknesses of the theory may be better known than the theory itself: (1) In many societies, it is hard to identify a 'sovereign' in Austin's sense of the word (a difficulty Austin himself experienced, when he was forced to describe the British 'sovereign' awkwardly as the combination of the King, the House of Lords, and all the electors of the House of Commons). Additionally, a focus on a 'sovereign' may make it difficult to explain the continuity of legal systems: a new ruler will not come in with the kind of 'habit of obedience' that Austin sets as a criterion for a system's rulemaker. However, one could argue that the sovereign is best understood as a constructive metaphor: that law should be viewed as if it reflected the view of a single will (a similar view, that law should be interpreted as if it derived from a single will, can be found in Ronald Dworkin's (1931–) work). (2) A 'command' model seems to fit some aspects of law poorly (e.g. rules which grant powers to officials and to private citizens—e.g. the rules for making wills, trusts, and contracts), while excluding other matters (e.g. international law) which most people are not inclined to exclude from the category 'law'. (3) More generally, it seems more distorting than enlightening to reduce all law to one type. For example, rules that empower people to make wills and contracts perhaps can be recharacterized as part of a long chain of reasoning for eventually imposing a sanction (Austin spoke in this context of the sanction of 'nullity') on those who fail to comply with the relevant provisions. However, such a recharacterization misses the basic purpose of those sorts of laws—they are arguably about granting power and autonomy, not punishing disobedience. (4) A theory that portrays law solely in terms of power fails to distinguish rules of terror from forms of governance sufficiently just that they are accepted as legitimate by their own citizens.

See Bentham, Jeremy; Blackstone, William; command theory of law; gunman situation writ large; Hart, H. L. A.; Hobbes, Thomas; international law; legal positivism; reductionist theories of law; utilitarianism; will theory (of rights)

authority The term has a variety of related meanings within legal and political theory. First, a person or institution in certain situations is said to 'have authority' over other people to compel compliance with commands or promulgated norms. Second, one 'is an authority' on a subject if one's expertise makes one a reliable source of information on that subject. Third, a person may derivatively have the authority to do something if the moral or legal system grants that person permission or the power to do it. The first and second sense of authority are often distinguished under the terms of 'practical' (power) versus 'theoretical' (expertise) authorities—reasons for action as against reasons for belief. The third sense of authority is usually dealt with under the rubric of rights (as in 'X has the right/authority to do A').

Theorists often distinguish de facto from de jure authority, where the former speaks to actual power or influence, and the latter to a legal or moral justification for such power or influence.

Robert Paul Wolff raised a famous paradox in his *In Defense of Anarchy* (1970) regarding how practical authority could ever be legitimate: authority involves deference to another, and how can it be morally right, or consistent with autonomy, to obey someone else, *regardless* of whether one believes that other person to be right or wrong? To do something just because one has been told (commanded) to do so could be seen as an abandonment of one's right and obligation to decide for oneself, considering all relevant reasons, what is to be done. A variety of responses have been offered to Wolff's challenge. One, based on Joseph Raz's (1939–) work (e.g. *The Morality of Freedom* (1986)), is that there are occasions when we know that we are more likely to do the right thing (we are 'likely better to comply with reasons which apply' to us) by following someone else's directive rather than deciding for ourselves. This may be because we know the other person to be an expert on the subject, because we know that our judgement is temporarily less than optimal (e.g. because we are biased, fatigued, or intoxicated), or because the other person is a salient source of co-ordination on some matter on which co-ordination is necessary to achieve an important social good.

Various sorts of jurisprudential theories have turned on the purported role of authority within law. For example: (1) theorists argue about the role of authority in how courts should interpret statutes (e.g. as 'faithful agents' trying to determine the intention(s) of the legislature, for it is the legislature's authoritative choices, even when not entirely clear, that should, under this argument, be given priority); and (2) Joseph Raz's authority-based argument for 'exclusive legal positivism'. Raz's argument, in brief, is that law, by its nature, purports to be a legitimate practical authority for its citizens. However, to be an authority, Raz argues, legal rules must be able to guide without evaluation in terms of the underlying reasons for and against an action. Thus, Raz concludes, the validity and content of law must be ascertainable without resort to moral evaluation (the basic position of exclusive legal positivism).

See **interpretation; legal positivism; rights**

autonomy Self-government, or *the capacity* to govern oneself. The concept of autonomy is central to many moral and political theories, though the nature and possibility of autonomy remain highly contested. For example, for some Kantian theorists, autonomy is evidenced only by actions grounded on reason; actions motivated by desire are not considered autonomous. Some communitarian and feminist theorists criticize the possibility or desirability of autonomy, on the basis that our actions never completely derive from our own will, but are inevitably conditioned by our position in society.

Within legal theory, discussions of autonomy often arise within the context of debates about the legislative enforcement of morality, with those who believe that autonomy is a central value urging a strong presumption against state action that constrains the range of life choices available to citizens.

See **consent; morality, legal enforcement of**

autonomy of law The 'autonomy of law' refers to a number of related but distinct claims: (1) that legal reasoning is different from other forms of reasoning; (2) that legal decision-making is different from other forms of decision-making; (3) that legal reasoning and decision-making are sufficient to themselves, that they neither need help from other approaches, nor would they be significantly improved by such help; and (4) that legal scholarship should be about distinctively legal topics (often referred to as 'legal doctrine') and is not or should not be about other topics.

A claim about the autonomy of law could be understood in three different ways: descriptively, analytically, and prescriptively. Descriptively, the question is what level of autonomy is assumed or encouraged by current practices within a particular legal system. The form of judicial reasoning and the approach to legal education within a community may be more or less autonomous. The general trend in both England and the United States, and in both legal reasoning and legal education, has been *away from* legal autonomy, towards a more interdisciplinary approach. Analytically, the question is whether law, by its nature, either *necessarily is* or *necessarily is not* autonomous. For an analytical claim, one would investigate the ways in which legal reasoning is purportedly autonomous, and see whether such claims stand up to close scrutiny. Prescriptively, one can argue that current practices should (or should not) be changed to incorporate greater or lesser dependence on other disciplines, either in judicial decision-making or in legal education. (A desire for greater use of other disciplines can, but need not, be connected with an argument about the non-autonomy of legal reasoning and the (limited) value of traditional doctrinal legal scholarship. One could argue that legal doctrinal analysis *requires* no supplement, but would none the less be improved by ideas from other disciplines.)

Obviously, there are connections between the analytical claim regarding autonomy and the descriptive and prescriptive claims. If one believes that legal reasoning either *must be* or *cannot be* autonomous, then this obviously constrains what one can sensibly prescribe for the practice, and must also affect the description of the practice (e.g. it may be, as some of the American legal realists argued, that judges portray their decisions as autonomous when, according to the realists' analytical view, that cannot be the case, and thus the judges must be attempting to deceive others, or at least are unintentionally deceiving themselves).

While it could be argued that the legal profession seems to depend on a language and a way of thinking entirely foreign to common sense and common language, this is only the appearance of one extreme of the practice. At the other extreme, those who claim that legal reasoning is in no way distinctive do not necessarily claim that there is no need for legal experts, and no such thing as legal expertise. For even if there is no special way of reasoning legally, decisions about what the law requires would need a knowledge of the sources of law, a set of rules and principles that (in most societies) are extensive and separate from the rules and principles of other normative systems (e.g. conventional morality or religion).

If there is an argument to be made for an approach to decision-making that is distinctively legal (both separate from non-legal forms of decision-making, and common from one legal system to the next), it would probably be one that emphasized certain aspects of (most) legal systems: institutional decision-making, a hierarchy of decision-makers, and an effort to systematize the rules. And because law is intended as a practical guide for action, there is a pressure in the interpretation and application of legal norms towards consistency, coherence, stability, predictability, and finality. Those pressures are sometimes at tension with the desire that the outcomes be fair and just (with 'justice' here referring to those aspects of justice that go beyond 'following the rules laid down'—going beyond meeting reasonable expectations and reasonable reliance). These tend to combine into rules of precedent, statutory interpretation, and constitutional interpretation. Though such rules tend to vary from one legal system to another, rough convergences can be found, and the form of reasoning can be contrasted with other social practices and social institutions that do not operate under similar constraints and pressures.

A similar conclusion might be reached from a different approach: what is distinctive about legal reasoning and decision-making is that it is primarily, though not exclusively, guidance by way of rules. The peculiar normative status of rules (and promises and agreements) is that when there is a reason to be governed by and through rules, one has a reason to do as the rule states independent of the content of the rule (though this is only a presumptive conclusion, which can be overcome when contrary reasons of a sufficient weight are present—thus, one can have reasons to disobey an unjust rule, just as one can have reasons to disregard a promise to do an evil act). In such situations as common-law judging, where the rule-applier also has the power to modify the rule, the tensions between following the rule earlier laid down, even when not optimal, and promulgating the optimal rule, together lead to a distinctive structure and style of analysis and argumentation (though other rule-governed institutions may have similar forms of argument and decision).

See American legal realism; autopoiesis; formalism

autopoiesis An approach to law developed by Niklas Luhmann (1927–98) and Gunther Teubner (1944–   ) and others, under which social systems, including law, are seen as (relatively) autonomous. Autopoiesis is the idea that many systems (both biological and social) have significant feedback or recursive mechanisms that allow the self-regulation of the system. 'Autopoietic law' starts from the notion that legal systems often are significantly self-regulating, self-reinforcing, and self-sustaining. Law is created, transformed, and justified according to its own rules; and autopoietic law discusses what follows from this fact. It is important to note that, at least in Luhmann's version of autopoiesis, 'law' and 'legal system' refers primarily to the 'discourse' of law, not to some set of institutions. In particular, Luhmann focuses on the creation of meaning—in the case of law, the way that things are defined as either 'lawful' or 'unlawful'. The claim is not that law is 'autonomous' in the sense of being unaffected by external forces (e.g. political movements and cultural changes); autopoietic law accepts that such forces affect law, but the effects are transformed into legal terms (distinguishing what is 'lawful' and 'unlawful') by the normal legal processes. Under this approach, there is a sense, not always fully delineated, in which law 'acts', 'thinks', or develops 'on its own'.

See **autonomy of law; Luhmann, Niklas**

B

bad man The term usually refers to a brief statement in Oliver Wendell Holmes, Jr.'s (1841–1935) 1897 lecture, 'The Path of the Law', published in the *Harvard Law Review* the same year. Holmes offers, in contrast to a moralistic view of the law or one viewing it as a matter of logical deduction, 'the view of our friend the bad man', who 'does not care two straws for the axioms or deductions', but who 'does want to know what the . . . courts are likely to do in fact.' Holmes adds: 'I am much of his mind. The prophecies of what the courts will do in fact, and nothing more pretentious, are what I mean by law.'

The 'bad man view of law' has become a shorthand for a predictive theory of law, one equating 'what the law is' with predictions of how courts will decide cases. As an analytical theory of law, such an approach has obvious weaknesses: e.g. that it understates the role that the law plays in giving reasons for action, including giving reasons for judges' decisions. Judges (at least those who are not subject to review by a higher court) can hardly be said to be deciding cases based on predictions of what the courts (that is, they themselves) will do.

However, it is probably better to understand Holmes as putting forward not a theory about the nature of law, but rather general advice about the attitude that both practitioners and theorists should bring to the law: where a focus on the end-results, the consequences of legal action, might immunize us from some of the distorting ways law is portrayed (and portrays itself).

See **Holmes, Oliver Wendell, Jr.; predictive theory**

base and superstructure A concept from Marxist theory: that the economic structure of society is foundational, and what determines all other aspects of that community. Thus, Marxist theory treats politics, morality, culture, and religion, the conventional focus of social theorists and historians, as mere 'superstructure' reflecting the underlying economic relations and forms of production. Marxist legal theories have often treated law as if it were nothing more than a reflection of the underlying economic base (a few Marxist theorists treat law, or aspects of the law, as already part of the economic base). Some modern neo-Marxist theorists have, following the work of Antonio Gramsci (1891–1937), argued that law is relatively autonomous from the community's economic base, but serves the interests of the powerful *indirectly*, by legitimating unjust institutions, by giving the government's actions and the social structures the appearance of neutrality.

See **Gramsci, Antonio; Marx, Karl; Marxist theories of law**

baseline problem A shorthand term for the difficulty of figuring out the standard against which a state of affairs is to be analysed. Baselines are obviously relevant for making judgements about what is normal or unusual (and central to Aristotle's notion of corrective justice was the returning of two parties to a baseline status quo from which some event or transaction had dislodged them, giving a benefit to one and an injury to the other). The general context can also affect judgements such as whether government is being neutral in its actions and whether its treatment of disparate persons or groups is equal, or whether a choice was voluntary or consensual, and whether an expectation or judgement was reasonable.

A somewhat different example of a baseline problem is exemplified by damages questions within contract law. In determining the extent to which the innocent party has been harmed by an unjustified failure to perform, should the court look at where the innocent party would have been had the contract been fully performed, or where the innocent party would have been had the contract never been entered into in the first place?

See **corrective justice; equality**

basic goods In John Finnis's (1940–) natural law theory, 'basic goods' refer to those things desired for their own sake and not as the means to some other objective. In *Natural Law and Natural Rights* (1980), Finnis listed seven: life, knowledge, play, aesthetic experience, sociability (friendship), practical reasonableness, and 'religion'. Within Finnis's analysis, no basic good is more fundamental or more important than another.

Basic goods play a foundational role in Finnis's system of moral thought. Seeking basic goods as one's ultimate objective shows one's actions to be intelligible, but not necessarily moral. Within Finnis's analysis, much of the work of distinguishing moral from immoral choices comes at a higher level, with 'intermediate principles', which determine the permitted ways of choosing and mixing basic goods.

See **natural law theory**

Basic Norm Also known by the original German term, *Grundnorm*, the Basic Norm is a central element of Hans Kelsen's (1881–1973) analysis of law.

Legal rules are norms, in the sense that they are statements of what citizens ought and ought not to do. Following the division of 'is' and 'ought' (usually attributed as original to David Hume (1711–76)), the specific normative statement of a legal rule can be grounded only by a more basic or general norm (e.g. 'whatever Parliament passes is valid law'). If one assumes that norms are justified by some more general or basic norm, then this chain of normative validity must stop somewhere. There must be a norm whose validity is assumed in some sense rather than derived from another norm. Kelsen analysed the legal system as a system of norms, and he called the foundational norm of the system the 'Basic Norm'. Since tracing back the validity of a current legal norm can go first to a constitutional document, and from there to prior constitutions that justified the later one, Kelsen sometimes equated the Basic Norm with the norm '[act according to the] historically first constitution' of the system.

The ultimate significance of the Basic Norm is that legal systems, like all normative systems (including morality and religion) are grounded on some foundational normative claim that, by definition, can have no further proof or foundation.

Many commentators have discussed the parallels between Kelsen's Basic Norm and H. L. A. Hart's (1907–92) 'rule of recognition', with both serving as foundational norms in legal systems. However, the similarities can be overstated; the two concepts operate within quite different theoretical structures. Kelsen's Basic Norm is held (under a neo-Kantian analysis) to be presupposed by citizens when they view the law as normative (as creating binding obligations); by contrast, Hart's rule of recognition is derived from the actions of officials in the interpretation and application of the system's laws.

See **Hume, David; Kelsen, Hans; neo-Kantian analysis; pure theory of law; rule of recognition**

Beccaria, Cesare Bonesana A Milanese theorist (1738–94) whose works ranged from monetary policy to epistemology, his most important work was *On Crimes and Punishments* (1764), which argued for a more enlightened and more rational approach to punishment. Beccaria applies an approach later labelled 'utilitarianism' (and Beccaria's phrase, 'the greatest happiness shared amongst the greatest number' would seem to be the inspiration for Jeremy Bentham's (1748–1832) better-known summary of utilitarianism, 'the greatest good of the greatest number'). Like many more recent theorists, Beccaria combined retributive and consequentialist elements in his prescriptions: that only the guilty should be punished, that punishments should be proportionate to the harm caused, and that excessive or cruel punishments (including torture) should not be used.

See **Bentham, Jeremy; punishment; utilitarianism**

behavioural law and economics   A relatively recent variation on, or challenge to, law and economics. Behavioural law and economics argues that the view or assumption of rationality on which neo-classical economic thinking (and traditional law-and-economics thinking) depends, is empirically false. The 'rational person' model assumed that individuals are self-interested, have stable and well-ordered preferences, and act in a way that offers the greatest net benefit given their preferences. A similar challenge appears within mainstream economic thought, under the rubrics of 'behavioural economics', 'transaction cost economics', and 'new institutional economics'. An influential theorist in this approach was Herbert A. Simon (1916–2001), who won the 1978 Nobel Memorial Prize in Economics, in part for this work.

The behavioural (legal) economists point to tests that seem to show that individuals frequently act altruistically, their preferences can be intransitive (preferring A to B, and B to C, but C to A), they systematically over- and underestimate the odds of various occurrences, and they can place a greater value on objects once they own them than they would if they did not own them (the 'endowment effect').

Classical economists have offered various responses to behavioural economists: e.g. that the alleged defects of the 'rational man' model have been overstated; that some of the insights of behavioural economics can be incorporated into classical economic models; and that markets can be rational even when individuals are not.

See **bounded rationality; law and economics; rational choice theory**

benefit theory (of rights)   *See* **interest theory (of rights)**

Bentham, Jeremy   An English legal and political commentator (1748–1832) whose work has influenced legal philosophy in many different ways. Though perhaps today best known as one of the founding theorists of utilitarianism, his wide-ranging writings were influential on topics as diverse as usury laws, prison reform, and legal codification.

His utilitarianism was summarized in *A Fragment on Government* (1776): 'it is the greatest happiness of the greatest number that is the measure of right and wrong'. (This phrasing has become well known, though this is actually an imprecise, and somewhat misleading summary of the theory.) Bentham's approach intended to reduce moral and political analysis to uncontroversial grounds: that we all seek pleasure and avoid pain (and with positive feelings, more is considered better than less, and with negative feelings, the opposite). Bentham added: 'each to count for one, nobody for more than one' (attributed to Bentham by John Stuart Mill (1806–73) in Mill's *Utilitarianism* (1861)), an idea seemingly obvious now, but perhaps seen as radically egalitarian in Bentham's time. For Bentham, and many of his followers, we are to guide our lives according to what will maximize social utility, and lawmakers should be similarly guided in creating and modifying the rules of a community. Bentham used utilitarianism primarily as a basic tool for legislative reform (laws should be enacted or reformed to maximize the greatest good for the greatest number) but also as a descriptive or analytical tool for explaining the behaviour of others (and predicting the probable effect of using rewards and punishments in governmental actions).

Along with its part in developing utilitarianism, Bentham's work plays a role in many other aspects of legal theory: (1) Bentham, along with John Austin (1790–1859), helped to develop modern legal positivism (Bentham distinguished 'expository' and 'censorial' jurisprudence), though there are significant differences between the theories of Austin and Bentham and such later significant legal positivists as H. L. A. Hart (1907–92) and Hans Kelsen (1881–1973). (2) More specifically, Bentham, along with Austin, developed 'command theories of law' (analysing laws as essentially expressions of the will of the lawmaker— 'commands of the sovereign'). (3) Based on his utilitarian views, he argued for an approach to punishment different from the retributive model dominant in his day. (4) Bentham was a sharp critic of Sir William Blackstone (1723–80), in particular Blackstone's celebration, in *Commentaries on the Laws of England* (1765–9), of common-law reasoning; Bentham was a critic of judicial legislation, and a strong supporter of codification—a term he apparently coined; Bentham compared judge-made common law to the way people train dogs—punishing, without warning, only after the action is done. (5) Bentham was an early supporter of an interest theory of rights (equating legal rights with being the intended beneficiary of another person's legal duty), which remains, along with the will theory, one of the most common conceptual approaches to rights. (6) Bentham was a critic of the idea of 'natural rights' (what today might be called 'human rights'), calling the idea of moral rights (rights not grounded in a legal rule) 'nonsense' and the concept of natural rights 'nonsense on stilts'. (7) Bentham, in conversation and in some of his writings, took a position that anticipates certain forms of pragmatism, focusing inquiries away from theory and towards the question of 'does it work?'

While some commentators consider Bentham to be an abler and subtler thinker than Austin, Austin was more influential in the development of legal positivism and of analytical jurisprudence in general. This was primarily because the Bentham text most focused on legal theory, *Of Laws in General*, though completed in 1782, was not published until well into the twentieth century.

See **Austin, John; Blackstone, William; command theory of law; common law; interest theory (of rights); Mill, John Stuart; utilitarianism**

Berlin, Isaiah   Sir Isaiah Berlin (1909–97) wrote widely in the areas of political theory, moral philosophy, and the history of ideas. His importance within philosophy of law comes primarily from his work, *Two Concepts of Liberty* (1959), which emphasized the differences between positive and negative liberty. Negative liberty is 'freedom from', freedom from interference by others, in particular freedom from legal restraints. Positive liberty is 'freedom to', the extent to which one can choose for oneself, the opportunities one has, including those given to one by law or society. This distinction remains highly influential, despite criticism by some (e.g. Gerald C. MacCullum, Jr.) that it is either untenable or unhelpful.

See **liberty**

Betti, Emilio   Italian legal philosopher (1890–1968) who was a significant figure in debates about hermeneutics and interpretation. He is often associated with an intentionalist or originalist approach to interpretation, and he was an important early figure in the effort to apply hermeneutic theory to law. Betti argued that 'cognitive meaning' of a (legal) text should be distinguished from its 'normative meaning'—how it guides behaviour or resolves disputes; he similarly argued that a legal historian's interest in or understanding of a text will differ from a judge's. Betti's approach to hermeneutics sharply differed from that of Hans-Georg Gadamer (1900–2002) (who rejected a view of a text as largely autonomous, and any distinction between intentional meaning and cultural significance), and each offered criticisms of the other's approach.

See Gadamer, Hans-Georg; hermeneutics

bilateral monopoly A term from economics to describe dealings where there is only one available buyer of a good or service *and* there is only one available seller. Examples or approximations arguably occur whenever parties are in an ongoing economic or non-economic relationship, the common example being negotiations between a company and its union, but with many commentators also mentioning 'negotiations' within a marriage.

Negotiations within bilateral monopolies have distinctive forms and strategies, which have been discussed at length within the game theory literature.

See game theory

Blackstone, William An influential figure in English legal history, Sir William Blackstone (1723–80) was, among other things, a Fellow of All Souls College, Oxford, Vinerian Professor of English Law at Oxford, a Member of Parliament, Solicitor-General to the Queen, and a judge both at King's Bench and at Common Pleas. His *Commentaries on the Laws of England* (1765–9), based on lectures Blackstone had given at Oxford, was an important summary and rationalization of English law, displaying the historical basis of many doctrines and presenting the common law in a systematic fashion. Blackstone's influence extended far beyond England. For example, in the early years of the United States, American legal education frequently centred on a detailed reading of the *Commentaries* and critical discussions of that work.

The *Commentaries* was almost as important for the criticisms it evoked: from Jeremy Bentham (1748–1832) (e.g. in *A Fragment on Government* (1776)), who argued that the text was too accepting of the laws in force, and too supportive of judicial legislation; and from John Austin (1790–1859) (e.g. in *The Province of Jurisprudence Determined* (1832)), who attacked the *Commentaries'* natural-law views (with Blackstone writing, 'no human laws are of any validity, if contrary to [the natural law]'). Austin's attack, though perhaps not entirely fair (there are more charitable ways of interpreting Blackstone's text than the one chosen by Austin), became a key point in Austin's explication of his legal positivist approach to law.

See Austin, John; Bentham, Jeremy; common law

Bodin, Jean Jean Bodin (1530–96) was a French scholar who wrote extensively on a wide variety of subjects, including free trade, philosophy of history, comparative religion, and the influence of climate on society. Bodin is considered by some the first French political scientist—the first to treat public law and policy in a scientific way (e.g. in what is arguably his best work, *The Six Books of a Commonwealth* (1576)). Within English-language political and legal theory, he may be best known for his writings on sovereignty. Like Thomas Hobbes (1588–1679) (whom Bodin influenced), Bodin's writings were shaped by his experience of civil war, and like Hobbes, Bodin favoured a strong—indeed near-absolute—monarch. Bodin argued that the concentration of power in a single figure or group was not only the best path to peace, but was required to have a coherent legal and political system. Bodin's sovereign was to be kept in check by the political institutions around the sovereign. Bodin also asserted that the sovereign was subject to natural law, which could significantly constrain what policies he or she could implement, though this natural-law duty was enforceable only by God.

See **Hobbes, Thomas; sovereign**

bounded rationality A term used in the internal and external criticisms of economic analysis, referring to the varying kinds of cognitive limitations in the way that many or most people make decisions, evaluate options, and deal with uncertainty, relative to the 'rational utility maximizer' posited by neoclassical economics. The term has a narrow meaning, associated with the work of economist Herbert A. Simon (1916–2001), who won the Nobel Memorial Prize in Economic Science in 1978, in part for his work in this area. This narrow meaning refers to the limits on most people's abilities to analyse data and remember facts, and the (reasonable) methods we use to respond to these limitations. In this sense of the term, we have 'bounded rationality' in that we do not truly maximize the satisfaction of our preferences, but rather act on limited information, after truncated reflection, and in ways that may not be entirely consistent with earlier decisions.

Sometimes the term 'bounded rationality' is used more broadly, and this broader usage is often associated with the cognitive psychology work of Daniel Kahneman (1934–) and Amos Tversky (1937–96). Under the broader usage, the term refers to all the ways in which actual human thinking and behaviour differs from what would be predicted by the 'rational actor' model of economics, with special emphasis on the habits and tendencies of thought that lead us systematically to overestimate or underestimate certain kinds of risks. Kahneman received the Nobel Memorial Prize in Economic Science in 2002 (along with Vernon L. Smith) for the work he did, alone and with Tversky and others, to document bounded rationality (broadly understood) through experiments.

See **behavioural law and economics; rational choice theory; rationality; satisficing; voluntariness**

C

Cardozo, Benjamin N. Benjamin Nathan Cardozo (1870–1938), influenced American law both through his thoughtful and well-crafted opinions while a judge and by his writings about the judicial process. While Cardozo served both on the highest court of New York State, the New York Court of Appeals, and on the United States Supreme Court, most of his well-known opinions, paradoxically, are from the New York court.

Cardozo's most important book is arguably *The Nature of the Judicial Process* (1921), in which he presents the judicial role as a creative part of a process for making law serve social needs. While such views may seem commonplace now, they went against the formalist views prominent at the time, but were consistent with many of the ideas being put forward by the American legal realists. Ironically, many of Cardozo's opinions, including some of his better-known decisions, read more like the work of a formalist than that of a legal realist, though this may only reflect Cardozo's beliefs about how decisions should be presented.

See **American legal realism; formalism**

causation While causation raises a series of interesting questions in mainstream philosophy (e.g. David Hume's (1711–76) challenge to the conventional understanding of causal necessity), its discussion in legal philosophy usually concerns the way in which the concept of causation is reshaped by and within legal doctrine to reflect ideas and intuitions of moral responsibility and policy concerns.

In law, as in moral philosophy, discussion of 'causation' is closely connected with the attribution of responsibility or blame for an incident or condition, though within a broader or more empirical sense of 'causation', the incident or condition was the product of a large, perhaps infinite number of actions and circumstances.

The most obvious example of the way the idea of causation has been modified by its use within a legal context is the distinction between 'causation in fact' (also known as 'but-for causation': the assertion that without the action in question, the harm would not have occurred) and 'proximate cause' (also known as the test of 'remoteness', necessary for legal liability) in Anglo-American tort law. The difficulty with causation in fact for the determination of civil or criminal legal liability is that in many cases it will point to too many causes for a single event. In a handful of cases it may lead to a paradoxical result of 'no liability' (e.g. where two causes—say, two fires—combine, and cause damage by their combination that each would have been insufficient to cause alone). The problem of liability for too many causes or causes that are too remote was supposed to be solved by the concept of 'proximate cause', though theorists differ in their efforts to articulate that idea. Some commentators see the decision of what is or is not proximate cause as simply a (thinly disguised) policy decision, while other commentators explain the doctrine in terms of foreseeability of the harm.

There are other legal limitations on liability connected directly or indirectly with causation: e.g. the way many legal systems are more likely to call an action 'the cause of a harm' than to characterize an omission in the same way. Many of the complications of legal causation were considered in H. L. A. Hart and A. M. Honoré's *Causation in the Law* (1st edn., 1958; 2nd edn., 1985).

A central theory of the law and economics movement, the Coase theorem, turns on what Coase calls 'the reciprocity of causation' in accidents. While tort law assumes that in many accidents or nuisances, one party will clearly be the culpable party (e.g. 'the train *caused* the fire on the nearby farmland', or 'pollution from the factory *caused* the discoloration of clothing at the neighbouring laundry'), Coase asserted that the accidents or nuisances were more properly understood as costs deriving from the intersection of activities: causation is 'reciprocal' in the sense that (e.g.) the fire would not have occurred without the trains, but it also would not have occurred without the farmer having planted so close to the tracks. Once both parties are seen to have jointly caused the harm, Coase could shift the focus to what combination of activities (and what combination of entitlements) will lead to the greatest social wealth. On a roughly similar basis, some economically minded legal commentators have suggested that legal rights and liability be distributed on the principle of which distribution would have the best long-term consequences (e.g. by encouraging optimal levels of prevention) rather than by any abstract sense of 'fault' or 'responsibility'.

See **Coase theorem; necessary and sufficient conditions; tort law**

central cases An approach to a persistent problem in social theory: how to construct a descriptive theory about a practice or institution which varies substantially in its different instantiations. Rather than discussing what all instantiations have in common (their lowest common denominator), a central cases approach chooses characteristics that may appear fully only in the most developed, mature, or sophisticated instantiations of the category. Thus, a business friendship is a peripheral example of 'friendship' and not the best focus for studying friendship. Similarly, John Finnis (1940–   ) argues for a 'central case' analysis of law (in *Natural Law and Natural Rights* (1980))—preferring a focus on a more sophisticated legal system over a simpler customary order, and on a legal system that is sufficiently just for its legal obligations to be presumptive moral obligations, rather than on evil legal systems where that would not be the case. Finnis traces the idea of central cases through the work of Alfred Schutz (1899–1959), Max Weber's (1864–1920) concept of the 'ideal type' and Aristotle's idea of 'focal meaning'.

See Weber, Max

chain novel A metaphor used by Ronald Dworkin (1931–   ), primarily in his later works (e.g. *A Matter of Principle* (1985)), using a quasi-literary image to explain the way that judges can be both constrained and free in their decision-making. In this image, judges are like a chain of novelists, all working, in turn, on the same novel. What has already been written in the novel (or decided in the prior cases) constrains what the later writers can say (or judges can decide), while still leaving a significant amount of freedom. The analogy is arguably the strongest with judges deciding common law cases, but it is meant to apply more generally.

See common law

choice theory (of rights) *See* will theory (of rights)

Cicero The significance of the Roman orator Marcus Tullius Cicero (106–43 BC) for jurisprudence is that in his works *The Republic* and *The Laws* he gave some of the first detailed discussions of the position later known as natural law theory. He wrote: 'True law is right reason in agreement with nature; it is of universal application, unchanging and everlasting' (*The Republic*). It is likely that these views were not original with Cicero, but adapted by him from the Greek Stoics.

See natural law theory

civic republicanism   Sometimes just known as 'republicanism' (but not connected with the American 'Republican' political party), this approach to social life and political theory values civic virtue, i.e. citizens' participation in the public and political life of the community. Under this approach, it is also a duty of the government to encourage civic virtue among its citizens. The relevance of such ideas to law and legal theory tends to be indirect: a few commentators have ascribed civic republican ideas to the Framers of the US Constitution, and have suggested that therefore the document should be interpreted in a way that reflects those values; other commentators have suggested that legislation and judicial decision-making should reflect these values, regardless of their place in the history of particular countries.

Much of the discussion of civic republicanism in recent decades derives from J. G. A. Pocock's book, *The Machiavellian Moment: Florentine Political Thought and the Atlantic Republican Tradition* (1975). Sympathetic commentators trace the republican tradition in different ways, emphasizing alternatively Aristotle, Machiavelli (1469–1327), and Montesquieu (1689–1755), among others.

One might note the tension between ideas such as civic republicanism, which depend on a robust notion of 'the public good', and approaches such as public choice theory, which, in some versions, is sceptical about 'the public good', either as a viable concept, or as something that can be obtained given human weaknesses.

civil law   *See* common law

Coase theorem   The term refers to part of the argument presented in Ronald Coase's (1910–   ) article, 'The Problem of Social Cost', which, by most accounts, was seminal to the modern law and economics movement. Coase argued against a welfare economics justification for state regulation (Coase's particular target was Arthur Cecil Pigou's *The Economics of Welfare* (4th edn. 1932)). Some economists had argued that businesses that impose costs on third parties ('externalities'), through pollution or other nuisances, should be forced to 'internalize their externalities', either through tort law liability or state sanction, for otherwise they would be receiving a kind of subsidy that would lead to an inefficient distribution of goods and services. Coase argued that this view was based on a series of misunderstandings. What is now known as the Coase theorem is in fact an intermediate step in the article's analysis: that in a world without transaction costs, the distribution of legal rights (e.g. to pollute or to prevent pollution) would not matter, because the party who valued the right the most could always buy the right from a lower-valuing user if the higher-valuing user did not have it to begin with.

Thus, if railroads create sparks that can damage nearby farmland, conventional analysis would predict that the amount of damage caused would depend on whether the railway has the right to give off sparks with impunity, or whether the farmers have the right to enjoin the activity, or at least to recover compensation for the damage caused. Coase pointed out that the initial distribution of rights is not the proper focus, because though the law makes the initial distribution of rights, those rights can and will be reallocated through voluntary ('market') transactions, until the rights end up with the parties that value them the most. For example, if the farmers begin with the right to recover in nuisance for damages caused by sparks, but the right to give off sparks is more valuable to the railway than the right not to be damaged is to the farmers, the railway will pay the farmers for the right.

A later conclusion of the same analysis in Coase's article is that in the real world, where there *are* pervasive transaction costs, the initial distribution of legal rights *does* matter, because high transaction costs may prevent a higher-valuing user from buying the right from a lower-valuing user.

The lesson law and economics theorists derived from Coase was that law often was largely irrelevant to analysis, in so far as efficiency is concerned, because parties could contract around the existing legal regime. A somewhat different conclusion some commentators have drawn is that lawmakers should be in the business of reducing transaction costs where possible. Many of the important later works in law and economics focused their study of (alternative) legal rules on a consideration of the effect they have had or would have on transaction costs.

See causation; externalities; law and economics; market failure; transaction costs

coercion *See* duress

coherence theory Within philosophy, some theorists have argued for coherence theories of truth (as against correspondence theories of truth). Coherence theories test propositions against other propositions already held, rather than against foundational axioms. Within legal theory, coherence theories have played a role in a number of debates, including the nature of 'truth' for legal propositions, and the work of Ronald

Dworkin (1931–). Dworkin's interpretive approach to law is not, narrowly speaking, a coherence theory of law, but aspects of the theory seem to approximate a coherence approach. In Dworkin's interpretive approach to law (e.g. *Law's Empire* (1986)), the determination of what the law is (what the law requires) on some topic is determined by the constructive interpretation of past official actions. The 'fit' of a legal proposition to other past official actions plays a role in determining whether the legal proposition in question is true or not, but 'fit' alone is not conclusive. Additionally, in Dworkin's discussion of 'Integrity' (in the same text), he emphasizes the importance of the community 'speaking with one voice' through its laws.

There is ongoing debate among commentators whether a proper understanding of legal reasoning, legal interpretation, and common-law reasoning requires reference to coherence theories. Those who see a role for coherence theories often view legal reasoning (especially common-law reasoning) as an ongoing effort of law to 'work itself pure'—to create an ever clearer, more consistent, and perhaps morally more attractive explanation and justification for the existing set of legal rules.

One problem with coherence arguments (whether regarding the nature of truth, the nature of law, legal reasoning, or legal interpretation) is that there is no agreed understanding of 'coherence'. There is an intuitive sense that it is something stronger (or more 'principled') than mere consistency, but that 'something more' has been notoriously hard to articulate.

See **common law; constructive interpretation; correspondence theory of truth; fit; integrity; legal reasoning; precedent**

collective action problem A term from economics for a basic problem of societal ordering and political theory: where certain public goods require the co-operation of many people and, if achieved, will benefit everyone, the benefit cannot be confined to those who contributed to achieving the public good. So how does one prevent free riding, people enjoying the benefits without paying the cost? Examples of goods that raise collective action problems might include national security and clean air and water.

See **free rider; prisoner's dilemma**

command theory of law Command theories equate law with the commands of the sovereign. The most prominent example is the work of John Austin (1790–1859), though Jeremy Bentham's (1748–1832) approach to law could also fit this category.

The strength of command theories is that they capture the coercive aspects of law, and the importance of the power of the state. Their weakness is in the problem of any theory that tries to reduce the variety of legal experience to one category, whatever that category might be. Not only do command theories have difficulty accounting for power-conferring rules, they also can have difficulty accounting for the basic structure of the legal system itself—the rules that constitute the roles and institutions of the system, and have to guarantee its continuity over time.

See **Austin, John; Bentham, Jeremy**

commodification The term has a series of overlapping meanings relating to (the legal recognition of) the exchange of certain things for money or other things of value; or giving a market (monetary) value to some object or service that usually is kept outside the market. Thus, the sale of donor eggs for use in in-vitro fertilization, or the sale of a living person's 'extra' kidney for use in donation to a needy recipient, would be examples of the first type of commodification. The valuation of home-maker services for the determination of an equitable division of property at divorce is an example of the second kind of commodification.

The argument is that the sale of body organs, blood, or sperm and eggs is inappropriate because it dehumanizes the person offering parts of his or her body for sale, and indirectly dehumanizes all of us, as we are now encouraged to see our own bodies and those of other people as mere objects available for money in the marketplace. Similar arguments are also made for prostitution and surrogacy as the sale of bodily services, though in each case other, conventionally more legitimate forms of physical labour can be distinguished only by focusing on the sexual or reproductive nature of the service in question.

See **property law**

common law A form of judicial decision-making and lawmaking dominant in Britain and a number of its former colonies, including the United States, Canada, Australia, and New Zealand, whose origin can be traced back to the Norman Conquest of England in 1066. In this broad sense of the term, 'common law' is often contrasted with 'civil law', an approach to law derived from ancient Roman law, which depends more on the interpretation of authoritative codes, and where judicial decisions are purportedly not a significant source of law.

Within common-law legal systems, 'common law' sometimes refers to more specific matters: (1) 'common law' versus 'equity'—where the latter refers to legal standards initially developed by the Court of Chancery, standards that tended to be less precise and more justice-based than the clear-line rules developed by the general court system; and (2) 'common law' versus legislation—contrasting statutory law with judge-made law, a distinction more commonly used when statutory law was less common than it is today, and tended only to modify existing judge-made law.

Common-law reasoning and decision-making has created many difficulties for legal theories, for there are problems in characterizing what the judges are doing (e.g. making law or finding law, and, if 'finding law', where is/was the law that is being found?). Historically, some commentators saw common-law reasoning as 'immemorial custom' (or 'law preserved in the memory of man', John Davies (1615)) restated by judges, or an 'artificial perfection of reason gotten by long study, observation, and experience' (Sir Edward Coke (1628)). This view of the common law (or of law generally) begins to converge with certain variations of natural law theory, under which eternal and perhaps divinely based moral principles underlie man-made legal pronouncements.

More modern characterizations see common-law reasoning as the gradual consideration (and reconsideration) of moral and practical problems through the application of moral intuition to fully stated facts (and arguments for both sides by adversarial advocates).

Common-law reasoning has also been seen as raising the problem of the actual or perceived retroactive character of applying the newly developed (or newly discovered) norms to the dispute before the court. Jeremy Bentham (1748–1832) described judge-made law as being 'Just as a man makes law for his dog. When your dog does anything you want to break him of, you wait till he does it, and then beat him for it. This is the way you make laws for your dog: and this is the way the judges make law for you and me' ('Truth versus Ashhurst' (1792)).

See analogical reasoning; Bentham, Jeremy; Blackstone, William; coherence theory; custom and customary law; Levi, Edward H.; natural law theory; precedent; *stare decisis*

communicative rationality, theory of A theory connected with the work of German philosopher Jürgen Habermas (1929–), and presented in *The Theory of Communicate Action* (1981), as well as in later texts. In that work, Habermas contrasts 'communicative action' with 'instrumental action' and 'strategic action'. 'Communicative action' involves efforts towards mutual understanding. To the extent that agreements are obtained by consensus and uncoerced persuasion, rather than by deception or coercion, they are legitimate. The idea of communicative rationality (which Habermas describes as a 'recasting' of 'the classical understanding of practical reasoning' (*Between Facts and Norms* (1992)) points to standards of correctness being derived from all parties to a discussion, rather than from some foundational truth assumed, discovered, or imposed. (Habermas's theory of communicative rationality, at least in the 1981 text, could also be seen as an effort to bring together more individualistic forms of analysis of social action with forms of analysis based on 'systems theory'.)

For Habermas, communicative rationality is the appropriate standard and approach both for practical (social and political) questions and for theoretical (scientific) questions. In his own terms, it is equally applicable to physics and to morality. Communicative rationality can be seen as reflecting an ideal in which arguments would be subject to detailed criticism and justification (in contrast to most practical situations, where there is frequently no time for detailed justification, and there is often quick recourse to claims of authority or threats of sanctions for deviation from a norm).

See **ideal speech situation**

communitarianism Approaches to justice, morality, and social ordering that emphasize the importance of community to individual identity, individual fulfilment, and the social good. Communitarians often stake out their position in contrast to what they characterize as unduly individualistic views of individuals, ethics, and justice. Communitarianism also tends to emphasize the value (to both individuals and society) of active engagement in civic and political life.

See **liberalism**

conceptual analysis Conceptual analysis seeks the truth about aspects of our world through breaking down the logical structure, or the necessary and essential attributes, of ideas and categories. Much of modern analytical jurisprudence purports to be the analysis of concepts (as exemplified by some of the genre's more familiar titles, e.g. H. L. A. Hart, *The Concept of Law* (1961) and Joseph Raz, *The Concept of a Legal System* (1970)), in particular, the concepts of 'law' and '[legal] right'.

Conceptual claims can be contrasted with empirical and causal claims, which are in principle testable, through controlled experiments, careful observation, or the analysis of past events. The relationship between conceptual claims about (e.g.) the nature of law or the nature of rights and empirical data is far more complicated.

The move towards naturalism in philosophy, led by the work of W. V. O. Quine (1908–2000) and others, has undermined conceptual analysis within mainstream philosophy. Many argue that it no longer makes sense to think of analysing the intricate meanings of term rather than investigating the world—for example, that 'the concept of knowledge' should be investigated in connection with the way people actually form beliefs and act upon them. Some commentators have argued that legal philosophy should similarly abandon conceptual analysis, though it remains central to analytical jurisprudence.

See analytical jurisprudence; necessity

conceptualism A pejorative term, used most commonly by the American legal realists and their followers, against opponents accused of improperly deriving conclusions from the mere nature of abstract concepts (e.g. 'contract' and 'property'). For example, the argument was sometimes made that courts must invalidate zoning and other regulations on the use of land, because such regulations were contrary to the nature of 'property'. The charge of 'conceptualism' is often connected to, or interchangeable with, the charge of 'formalism'. ('Conceptualism' should be contrasted with 'conceptual analysis': conceptual analysis is an effort to determine the nature or essence of some object or practice—where this degrades into 'conceptualism' would be where someone would claim that significant questions of law or policy should turn on a purported analysis of a term.)

See American legal realism, formalism

Condorcet jury theorem A theory proved by Marie Jean Antoine Nicolas de Caritat, the Marquis de Condorcet (1743–94), that if individual voters have a greater than 50 per cent chance of being correct, the greater the number of voters, the greater the chance that the collective (majority) decision will be correct. This theorem has implications not only for juries, but also for democratic theory. The full recognition of the significance of this argument did not come until more than 150 years after it was published, but it has become central to discussions within social choice theory.

See public choice theory; social choice theory

Condorcet's voting paradox   The paradox discovered by Marie Jean Antoine Nicolas de Caritat, the Marquis de Condorcet (1743–94), showing how majoritarian voting can lead to indeterminate or 'cycling' group preferences. Voter 1 may prefer A to B and B to C; Voter 2, B to C and C to A; Voter 3, C to A and A to B. Given such preferences, a majority vote would prefer A to B, and B to C, but C to A. This same basic insight is at the core of Arrow's theorem and social choice theory generally. Condorcet's work on voting was largely ignored (or forgotten) until it was incorporated by Duncan Black (1908–   ) into a theory of public choice (e.g. in Black's *The Theory of Committees and Elections* (1958)).

See **Arrow's theorem; public choice theory; social choice theory**

consent   Within moral, legal, and political theory, consent is a normatively significant assent to some action, choice, situation, or authority.

As consent can be seen as reflecting a state of mind (whose external manifestations can be faked), one can distinguish 'real consent' from the actions that certain social or legal institutions take as evidence (sometimes conclusive evidence) of consent. For example: (1) one can promise to paint a friend's roof for £100, but privately have no intention of putting oneself under an obligation to perform on those terms; and (2) it can be argued that by staying in an organization and accepting its benefits, Smith had consented to being bound by its rules, even though Smith in fact had no such intention, belief, or attitude.

The moral significance of consent in part relates to a perspective on moral and political matters that emphasizes autonomy (an approach that can be traced back to the work of Immanuel Kant (1724–1804)). Because of the perceived importance of autonomy, and thus of consent, some theorists will build justifications on notions *related to* (or purportedly related to) consent: such as John Locke's (1632–1704) notion of tacit consent, and the idea of hypothetical consent (what one *would have chosen* had one been faced with a particular choice, or perhaps faced with a particular choice while having more or less knowledge than one currently has) found in theorists from John Rawls (1921–2002) to Richard Posner (1939–   ). The extent to which actions, rules, or principles can be justified by tacit consent or hypothetical consent is a matter of ongoing controversy.

The moral and legal force of a particular purported act of consent will often turn on the extent to which the actor was fully competent, had full information, and was not under significant external pressures. Legal doctrines and moral philosophers differ on which pressures (poverty, bribery, religious belief?) should be seen as undermining the force of the consent.

In criminal law and tort law, there are moral and legal questions raised about when a victim's 'consent' or 'assumption of risk' negates liability in the injurer (the Latin phrase, *volenti non fit injuria*, 'no injury is done to a willing person', is often quoted). Issues include whether the level of consent matters (assent could be given to an activity, such as rugby, where the risk of injury is well known, or assent could be given to the 'injury' itself, as in tattoos or sado-masochistic sexual practices); and whether some activities (e.g. intentional killing or enslavement) should be forbidden by public policy regardless of the consent of the parties (in many legal systems, sado-masochistic sex may also fall within the category of actions subject to criminal liability despite the consent of those involved).

See **autonomy; contract law; Locke, John**

consequentialism Moral theories under which judgements of actions and decisions depend on the consequences of those actions and decisions. The best-known form of consequentialism (a term apparently introduced by Elizabeth Anscombe (1919–2001)) is utilitarianism, but one can reject utilitarianism and still accept consequentialism. The alternative to consequentialism is a belief that actions and decisions should be based solely on the moral value of the 'will' or motive behind the action, regardless of the consequences ('deontology'), or that morality is best understood not through the evaluation of individual actions but through the development of an individual's character, in particular, the development of certain virtues ('virtue theory'). Consequentialism in turn has many variations: some theories focus on the consequences of particular acts, while others focus on the consequences of general rules or principles for action.

See **deontological; moral luck; utilitarianism**

constitutional theory Theorizing regarding the proper interpretation and application of a country's foundational law(s). In the United States, because of the strong doctrine of 'judicial review' (the ability of courts to invalidate otherwise valid laws based on conflicts between those laws and constitutional provisions), and the tendency of most policy questions to be turned eventually into constitutional disputes, constitutional law is centrally important—and thus, constitutional theory as well. While constitutional theories are usually strongly grounded in the text and drafting history of the particular foundational laws and in the culture and legal history of the country, such theories regularly touch on more general theoretical questions (e.g. basic principles of interpretation and the proper understanding of moral principles mentioned in the constitution). Many of the important questions within constitutional theory are those of applied political theory: for example, the proper relationship of different branches of government, what constraints there should be on majoritarian rule, which (if any) rights should be protected by constitutional provisions, and so on.

See adjudication, theories of; countermajoritarian difficulty; Ely, John Hart

constructive interpretation In Ronald Dworkin's (1931–) later work, in particular *Law's Empire* (1986), he argues that law, like art and literature, must be approached through 'constructive interpretation', an interpretation that makes the object of interpretation 'the best possible example of the form or genre to which it is taken to belong'.

The appropriateness of this form of interpretation for either art and literature or for law is highly contested. Among the alternative views is one that would focus on the author's or creator's intentions in the interpretation of a work of art. There are analogous views about law and legal interpretation: that constructive interpretation understates the importance of authority to the nature of law.

Also controversial is Dworkin's claim that constructive interpretation is equally applicable for lawyers and judges attempting to discern what the law is on a particular topic and for the legal theorists creating a theory of law. Most theorists believe that there should be a sharp divide between general theories about the nature of law and ideas about legal issues within a particular legal system.

See coherence theory; interpretation; interpretive theory of law

contract law Contract law involves the enforcement of certain forms of promises, agreements, and exchanges. As no legal regime enforces *all* promises or *all* agreements, questions are raised about the justifications for enforcing some and not others (and for differing levels of enforcement, as when some plaintiffs can seek lost profits while others are allowed only out-of-pocket expenses).

There are numerous other questions within contract law that have attracted the attention of theorists. For example, when should a court imply terms on a matter on which the parties have remained silent?

The treatment of such 'incomplete contracts' has evoked a number of disparate responses: e.g. some commentators argue that it is unjust to imply any terms for which the parties could not reasonably have been said to consent; while other commentators offer economics-based arguments that certain strategies of implication would increase efficiency; and some argue that terms should be implied that would encourage the maintenance of existing long-term relationships.

Contemporary discussions about the philosophical foundations of contract law usually divide (as do similar debates about tort law), according to whether the analysis should be approached from traditional moral philosophy or from economic analysis. From traditional moral philosophy, the analysis is generally in terms of autonomy and consent, and more specifically through ideas about promising and (to a lesser extent) corrective justice (by way of a remedy for a breach of a contract). Economic analysis, by contrast, tends to focus on *when* remedies are available, and *which* remedies are available, and to consider whether parties are being given the optimal incentives to act in accordance with the purposes ascribed (by lawmakers or judges) to the law.

As a matter of both historical development and theoretical justification, the relation of contract law and tort law is interesting. Obligations to users of a product or service were for a long time (in England and the United States) grounded and confined by privity of contract; only in the mid- to late nineteenth century were those constraints largely lifted. More recently, it has been argued that contract law has become, in some ways, a subset or variation of tort law—with obligations arising largely independently of the assent of the parties (e.g. promissory estoppel and certain mandatory or presumptive protective terms or warranties).

The role of contract, at least in the broader sense of agreement (to exchange), plays a crucial role in various places: e.g. in law and economics (where voluntary market exchanges are the model and the ideal on which most analysis is based) and in moral and political theories grounded on 'social contract'. What makes contractual/agreement models so consistently attractive for moral, legal, and political analysis is the way that party consent (even when the contracting parties are hypothetical actors) seems to get around the problem of justifying norms by a foundational moral claim.

See autonomy; consent; corrective justice; law and economics; social contract; tort law; unconscionability

conventional morality *See* morality, critical v. conventional

conventionalism The assertion that truth or meaning in some area derives ('merely') from the agreement in practice or belief among a population. While advocates of legal positivism frequently emphasize the importance of convention for their views of law, few legal positivists refer to their position as 'conventionalism'. This term is generally used in legal philosophy to indicate a disfavoured alternative to a theory being put forward, the favoured theory usually being one that gives a significant role to moral truth (although, as with other generally pejorative terms, such as 'formalism', there are theorists who accept the label defiantly).

co-ordination games A term from game theory where the largest (joint or individual) pay-offs to the players would come from their co-ordinating their behaviour. Because players have difficulty anticipating other players' strategies, co-ordination is hard to achieve. Additionally, the circumstances of the game (and of the real-life situations it models) often create incentives for selfish behaviour that can undermine both the joint returns of the participants and the long-term interests of each individual participant.

The problem of co-ordination and co-operation is a general problem, both strategically, for interacting individuals (whether those interactions are part of a commercial deal, or just between neighbours), and theoretically, for understanding how supportive interaction can be created and maintained in social, commercial, legal, and political life.

See co-ordination of behaviour; prisoner's dilemma

co-ordination of behaviour Many legal theorists view law as being primarily or essentially involved with the co-ordination of individuals' behaviour within society. Additionally, some theorists assert a tie between co-ordination, authority, and the obligation to obey the law. One line of analysis is that there is an obligation to obey the law when obeying the law makes it more likely that one will do the right thing than if one evaluated the situation for oneself. One such circumstance where obeying the law may be morally obligatory would be where co-ordination of citizen behaviour is necessary to obtain an important social good (e.g. safe water, clean air, safe roadways, etc.). Even those, such as Joseph Raz (1939–), who do not believe that law *generally* creates an obligation to obey, agree that there is an obligation to obey when law is effectively co-ordinating behaviour in these sorts of situations.

See co-ordination games

corrective justice   Corrective justice (also sometimes called 'rectificatory justice') refers to what is required to rectify the situation between two persons when one has harmed the other in some way. Corrective justice thus underlies the modern institutions of contract law, tort law (though both contract and tort law also allow forms of damages that may go beyond 'corrective justice'—punitive damages for tort law and expectation damages for contract law), restitution, and criminal justice. The division of justice into 'corrective' and 'distributive' goes back at least to Aristotle (*Nicomachean Ethics*, Book V). Aristotle thought of both forms of justice as reflecting an aspect of equality, with corrective justice being a return to the equality (baseline status quo) that existed between two parties prior to some injury or unjust enrichment, while distributive justice was the equal division of shares over a group of people (where 'equal' here means not absolute equality, but division according to relative criteria—whether merit, need, or some other measure).

The possible or necessary interaction of corrective justice and distributive justice (e.g. whether distributive inequities justify any modification of one's duties under corrective justice) remains a matter of active discussion in the literature.

See **Aristotle; baseline problem; contract law; distributive justice; justice; tort law**

correspondence theory of truth   The theory that a proposition is true if it corresponds with the facts—or, more broadly formulated, if it corresponds with reality. While this may seem both a commonsense view and obviously correct, modern philosophical theory has offered alternative accounts of truth: e.g. coherence and pragmatic theories of truth. Sceptical responses to correspondence theories usually derive from doubts about whether we have direct access to 'facts' or 'the way things really are', separate from our beliefs. The question about whether to apply a correspondence theory when talking about the truth of legal propositions has a somewhat different grounding, in that it is not clear to what the truth of 'X is guilty' or 'there was a valid contract between A and B' purportedly corresponds. This question has led some to a predictive theory of law (legal propositions are true if they correctly predict what a court will say on the subject), others to a coherence theory, and still others to metaphysically realist positions.

See coherence theory; realism; pragmatism; predictive theory of law

countermajoritarian difficulty A shorthand term for a concern raised primarily in American constitutional law, but with obvious applications for all legal systems that allow some form of judicial power to challenge or invalidate otherwise valid law on the basis that it is contrary to written or unwritten constitutional norms. The concern is that such judicial power seems contrary to the essentially democratic or majoritarian principles underlying the government. A wide variety of responses has been offered to this difficulty, including the assertion that such judicial power was itself justified by democratic action (the ratification of the Constitution). How troubling judicial review seems to be, and how adequate the various response, depends on one's perception of various issues, in particular the extent to which one thinks that judges can be constrained by the constitutional norms, and, independent of how constraining those norms *could be*, whether one thinks that judges in fact *have been* constrained in their past decisions, or are likely to be in future decisions.

See constitutional theory; Ely, John Hart; judicial legislation

criminal law The body of law dealing with state punishment for violation of legal norms. The focus of the criminal law is generally thought to be the maintenance of social order (in contrast, e.g. with tort law, which covers many of the same sorts of violations, but leaves enforcement to the individuals affected, on the basis that tort law is about the vindication of personal rights rather than public interests).

Criminal law is a doctrinal area of law with substantial intersection with legal philosophy, as it raises questions of responsibility, culpability, punishment, morality, and the proper role of the state (e.g. in situations where harm to others is not involved, should the criminal law none the less be used to enforce morality or to protect people from harming themselves?).

For example, on questions of culpability and punishment, the issue is whether law should focus on the action, the intention behind the action, or the character of the person acting (the approaches would lead to quite different conclusions, e.g. in cases of failed attempts to commit a criminal act, and in cases where the same negligent or reckless actions caused varying levels of harm). It is therefore not surprising to find important legal philosophers, such as H. L. A. Hart (1907–92), involved prominently in theoretical discussions of criminal law.

There is a significant overlap between theories of culpability and theories of punishment, though the two may be treated as separate subjects (e.g. for those who argue that punishment should be grounded primarily on some basis other than the actor's culpability).

Various theoretical approaches have also considered aspects of criminal law, from economic theorists such as Gary Becker (1930–   ), who have used economic analysis to try to show how the type and likelihood of punishment would predictably affect the rate of crime, to critical scholars of various schools who have tried to show that the criminal law rules and procedures are systematically biased against certain groups.

See harm principle; moral luck; punishment; retribution

critical latino/latina studies *See* critical race theory

critical legal studies A radical critique of law that, as a movement, was active in the United States from the early 1970s until the late 1980s (with some followers or supporters in other countries). Critical legal studies (CLS) combined leftist political positions with radicalized versions of the critical arguments first developed by American legal realism. Among CLS's themes were the radical indeterminacy of law, a criticism of the public–private distinction, and an argument that law works to further the interests of the powerful. The view that law was radically indeterminate, and that legal reasoning was just a cover for the clash of different interest groups or different ideologies was sometimes summarized by the slogan, 'law is politics'.

Pressures on the movement and tensions within it led to its breaking up or fading away. Many of the critiques developed by critical legal studies were taken up by other critical approaches, such as critical race theory, feminist legal theory, and postmodernist legal theory, while a number of the theorists prominent in CLS continued to work in much the same way that they had within CLS, long after there was no longer a self-identified group or movement by that name.

See American legal realism; fundamental contradiction; Gramsci, Antonio; Hale, Robert L.; hierarchy; ideology; indeterminacy; legitimation; Marx, Karl; nihilism; public–private distinction; scepticism; social construction; trashing

critical morality *See* morality, critical v. conventional

critical race theory A critical approach to law and society that focuses on the disparate treatment of different racial and ethnic groups, and that builds from the different experiences and perspectives of members of those groups. Critical race theorists have applied their ideas to a variety of topics, focusing on such issues as discrimination, unconscious racism, affirmative action (positive discrimination), and hate speech, which highlight the way race and ethnicity is experienced.

Because of critical race theory's focus on the distinctive experiences and perspectives of racial and ethnic minorities, it was perhaps predictable that it would lead to an ever-expanding list of categories of scholarship defined more narrowly, in terms of the experiences of particular racial and ethnic groups or sub-groups, such as 'critical latino/a theory' (also known as 'LatCrit theory'), 'Chicana/o studies', 'Asian critical theory', and the like (along with combinations such as 'critical race feminism'). While there may be general points to be derived regarding the social construction of various aspects of people's lives, questioning the neutrality or objectivity of the version of reality presented by powerful or majority groups, or the relationship between oppression and knowledge, most of the theorists within these movements tend to focus on the more particular—the connection between the experiences and harms of *this* group and certain observations about legal and social regulation. (While the focus is usually on the experience of a certain group within one country, there are occasional efforts to draw wider lessons for oppressed people everywhere.)

See affirmative action; discrimination; essentialism; hate speech; identity politics; narrative scholarship; queer theory; race; social construction; unconscious racism

cultural feminism *See* feminism

culpability *See* responsibility

custom and customary law In many societies, widespread or long-established custom is an important source of law. Even in countries where this is no longer generally the case, custom may still be recognized as the source of more localized rules for commercial transactions and standards of reasonable care; additionally, custom remains an important source of international law. Discussions of customary law have sporadically played important roles in legal theory: e.g. in debates over whether common-law decision-making was best understood as merely codifying 'immemorial custom' (a once-common position now rarely espoused); and whether legal positivist theories can adequately account for the legal status of custom (as custom seems to become law without promulgation by an authority, and prior to its recognition by a judge).

See common law; legal positivism

D

decision theory A form of analysis, usually more prescriptive or ideal than descriptive, regarding an individual's (or individual institution's) process of making decision(s) in the face of uncertainty and/or imperfect knowledge. Decision theory is often contrasted with game theory, in that the latter involves similar sorts of decisions, *but* in the context where the decision-maker is interacting with other actors, actors who are often facing similar choices.

See **game theory**

deconstruction A concept that comes from literary theory, in particular the work of Jacques Derrida (1930–   ), which has been adapted, in various forms, by theorists within postmodern legal theory, critical legal studies, the law and literature movement, critical race theory, and feminist legal theory. Deconstruction emphasizes the contradictions and conflicts within texts, and denies the traditional hierarchies within language, meaning, and communication (e.g. speech over writing).

Deconstruction is important to law and legal theory to the extent it undermines the possibility of 'clear' or 'correct' interpretations of legal texts, be they statutes, constitutions, contracts, or wills.

See **indeterminacy; law and literature; postmodernism; scepticism**

default rule or term The reference to 'default' rules or terms has its origin in computer programming, which indicates an option that will be used if the programmer or user does not expressly choose an alternative. The term has been used frequently in recent years in theoretical discussions of law, particularly relating to contracts, and primarily within analyses by law and economics scholars. Through statutes (e.g. the American Uniform Commercial Code) and judicial case-law, there are certain issues (e.g. regarding when performance is due or whether the seller would be responsible for consequential damages) for which terms will be implied if the agreement is silent on the matter, but the parties have the right to agree to different terms ('to contract around' the default rule). Law and economics theorists have discussed at great length the optimal approach to such default rules, with some arguing for the one that most parties would agree on in any event (a 'majoritarian default'), others arguing for the most efficient term (whether or not it is the term most would agree to), and still others arguing that default terms should sometimes be set, in situations of 'asymmetric information', against the interests of the parties with greater information (a 'penalty default'), forcing those parties to disclose information in order to justify contracting around the default rule (the argument being that such disclosures would increase efficiency or fairness). The *Hadley* v. *Baxendale* rule, that only the usual or expected level of damages can be recovered, unless the buyer informs the seller of the buyer's unusually high level of potential loss, is frequently described as a 'penalty default' rule.

See **contract law; law and economics**

defeasibility Capable of being defeated: this refers to the ability of a conclusion to be justified by certain criteria being met, yet subject to being 'defeated' or rebutted if further criteria are met. Some commentators (in particular, H. L. A. Hart (1907–92), in some of his earliest works) argue that the defeasibility of legal concepts is important to understanding law's nature. An example of such defeasibility is how certain criteria would be sufficient to show that an agreement was a 'valid contract', but that a contrary conclusion could be reached if the court learned that one of the parties was legally incompetent, if the contract had been the product of fraud, or if some other comparable doctrinal defence applied.

See **Hart, H. L. A.**

deontic logic The logical relations that apply to norms, including legal norms. Discussions of deontic logic go back at least to the work of G. W. Leibniz (1646–1716), but much of the foundational work in the field was done in the twentieth century, by such commentators as Georg Henrik von Wright (1916–2003).

As von Wright (and others) have pointed out, part of the confusion in determining the nature and extent of logical relations between norms has been caused by conflating discussions of prescriptions ('norms') and discussions of what is the case within established normative systems such as law ('norm propositions'). For example, it can be argued that, at the level of norms, one cannot be both required to do X and forbidden to do X, and that any action can be classified as either permitted, required, or forbidden. By contrast, it seems likely that most legal systems will have contradictory norms and may have gaps (though Hans Kelsen (1881–1973), at times, seemed to argue that legal normative systems are necessarily 'gap-less' and without contradiction). Additionally (as von Wright and others have argued), one can distinguish a normative analysis focused on 'what ought to be the case' from one focused on 'what ought to be done'.

The debate over deontic logic has connections to Hans Kelsen's work, as Kelsen argued (1) that the enactment of later norms automatically invalidated inconsistent earlier norms; but (2) that a judge's application of a general norm to an individual case necessarily involves the creation of a new norm. Also, some commentators have connected deontic logic to the argument between inclusive and exclusive legal positivism, asserting that under exclusive legal positivism's sources thesis, legal norms would not be validly created by the application of deontic logic to existing valid laws; those new norms would only become valid parts of a legal system when promulgated by some authoritative source. The above points also show the connection between deontic logic and the general question about the relative roles of 'will' and 'reason' in legal validity.

See **Kelsen, Hans; legal positivism; Wright, Georg Henrik von**

deontological Deontological theories of morality or ethics focus exclusively, or primarily, on the intrinsic moral status of actions, as contrasted with theories (such as utilitarianism) that focus on consequences. Deontological theories often derive from, or are otherwise connected to, the work of Immanuel Kant (1724–1804).

See **Kant, Immanuel**

derivative dependency *See* inevitable and derivative dependency

desert The notion of treating people according to what they are due, as a matter of 'desert' (which, depending on the theorist, may itself be grounded on aspects of character, intentions, or actions), is considered a central element of justice, especially distributive justice. Desert is often tied to effort or to merit. While it is possible to see the definition of 'merit' as restating the question of desert, this need not be the case. For example, some commentators have urged a sharp separation of desert and merit (often in the context of advocating some plan of affirmative action), arguing that people's abilities are directly or indirectly a matter of mere fortune (the 'accident' of having good genes, or being born to an affluent and supportive family, etc.), and therefore do not warrant having more resources than someone else who was not so fortunate.

See affirmative action; justice

determinacy *See* indeterminacy

determinatio A concept found in the work of St Thomas Aquinas (1224–74), and further elaborated by later natural-law theorists, including John Finnis (1940–   ). *Determinatio* refers to a relation of a more specific rule/norm to a more general rule/norm, where the relationship is looser than a direct derivation or entailment, involving some amount of choice of discretion in selecting the more specific rule/norm. According to Aquinas and Finnis, legislators must enact certain laws, and in a particular form, because such is required by the natural law, while for some other topics, only the general nature of the law's content is determined by natural law principles; the legislators have some choice as to the precise content (e.g. that the natural law might require legislators to create an automobile speed limit to protect the peace and order of citizens, but that there might be a range of equally moral, equally just maximum speeds among which any choice would be legitimate).

See Aquinas, Thomas

deterrence A justification for punishment based on its effects on future behaviour, in particular the prevention of crime. Theorists frequently distinguish the 'general deterrent effect' of punishment (the extent to which the punishment of one person prevents the commission of crime by others) from its 'specific deterrent effect' (whether the punishment deters future criminal behaviour by the person being punished). It is not easy to prove or disprove the deterrent effect of punishments, a matter exemplified in the highly contested narrow issue of whether capital punishment creates a greater deterrent value for murder than life imprisonment.

See punishment; rehabilitation; retribution

Devlin, Patrick Patrick Arthur Devlin (1905–92) was a highly respected English judge, who rose to the House of Lords, though he resigned from the judiciary (in 1963) shortly after reaching that position. His main significance for legal theory was his response to the Wolfenden Committee, whose 1957 report recommended decriminalizing homosexual acts and prostitution. The report's conclusions were grounded on John Stuart Mill's (1806–73) 'harm principle', that criminal prohibition was justified only to prevent harm to others, and the report distinguished 'public morality' from 'private morality'. (The Street Offences Act 1959 and later legislation followed the Wolfenden approach to prostitution, leaving private acts legal, but criminalizing almost all public manifestations of prostitution, such as soliciting or procuring. The partial decriminalization of homosexual activity had to await the Sexual Offences Act 1967.)

Devlin's 1958 Maccabaean Lecture to the British Academy, later expanded to book form (*The Enforcement of Morals* (1965)), responded to the Wolfenden Report, arguing that a shared morality is what keeps a society together, and that society has a legitimate interest in protecting its shared morality for much the same reason that it can legitimately protect itself against those who commit treason. Devlin's argument restates elements of James Fitzjames Stephen's (1829–94) criticism of John Stuart Mill, while diverging at key points from Stephen's 'perfectionist' view.

H. L. A. Hart (1907–92) responded to Devlin's Maccabean Lecture in *Law, Liberty, and Morality* (1963). In that book, Hart defended a modified version of John Stuart Mill's 'harm principle'; against Devlin's particular position, Hart argued primarily that there was no reason to believe that a mere change in a society's conventional morality would threaten that society. If conventional morality changes over time, and these changes usually occur without significant harmful effects, it is not clear why society should be interested in protecting the *old* conventional morality against the *new* shared beliefs that were taking over. Additionally, in a society of diverse political and religious beliefs and ethnic backgrounds, it may be unhelpful (or absurd) to speak of a single 'shared morality', or to refer to all contrary perspectives as 'similar to treason'.

See harm principle; Hart, H. L. A.; Mill, John Stuart; morality, critical v. conventional; morality, legal enforcement of; Stephen, James Fitzjames

Dewey, John An American philosopher (and educator and social reformer) (1859–1952), who was prominent in the pragmatist movement in philosophy. While pragmatism generally influenced many of the American legal realists, Dewey's influence was more direct, through articles he wrote for law reviews—'Logical Method and the Law' for the *Cornell Law Quarterly* (1924), and 'The Historic Background of Corporate Legal Personality' for the *Yale Law Journal* (1926).

See American legal realism; pragmatism

difference principle One of the two principles of justice John Rawls (1921–2002) argues for in *A Theory of Justice* (1971). The principle states: 'social and economic inequalities are to be arranged so that they are ... to the greatest benefit of the least advantaged'. Rawls argues that the bargainers in his 'original position' (who negotiate behind a 'veil of ignorance', unaware of their values, preferences, or circumstances) would choose this principle over either a strict equality in the distribution of income and wealth, utilitarianism, or unconstrained inequality.

See justice as fairness; maximin principle; original position; veil of ignorance

discretion The right or power to select among a range of alternatives. The meaning of discretion is important in evaluating the claims of those who assert (or deny) that judges have discretion in deciding (difficult) legal questions. Ronald Dworkin (1931–) (in *Taking Rights Seriously* (1977)) distinguished between 'weak' and 'strong' senses of discretion. Dworkin suggested that we sometimes use discretion in a 'weak' sense when speaking of situations where the application of some criterion requires the application of judgement, or where a decision-maker had final authority in a matter. These were to be distinguished from a 'strong' sense of discretion, under which the decision-maker is not (completely) bound by standards.

discrimination The treatment of persons due to characteristics (e.g. race, gender, religion, sexual orientation) that do not seem relevant to the choice or transaction in view. The nature of discrimination, its pervasiveness, and how it can be fought are issues central to critical schools grounded on difference, such as feminist legal theory and critical race theory.

Some critical race theorists have argued that discrimination is often the effect of racist beliefs held at a deep or 'unconscious' level.

Those who do economic analysis of law approach the problem of discrimination by trying to determine within their own models of human behaviour why it occurs, given that discrimination appears 'inefficient' and (thus) 'irrational'. Gary Becker (1930–) (in *The Economics of Discrimination* (1957)) took discrimination to be merely a result of individuals' taste ('a taste for discrimination'), simply one preference to be put into the analysis with other (perhaps equally irrational or unpleasant) preferences. Other economic analysts have written about 'statistical discrimination', the fact that discrimination may sometimes be 'rational', where the personal characteristic in question is a somewhat useful proxy for other relevant information, and more reliable information would be too expensive to acquire (one example often given is the treatment of male and female employees differently in an industry where men have been more likely to stay in the job longer after having received firm-specific training).

See critical race theory; feminist legal theory; race; unconscious racism

distributive justice Refers to the principles that guide the distribution of goods or burdens among a group of recipients. This is in contrast to claims of justice arising from the correction of dealings between two parties ('corrective justice'), just punishment of wrong actions ('retribution'), and the proper following of rules laid down earlier ('formal' or 'legal' justice).

In recent political theory, the term 'distributive justice' has been applied primarily to a government's distribution or redistribution of goods and burdens among its citizens.

See Aristotle; corrective justice; justice

dominance feminism *See* feminism

double-effect, principle of The notion that we should judge differently consequences intended and consequences not intended but clearly foreseen. At its most extreme, the principle (or 'doctrine') of double effect would absolve actors from unintended consequences even when these consequences are severe and known to be all but certain. The principle is commonly associated with Catholic theology. A common context for the discussion of this principle is medical treatment for seriously ill patients, with some moral (and theological) theorists arguing that while it is improper to give treatment which has the purpose of causing death, it is proper to give treatment for other purposes (e.g. relieving pain), even when that treatment is known to have the further consequence of speeding death.

Duguit, León French social theorist (1859–1928) whose primary focus was the sociological concept of 'social cohesion' or 'social solidarity'. Duguit viewed social solidarity as a natural tendency of people living within society, and law as an integral aspect of the maintenance of that solidarity. As part of this approach, Duguit distrusted both concepts of state sovereignty and strong state power and claims of individualism and individual rights. He viewed legal rules not as imposed from the sovereign, but as reflecting the tendencies or consciousness of the community.

duress In many legal systems, a showing that an action was done under strong compulsion or coercion may remove or lessen civil or criminal liability for the action. For example, in English and American law, a contractual obligation may be excused if the contract was entered because of 'duress'. While duress was once understood narrowly to mean the use or threat of physical force, in recent decades it has been expanded to include what is called 'economic duress' or 'duress of goods'. While it was easy to draw a relatively sharp line as to what constituted (physical) duress in the traditional sense, the modern doctrine requires a relatively subtle and hard to discern distinction between (economic) duress and acceptable types of hard bargaining or taking advantage of one's superior bargaining situation. Similarly, where the coercion is one of 'hard choices', but not of threat to life and limb, talk of duress 'overcoming free will' seems either inaccurate or unhelpful. Where the consequences of not acting in a certain way become more onerous, the sense in which one's actions are 'voluntary' or 'consensual' diminishes. At the same time, many commentators argue that there are good moral and policy reasons for holding people criminally or contractually responsible even for choices and actions that may not have been entirely voluntary.

The American legal realist Robert Hale (1884–1969) argued that coercion and power imbalances were a pervasive aspect of market and labour transactions, though he intended this argument not as a basis for refusing to hold people to their agreements, but as a basis for a change in government policies in order to equalize bargaining power.

See **autonomy; consent; Hale, Robert L.**

duty That one 'ought', under the rubric of some normative rule or system (moral, legal, or otherwise—even games create obligations of sorts), to bring about some state of affairs (e.g. a legal duty to pay a certain amount in taxes), or at least to refrain from interfering with some other person as regards some activity (e.g. a duty not to interfere with another person's freedom of religious belief).

The concept of 'duty' (also called 'obligation'—some philosophers purport to distinguish 'duty' and 'obligation', but such distinctions are rare in mainstream philosophical writing, and rarer still in legal philosophy) is foundational in both moral and legal analysis, and difficult to explain in terms more basic.

Questions regarding 'duty' arise in a variety of contexts within legal philosophy: e.g. whether 'rights' have independent significance, or are best understood merely as the correlates of certain kinds of duties; and whether the law should be defined in terms of duty-imposing rules (as John Austin (1790–1859), among others, argued).

In American tort law, doctrines have developed connecting the notion of 'duty' with foreseeability (*Palsgraf* v. *Long Island Railway* (New York, 1928)).

See **Hohfeld, Wesley N.; rights**

E

easy cases *See* hard cases

economic analysis of law *See* law and economics

economic rent Payments made to obtain the use of a resource above what would be (or should be) required to obtain the use of that resource (that is, its value in a competitive market, or its 'opportunity cost'—its value by an alternative user). In principle, a state of perfect competition would also be one in which no rents are made by any resource (natural or human). Rents can sometimes be equivalent to profits, but need not be, if the next best use of a resource already includes some profit.

The term is conventionally associated with David Ricardo (1772–1823), though Ricardo himself attributed the concept to Thomas Robert Malthus (1766–1834).

See **quasi-rent; rent-seeking**

efficiency A key term in economic analysis, but one for which there does not seem to be a precise definition accepted as a matter of consensus. Roughly, the term refers to that choice or state of affairs which, compared with the alternatives, maximizes the total level of utility, welfare, or wealth (given the same starting place or set of inputs).

There are related concepts that are defined with greater precision. 'Pareto efficiency' (also known as 'Pareto optimality') refers to a state of affairs where no change to another state of affairs would be treated by all as either preferable or indifferent (for a given collection of goods and individuals, there are usually *a number* of different distributions which would be 'Pareto efficient' or 'Pareto optimal'). Secondly, a move from one state of affairs to another is 'Kaldor-Hicks efficient' if those who benefited by the move *could* compensate those made worse off for all their losses while the first group still remains better off. In Kaldor-Hicks analysis, the 'could' is understood narrowly—a compensation that could happen, but *does not* (if the better-off *did* compensate those left worse off for all their losses, while themselves remaining better off, the result would seem to be a 'Pareto superior' move—with everyone either preferring the second state of affairs or being indifferent).

See **Kaldor-Hicks analysis; Pareto efficiency; law and economics**

Ely, John Hart John Hart Ely (1938–2003) was a constitutional law scholar who taught at Yale University, Harvard University, and the University of Miami, and also served as Dean of the Stanford Law School. His book, *Democracy and Distrust: A Theory of Judicial Review* (1980), offered a justification of judicial review (the judicial invalidation of legislation based on constitutional rights) that was grounded on reinforcing democratic processes. Ely's theory can be seen as an elaboration of a famous footnote in a Supreme Court decision, footnote 4 of *United States* v. *Carolene Products Co.* (1938), where the Court suggested that greater scrutiny of legislation might be warranted where the enactment is directed 'against discrete and insular minorities' and works 'to curtail the operation of those political processes ordinarily to be relied upon to protect minorities'. Ely's theory attempted to give a justification for judicial review that was grounded in, rather than in obvious tension with, democratic values.

See **constitutional theory; countermajoritarian difficulty**

epistemology The study of how we know things, or the justifications for assertions. Questions regarding the nature and foundations of (legal) knowledge will also be connected to issues about the nature of (legal) truth. Thus, questions of epistemology and justification can arise in a number of areas within legal theory, including questions regarding judicial reasoning, legal reasoning, the right answer thesis, etc.

equal concern and respect In Ronald Dworkin's (1931–   ) earlier works, in particular *Taking Rights Seriously* (1977), he emphasized what he described as citizens' rights to be treated by their governments with 'equal concern and respect' (and governments' corresponding duty to offer such treatment). This view is somewhat more precise than a general claim of equality, but still leaves substantial room for debate. For example, commentators have disagreed on whether legislation enforcing moral norms against those who might otherwise be inclined to act differently is consistent with, or in violation of, 'equal concern and respect', and there has been similar controversy over Dworkin's claim that considering people's negative external preferences (preferences that certain other people should *not* obtain their preferences—usually the result of individual animus or group prejudice) within a utilitarian calculus is contrary to 'equal concern and respect' for the disliked individuals or groups.

See equality

equal-treatment feminism *See* feminism

equality A basic concept in moral, political, and legal theory, but about which there is little agreement. Within adjudication, 'treating like cases alike', a central notion of common-law adjudication, leaves open the crucial issue of which considerations are relevant in deciding whether two cases are in fact 'alike'. Similarly, in 'equal treatment' of people, it is a matter of great controversy whether relevant characteristics are quite general (e.g. all rational creatures, all human beings, or all citizens) or more specific (e.g. some particularized test of merit or need), and whether the focus should be on 'outcomes' or 'circumstances'. Thus, both advocates and opponents of beneficial treatment for historically disadvantaged groups ('affirmative action' or 'positive discrimination') refer to 'equality' to justify their positions.

Within political theory, it is often thought that equality conflicts with liberty, that it is a worthy goal, but can be achieved only by significant intrusions into people's freedom to act, or their ability to keep what they have earned.

Some have argued that equality is an empty notion, in the sense that it adds nothing to the view that treatment should be according to specified standards. If everyone with red hair is to get a large bonus, then everyone who is equally red-haired (or equally *not* red-haired) should be, and will be, treated in the same way. Likewise, if one's view is that all citizens of Germany, or all women, or all living human beings deserve treatment in a particular way, all individuals *within the relevant class* would warrant *equal* treatment.

See **affirmative action; baseline problem; equal concern and respect**

equilibrium A term that has different meanings in different contexts within legal philosophy. For example, within game theory, 'equilibrium' usually refers to 'Nash equilibrium', a stable point in a 'non-cooperative game', a situation, resulting from a combination of players' strategies, under which no players could improve their position by changing their strategy. Equilibrium in game theory does not refer, as it does in conventional speech, to a stable result (the term that approximates this in game theory is 'outcome').

The term 'reflective equilibrium' is used within moral theory and theories of justice, indicating an approach to moral reasoning by which moral intuitions and moral theories are regularly tested, one against the other.

See **game theory; Nash equilibrium; reflective equilibrium**

equity   The basic principle of equity refers to the deviations from strict compliance with rules that is required by 'true justice' or 'ideal justice' (as contrasted with 'legal justice'—which is justice according to the strict application of the rules laid down). In particular, it is the idea that in unusual circumstances, the principles of justice (or the reasons and purposes motivating or underlying the rule) may require deviation from the strict application of the rule. The idea of equity in this sense goes back at least to Aristotle (*Nicomachean Ethics*).

A different but related sense of equity comes from the rules and principles developed by the Chancellors of England, later English Courts of Equity, and contemporary courts of equity sitting elsewhere (e.g. the United States). Recourse could be had to the Chancellor or to courts of equity to relieve parties from injustices caused by the strict application of common-law rules. Over time, (1) the courts of equity developed standards and principles whose application could seem as strict or as blind as those of the common-law rules; and (2) in both England and the United States, law and equity are no longer separated, in the sense that individual courts are empowered to apply both kinds of standards and to grant both kinds of remedies.

See **Aristotle; justice**

essentialism   Generally, a term of criticism, claiming that others falsely believe that some category has a fixed nature, when in fact the category has the shape it does due to human choices. Among critical theorists, the focus of arguments regarding essentialism is usually on the extent to which the sexes, or various racial or ethnic groups, could be said to have a basic nature, or a distinct way of thinking, analysing, or experiencing the world. Within analytical debates, questions about essentialism are often raised regarding whether it makes sense to talk about 'the nature of law' or 'the nature of property', or the like. 'Essentialism' is often contrasted with 'nominalism' or 'social construction'.

See **critical race theory; feminist legal theory; intersectionality; queer theory**

ethical (legal) positivism *See* legal positivism

evil regimes While arguably common in real life, pervasively evil regimes make only infrequent appearances in legal theory, usually in questions about the obligation to obey the laws (whether a moral obligation ever extends to the rules promulgated by evil regimes), and about the criteria for 'law' (whether the rules of pervasively evil regimes can be 'law', or fail to qualify as law because of their iniquity).

In the *Harvard Law Review* in 1958, H. L. A. Hart (1907–92) and Lon Fuller (1902–78) debated whether the rules in force in Nazi Germany should be called 'law' or not. Hart argued that nothing is gained in moral reasoning and much may be lost in clarity to confuse the conclusion 'valid law but evil' with the conclusion 'not valid law'. Fuller's position was that there were forms of guidance so lacking in the procedural forms and protections of law that it was appropriate to conclude that those acts of power and arbitrary will were 'not law'.

Another response to this debate was formulated later by Ronald Dworkin (1931–) ('Legal Theory and the Problem of Sense' (1987)): that we can understand the point of the assertions on both sides—that the Nazis *had law*, in the sense that their institutions and procedures were roughly similar to the institutions and procedures in our own legal systems; and that the Nazis *did not have law*, in the sense that their rules were so unjust, both in content and as applied, that they did not create the moral obligations that the legal processes of more just regimes normally do. (Dworkin also argued that judges in pervasively evil regimes may have a moral obligation to lie regarding what the law requires.)

See obligation to obey the law

evolutionary psychology The belief that a variety of traits or inclinations are largely or entirely due to our genes, or that a particular trait or inclination has developed, survived, or become dominant because of its evolutionary advantage (most likely its advantage at some point in our distant past). This general view, which once went under the label 'sociobiology' (and, under that label, was associated with the American scientist Edward Osborne Wilson (1929–)), is frequently held to have implications for law and legal theory, regarding issues of culpability (should one be punished for what one 'could not help', being genetically predetermined?) or to the related question of how amenable certain behaviours are to reform through state action. Many commentators take a cautious approach in this area: without in any way denying the great importance of genetics to human behaviour, it is extremely complicated to determine the level of genetic determination, and tricky to ground significant policy recommendations on the uncertain data in this area.

ex ante v. ex post Looking at issues from a perspective earlier in time (*ex ante*) as opposed to a perspective after the event (*ex post*). The difference in perspective is often emphasized by law and economics theorists, and seems especially salient in discussing optimal remedies. For example, in tort law cases, the remedies that may seem optimal after the fact (e.g. because they fully compensate an injured party for that party's losses) may be less than optimal taking into account the 'before-the-fact' perspective of either the tortfeasor or the victim (or future actors), for it provides an inefficient level of incentives for one or both to take precautions. The result which may be fairest to the parties to the dispute, viewing their facts in retrospect, may vary from the rule which will have the best consequences for other parties in the future.

See law and economics

exclusionary reasons *See* reasons for action

exclusive legal positivism *See* legal positivism

expressive theory of punishment *See* punishment

external preferences In some of Ronald Dworkin's (1931–) earlier works (e.g. *Taking Rights Seriously* (1976)), he offered a critique of utilitarianism that focused on the fact that this approach in principle takes into account all individual preferences, including unsavoury preferences. 'External preferences' are preferences regarding the assignment of goods or opportunities to others. External preferences we might not want to take into account in evaluating social policies might include preferences based on individual malice or group prejudice.

See utilitarianism

external scepticism A term used by Ronald Dworkin (1931–), in some of his later work (e.g. *Law's Empire* (1986)), to respond to critics who doubted the ability to speak of 'right answers' for difficult legal questions. Dworkin, rejecting such global claims, distinguishes between those who offer doubts and questions *within* a practice (like legal or judicial decision-making) and those who challenge the legitimacy or foundations of the whole practice. The former Dworkin calls 'internal scepticism' and treats as an appropriate response; the latter Dworkin calls 'external scepticism' and rejects as unhelpful and inappropriate.

See internal scepticism

externalities A term from economic analysis that refers to effects a transaction or activity has on those other than the parties to the transaction or the main actor(s). Though such effects can be either positive or negative, and theorists will refer to 'positive externalities' and 'negative externalities', sometimes the term 'externalities' is used to refer only to the latter.

The importance of externalities is that some theorists believe that the negative effects of transactions and activities otherwise consensual might justify state intervention. The Coase theorem was an important response to that view, arguing that it may be wrong to view social costs in terms of 'externalities' and that in many circumstances state intervention will not affect which activities occur.

The classic example of a (negative) externality, and the one prominent in the views Ronald Coase (1910–) criticized, is that of pollution: that an industrial activity might impose a cost or harm on its neighbours that the activity itself does not pay (unless that externality is 'internalized' by a fine, a tax, or a tort liability that corresponds to the level of harm imposed).

See Coase theorem; market failure

F

fairness A basic term within morality, indicating morally appropriate treatment, though what is required for treatment to be fair, and what deviates from that requirement, is pervasively controversial. Within legal theory, fairness is sometimes put forward as the key concept for understanding justice, as in John Rawls's (1921–2002) theory of justice. Rawls's theory, which he sometimes labelled as 'justice as fairness', analysed justice in terms of which principles hypothetical bargainers, ignorant of their place in society or their values, would choose for organizing society.

Within law and economics, some welfare economics theorists (e.g. Louis Kaplow (1956–   ) and Steven Shavell (1946–   )) use 'fairness' as a contrast to 'welfare', where 'fairness' stands for all claims of justice or morality not grounded in the preferences or welfare of individuals.

See **justice as fairness**

feminist legal theory An effort to bring insights from feminist theory to discussions about the nature of law and the need for legal reform. There are many variations of feminist legal theory, most of which share a focus on the allegedly patriarchal nature of legal doctrine or the application of law—that is, the way law purportedly favours the interests of men over those of women and works to maintain a hierarchical structure in which men have more power than women.

One early division within feminist legal theory was between 'equality' and 'difference' feminism. These were alternative ways to analyse the different treatment of men and women within law (and within society), and they led to somewhat different recommendations for legal (and societal) reform. Equality feminists believe that there will be justice in the treatment of the sexes when women are treated the same as men, in the sense of having identical treatment. Equality feminism is behind the idea of 'equal pay for equal work', as well as (more controversially) movements to get rid of provisions that seem to give favourable treatment to women. (Many feminists argue that provisions that purport to give favourable treatment to women frequently act against women's interests, by reinforcing stereotypes of women's weakness or their place being primarily in the home, or by making it more difficult or more expensive to hire female workers.)

Difference theorists argue that treating men 'the same' requires consideration for the ways that men and women are different. Identical treatment or identical standards are inappropriate, they argue, because it usually involves asking women to meet male standards (as exemplified in height or strength requirements) or in some other way 'be like a man' (e.g. to be willing to work long hours while leaving the care of children to others). The contrast between equality and difference feminists is perhaps sharpest in debates about maternity leave and pregnancy discrimination acts.

Cultural feminism (also known as 'relational feminism') asserts the importance of care and maintaining relationships instead of, or alongside claims of rights and autonomy, as essential parts of moral analysis. This approach, in large part, derives from Carol Gilligan's work (in particular, *In a Different Voice: Psychological Theory and Women's Development* (1982)), in which she argued that women tend to think morally differently from men—and that this approach is at least as important and valuable as more traditional (rights or justice-centred) approaches to moral thinking. Cultural feminism argues that the law currently reflects a particularly male view of what is important and what is experienced as a harm, and should be reformed to include female values of care-giving and the protection of relationships.

Catharine MacKinnon's (1946–   ) distinctive alternative approach to feminism has sometimes been labelled 'dominance feminism'. This position involves a rejection of equality feminism, difference feminism, and cultural feminism. The argument is that modern Western society involves pervasive oppression of women by men, and fighting that domination must be the focus of feminism. According to this approach, equality feminism is wrong because it legitimates asking women to meet male standards. According to MacKinnon, difference feminism also, to some extent, makes the error of legitimating a male standard of comparison (if women are 'different', it is relative to a male standard); and cultural feminism is also in error in that it mistakes long-term consequences of the oppression of women for women's 'real nature'. Under MacKinnon's approach, women's 'difference voice' (different values and different approaches to moral reasoning) are seen not as intrinsic, or intrinsically valuable, but rather as the result of domination—an adaptation to a subjugated state (analogous to Friedrich Nietzsche's

(1844–1900) discussion of 'slave morality' and Marxist arguments about 'false consciousness').

One can also find other variations of feminist legal theory that attempt to combine feminist legal theory with the insights or approaches of different schools of thought: e.g. 'postmodernist feminist legal theory' and 'critical feminist race theory', though there are sometimes internal tensions arising from these combinations (e.g. postmodernism's rejection of 'essentialism' and 'grand theory' may be in tension with much of what feminist legal theorists have espoused).

See discrimination; essentialism; gender v. sex; patriarchy; pornography; postmodernism

fit A concept that plays a central, if not always clearly defined, role within Ronald Dworkin's (1931–) approach to law. According to this approach, judges deciding cases—and other legal actors or commentators trying to determine what the law is on some matter—are to consider the 'data' of past official actions (statutes, judicial decisions, constitutional provisions, etc.), and theories that might 'explain' those actions. In comparing possible theories, they are to consider both how well the theories 'fit' the data, and the theory's moral value.

Under this approach, fit is to be balanced against moral value in judging which theory of the law is correct. How much weight fit was to be given in the balance is itself an interpretive question, with the answer probably varying from area to area (e.g. greater in commercial activity, less with civil liberties). Additionally, Dworkin sometimes referred to a 'threshold level of fit' that a theory would have to meet to be acceptable (to be an interpretation of the materials at all).

See coherence theory; interpretive theory of law

formal justice See justice

formalism The term is usually used in a pejorative sense, to describe analysis (in either articles or judicial opinions) that moves mechanically or automatically from category or concept to conclusion, without consideration of policy, morality, or practice. The argument against formalism (similar approaches were also sometimes criticized under the labels 'mechanical jurisprudence' and 'conceptualism') was that the move from category to legal conclusion was both unwarranted and unwise. Formalism was particularly the chosen target of the American legal realists writing in the early decades of the twentieth century.

Occasionally modern theorists will describe their own work as supporting 'formalism', but they almost always mean something quite different from what the legal realists were attacking. Sometimes what is meant by this more positive use of 'formalism' is what others call 'textualism'—an assertion that statutes or constitutions should be interpreted according to their plain meaning, and not (where this would be different) according to their underlying purposes or their drafters' intentions. Still other theorists use 'formalism' to refer to a cluster of views that includes not only textualism, but also a preference for rules over standards, interpretation (especially of constitutional provisions, but also, sometimes, of statutes) according to the lawmakers' original intentions, and/or a belief that doctrinal areas of law should be interpreted in ways that are consistent with their 'essence' or 'basic form'. A variation of this last positive view of 'formalism' is the use of the term to describe the way that the use of rules to make decisions and run institutions necessarily constrains the choices of decision-makers, a constraint that has advantages as well as disadvantages.

See **adjudication; American legal realism; autonomy of law; conceptualism; textualism**

Foucault, Michel   A French philosopher (1926–84) who, in the course of works on the history of ideas and social institutions (e.g. *The Order of Things* (1966) and *Discipline and Punish* (1975)) analyzed the way that power defines reason and pervades social relationships. Foucault's work does not discuss law extensively, and when it does the references frequently equate law with a centralized view of power that Foucault expressly rejected. However, his views about the complicated relationships of power and knowledge—views strongly influenced by the works of Friedrich Nietzsche (1844–1900), and that also have been compared to structuralism, though Foucault himself rejected that description—would seem to have applications to legal theory, in particular critical theories that present the legal system as distorted by social interests. A number of commentators have assayed such applications, with varying success.

See **Nietzsche, Friedrich**

Frank, Jerome N.   Jerome New Frank (1889–1957) was one of the most prominent thinkers in the American legal realist movement, with his best-known works including *Law and the Modern Mind* (1930) and *Courts on Trial* (1949). He was also a Chairman of the Securities and Exchange Commission and a federal appellate court judge.

Frank's approach is exemplified by the title of one of his articles, 'Are Judges Human?' (*University of Pennsylvania Law Review*, 1931). Frank urged lawyers and legal academics to focus on the myriad factors beyond the abstract legal rules that cause judges to decide cases the way they do—from various forms of prejudice or bias to psychological proclivities (Frank attributed judges' belief in an unchanging and infallible law to 'father-worship'). He also emphasized the importance of facts—the uncertainty in their determination and the large possibility of error—in success or failure at trial. This uncertainty in the determination of facts at trial Frank sometimes called 'fact scepticism'—to be contrasted with the 'rule scepticism' that was advocated by some of the other American legal realists.

See **American legal realism**

free law movement An approach to law whose adherents were primarily German thinkers at the end of the nineteenth century and the first decades of the twentieth century, but whose influence was arguably quite wide, perhaps affecting strongly the ideas of the American legal realists. The free law movement adopted ideas of François Gény (1861–1959) and Rudolf von Jhering (1818–92), theorists in the movement, who argued that the interpretation of German codified law will inevitably have gaps in its application, and that the judge should draw on knowledge of society or social consciousness in deciding cases. Among those associated with the movement were the Austrian legal sociologist Eugen Ehrlich (1862–1922) and the German jurist Hermann Kantorowicz (1877–1940).

See **American legal realism; Gény, François; Jhering, Rudolf von**

free rider A phrase used in economic analysis, particularly game theory, to refer to one party receiving the benefits of another party's efforts without paying for them. This is particularly problematic for public goods where (1) the effort of many is required to create or achieve the good; and (2) once the good is created or achieved, it cannot (easily) be confined to those who helped bring it about. The discussion of the free-rider problem is thus often connected with the problem of collective action.

While examples of the problem of collective action and free riders are discussed in a wide variety of classical thinkers (from Adam Smith (1723–90) to David Hume (1711–76) to Vilfredo Pareto (1848–1923)), the problem was arguably not discussed in general terms until the work of Mancur Olson (1932–98), in particular, his *The Logic of Collective Action: Public Goods and the Theory of Groups* (1971).

See collective action problem; game theory; public goods

Fuller, Lon L. Lon Luvois Fuller (1902–78) was an important figure in American Contract Law (where his casebook was the first to incorporate the insights of American legal realism, by beginning with remedies rather than contract formation) and alternative dispute resolution. Within legal philosophy, he was an early and insightful critic of some aspects of American legal realism, but his greatest influence came from his procedural natural law theory and his criticisms of legal positivism.

Fuller criticized legal positivism (perhaps unfairly) as treating law merely as an object for quasi-scientific study rather than as a process or a function; and as portraying law as 'one-way projection of authority', when it is better understood in terms of reciprocity between officials and citizens. His most important work, *The Morality of Law* (1964), puts forward an alternative vision, which Fuller characterizes as 'secular natural law'.

For Fuller, law is not merely an object or entity, to be studied dispassionately under a microscope; law is a human project, with the implied moral goal of allowing people to coexist and co-operate within society. It is not merely that law has an ideal, but that the law cannot truly be understood without understanding the (*moral*) ideal towards which it is striving (there are many human activities, from painting to jogging to boxing, that are hard to understand unless one knows the objective or ideal towards which the participants are striving). Law is the 'enterprise of subjecting human conduct to the governance of rules'. Law thus is a *process*, to be contrasted with the slightly different process of *managerial direction* (the latter can be specific rather than general, and is more attuned to attaining the objectives of the 'rulemaker'—as contrasted with law, whose purpose is primarily helping citizens to coexist, co-operate, and thrive—though, even with managerial direction, it is unwise to make rules that oppress or confuse).

Fuller's phrase, the 'enterprise of subjecting human conduct to the governance of rules', and a close examination of his eight criteria for the 'internal morality of law', both indicate that his focus, in those discussions, was on legislation. Fuller's approach to law can be seen as rejecting the notion that 'law' is best understood as an object that can be analysed down to its component parts. Instead, he would argue, law is better understood as being the official response to particular kinds of problems—in particular the guidance and co-ordination of citizens' actions in society.

Fuller argues that legal positivism sees laws mostly as a 'one-way projection of authority'—one party giving orders, and other parties complying. This is most obvious in John Austin's work, with its reduction of law to the commands of a sovereign, but later legal positivists are arguably not that different. This view of law, Fuller states, is a basic misunderstanding: for so much of law, so much of a fully functioning legal system, depends on there being a *reciprocity of duties between citizens and lawgivers*: 'the existence of a relatively stable reciprocity of expectations between lawgiver and subject is part of the very idea of a functioning legal order'. Only when citizens and officials co-operate, each fulfilling his or her own functions, can law work. For example, officials promise, expressly or implicitly, to enforce the rules as promulgated and to make the demands on citizens reasonable and consistent; to the extent that officials violate these duties, the smooth running of society will begin to break down.

Fuller's affirmative analysis develops from his evaluation of the shortcomings of legal positivism. In the place of legal positivism, he offers an analysis that focuses on law as a process, one that emphasizes the importance of the interaction between officials and citizens, and that makes more transparent the way in which a legal order can be instrumental to the attainment of other goods.

Fuller offers a list of eight 'principles of legality', that would serve as criteria for testing the minimal duties of a government, and also set the objective of excellence towards which a good government would strive. Fuller's eight criteria are:

- the rules must be general
- the rules must be promulgated
- retroactive rulemaking and application must be minimized
- the rules must be understandable
- the rules should not be contradictory
- the rules should not be impossible to obey
- the rules should remain relatively constant through time
- there should be a congruence between the rules as announced and as applied

Some of Fuller's eight principles are best seen as minimum requirements—for example, in the case of laws that require the impossible or contradict one another. Others, such as the minimizing of retroactive legislation, the full promulgation of laws, and the understandability of the laws, are best seen as ideals to which legal systems should always strive, but which may not always be achieved.

Rule systems that substantially comply with the eight requirements are '*legal* systems', *in the sense* that they are likely to succeed in guiding the behaviour of their citizens; rule systems that do not substantially comply with the eight requirements are not legal systems, as they are unlikely to be able to guide citizen behaviour.

A number of critics, most prominently H. L. A. Hart (1907–92), have objected to calling Fuller's eight criteria 'morality'—arguing that they are, at best, merely efficacy or efficiency, a morally neutral value as important to evil officials and governments as to virtuous ones (one could easily, Hart famously notes, have an '[internal] morality of poisoning'). If a legal system has evil ends, such as Nazi Germany or Apartheid South Africa, then following Fuller's guidelines will allow the government to be more efficient in achieving those evil ends.

While Fuller's argument for the moral status of his eight criteria is not as clear as it might be, the following arguments have been offered, each of which has some basis in Fuller's own work. (1) As others have noted, 'playing by the rules of the game'—or playing the game fairly, is itself an integral part of justice, even if by no means all of it (by analogy, many people believe that it is of some moral value to keep one's promise, even if it was a promise to do something bad). For example, if retroactive lawmaking is to be criticized, it is not at the level of efficacy, but at the level of justice and morality. (2) Certain kinds of evil are arguably less likely when proper procedures are followed: for example, courts may be more likely to come up with just decisions when judges know that they must give public reasons for their decisions (certain forms of corruption may be hard to rationalize). Also, as one commentator has observed, 'a wicked government's decision to act within the procedural constraints of the rule of law affords the general population at least some measure of security' (Robert P. George, *In Defense of Natural Law* (1999)). (3) Fuller once wrote that he could not believe that a legal system that was procedurally just would not also be substantively just. Certainly, a correlation exists (at least in the negative sense that countries that care little for one are likely to care little for the other), but there have also been countries that have promulgated evil in an efficient and meticulous way. On most accounts, Fuller's faith in a strong connection between procedural and substantive justice is an optimistic, but peripheral part of his theory.

See **Hart, H. L. A.; internal morality of law; legal process; natural law theory; procedural natural law; rule of law**

functional kind A category that is defined by a shared function (as contrasted with a shared structure). Some legal theorists, e.g. Michael Moore (1943–   ), have suggested that law might be best thought of as a functional kind.

functionalism The term 'functionalism' is used to describe those who equate 'law' with the serving of certain social functions. The term is sometimes used narrowly to describe a certain school of thought within the sociology or anthropology of law. At other times, the term is used more loosely, e.g. in describing some of the American legal realists (e.g. Felix Cohen (1907–53)) who emphasized a focus on the roles law plays in social life, as a contrast with what the realists saw as the more metaphysical view of legal formalism.

See **American legal realism; law and society**

fundamental contradiction An idea introduced by Duncan Kennedy (1942–   ) in his 1979 *Buffalo Law Review* article, 'The Structure of Blackstone's *Commentaries*', which was influential among some theorists within the critical legal studies movement. The argument, roughly, was that our strong desire simultaneously to join with others and to remain separate and independent from them creates a 'fundamental contradiction' that is reflected in tensions between individualism and altruism, and perhaps also in a tension between regulating behaviour through rules and through standards. These contradictions were said to be pervasive, making the choice between potential legal doctrines and legal rulings irrational or indeterminate. The argument has some similarities to arguments for legal indeterminacy derived from structuralism or deconstruction.

A number of critics have pointed out that (1) the 'fundamental contradiction' is simply asserted in the 1979 article; no proof, or even significant argument is offered for it; and (2) on its own, without further theoretical stage-setting of one kind or another, the 'fundamental contradiction' is probably inadequate to ground the specific or systematic claims about the nature of law that are sometimes made in its name. Kennedy himself 'renounced' the fundamental contradiction in a 1984 publication.

See **critical legal studies; scepticism; structuralism**

G

Gadamer, Hans-Georg German philosopher (1900–2002) whose most important work, *Truth and Method* (1960), contributed to modern hermeneutic theory. In particular, Gadamer argued that the interpretation of texts is done in a context in which both the authors and the readers are affected by the culture in which they are situated. According to Gadamer, we are all historically conditioned, and interpretation involves an effort to find a 'fusion of horizons' between the two different perspectives. Like other writers within the hermeneutic tradition, Gadamer has been cited and discussed by some theorists working on legal interpretation, but it has never been obvious how to translate Gadamer's abstract observations directly into useful prescriptions or insights for the interpretation of legal texts. Gadamer raises in a sophisticated way the basic problem of legal interpretation: the application of rules across time, when the problems have changed, as has the way of viewing the world.

Gadamer's work has also been relied upon by those (in the legal academy and elsewhere) who challenge the quest for objective or timeless truth and the objective of determinate meaning in interpretation, though Gadamer's claims at this more general level are subject to many of the standard objections raised against historicism and relativism.

Gadamer's approach to hermeneutics differed sharply from that of contemporary theorists in the area—e.g. that of the Italian hermeneutic theorist, Emilio Betti (1890–1968).

See **Betti, Emilio; hermeneutics**

game theory Game theory is a branch or variation of rational choice theory that analyses the choices and actions of actors who are aware that their decisions affect one another. In such circumstances, decisions are interactive and 'strategic'. (While aspects of game theory predate their work, the development of game theory is often attributed to John von Neumann (1903–57) and Oskar Morgenstern (1902–77), in particular, their 1944 book, *The Theory of Games and Economic Behaviour*.)

For the purposes of legal philosophy, game theory is significant in that it has provided an alternative for theorists who would otherwise analyse legal and policy issues in terms of classical economic theory. Additionally, some political theories and theories of morality and justice (e.g. that of David Gauthier (1932–)) are grounded in game-theoretical analyses.

Game theory has also been applied to issues of law and policy to try to use the idea of strategic behaviour to analyse the effects of current legal rules, and to determine how alternative legal or non-legal forms of regulation might better achieve social purposes.

> *See* bilateral monopoly; decision theory; equilibrium; free rider; Nash equilibrium; prisoner's dilemma; signalling; social choice theory; strategic behaviour

gaps in the law *See* legal gaps

gender v. sex Some theorists, including a number of prominent feminist, critical, and postmodernist theorists, distinguish between certain biological, phenotypical, and genetic attributes on the one hand, and the social category on the other, arguing that the second is largely socially or culturally constructed.

> *See* feminist legal theory; social construction

Gény, François French legal theorist (1861–1959) who argued, contrary to theorists who thought that French law was largely determined by the text of the Civil Code, that there would inevitably be gaps in the law not filled by the formal logic of the law, and that there thus was (and should be) substantial judicial creativity in the development of the law. Gény argued for legal interpretation in the light of 'social exigencies'. Gény's work influenced and overlapped that of the German free law movement.

> *See* free law movement

Gierke, Otto von Otto Friedrich von Gierke (1841–1921) was a German theorist, whose work on associations and association law was influential both on practical questions of legal regulation and on more metaphysical questions regarding whether collectives (including guilds and commercial corporations) can or should be treated as 'real' entities for ethical purposes as well as legal ones. Gierke's writings on *Genossenschaft* ('free legal association') are grounded in a reading of history as an ongoing struggle between such associations and imposed authority (*Herrschaft*).

Gramsci, Antonio Antonio Gramsci (1891–1937) was an Italian theorist working within the Marxist and Communist tradition. His ideas of 'legitimation' and 'hegemony' have been influential among critical theorists, especially some of the adherents of critical legal studies. The basic notion is that the force of ideas can cause the oppressed to accept as legitimate the structures and practices that oppress them. This argument offers a solution to the puzzle or paradox (from the perspective of traditional Left thought) of why workers and the poor often seem to support institutions and practices that (the argument goes) are acting against the interests of those classes.

See **critical legal studies; legitimation; Marxist theories of law**

Grotius, Hugo Hugo Grotius (1583–1645) was a Dutch philosopher of law whose work played a pivotal role in the natural law tradition and the development of international law. His volume, *The Laws of War and Peace* (*De iure belli ac pacis*) (1625) was an effort to rethink the principles of natural law in the light of the variety of views different people and different societies held regarding politics and religion. Grotius attempted to find principles of natural law grounded in reason, that people of different faiths could accept, and that could mediate across national boundaries. Modern international law is often thought to derive from the principles Grotius offered.

For some, Grotius's importance to the history of natural law theory comes primarily from a passing comment that seemed to declare the independence of natural-law principles from religion: 'What we have been saying would have a degree of validity even if we should concede that which cannot be conceded without the utmost wickedness, that there is no God'. The importance of this passing comment to the development of secular natural law (and natural rights) theories remains a matter of controversy (for example, some commentators assert that Grotius's comment was not particularly original, with similar statements having been made by a number of earlier theorists).

See **international law; natural law theory; Pufendorf, Samuel; Suárez, Francisco**

Grundnorm *See* **Basic Norm**

gunman situation writ large The phrase comes from H. L. A. Hart's (1907–92) criticism of John Austin's (1790–1859) command theory of law. The argument is that a theory of law that reduces law to power and sanctions will be unable to distinguish 'law' from a rule of terror by armed gangsters. Hart's point does not depend on our seeing all, or even most, legal systems as legitimate, but it does depend on there often being *citizens* or *officials* that see their own legal systems as legitimate, and therefore a legal theory that can take account of this 'acceptance' of a legal system by its citizens is, for that reason, a better theory.

Some have seen Hart's gunman critique as an argument that a theory of law must be able to *explain* the legitimacy of legal systems, and a few of those commentators have gone on to complain that Hart's own theory (law as combination of primary and secondary rules) no more guarantees moral or political legitimacy than did Austin's commands of a sovereign. However, this critique is probably based on a misunderstanding of the objectives of Hart and other legal positivists: to offer a morally neutral theory of law, leaving the moral evaluation of individual laws and whole legal systems to other forms of theorizing.

See acceptance; Austin, John; Hart, H. L. A.; legal positivism

H

Hägerström, Axel *See* Scandinavian legal realism

Hale, Robert L. Robert Lee Hale (1884–1969) was a American legal realist and progressive economist, who, though perhaps less well known than contemporaries such as Karl Llewellyn or Jerome Frank, has had a continuing influence on later critical theorists. His attacks on laissez-faire economics, in such articles as 'Coercion and Distribution in a Supposedly Non-coercive State' (*Political Science Quarterly* (1923)), made him a favourite among the later critical legal theorists. Hale's argument for the pervasive presence of coercion even in market transactions was the ground for later critical legal studies attacks on 'the public–private distinction'.

See **American legal realism; critical legal studies; duress; public–private distinction**

Hand formula A formula that purports to summarize the rule of negligence, put forward by the highly regarded American judge, Learned Hand, in the case, *United States* v. *Carroll Towing*, 159 F.2d 169, 173 (2nd Cir. 1947). Under this formula, one who causes harm is liable only if $B < PL$, where B is the cost of the precaution that would have been needed to prevent the harm, P is the probability that the harm would occur, and L is the extent of the loss.

See **law and economics; tort law**

hard cases Within discussions about judicial decision-making, and the related issue of whether there is always (or usually, or sometimes, or never) a right answer to legal questions, many scholars distinguish between 'hard cases' and 'easy cases'. Hard cases are those in which competently trained and thoughtful lawyers or judges might come to different conclusions about the result. In a sense, the difficulty or easiness of a case could be seen along a few variables: the extent to which all (competently trained) people would agree about the outcome, and, for any given evaluator, the quickness with which the conclusion is reached and the confidence or certainty with which the conclusion is maintained.

A standard view, supported by, among many others, H. L. A. Hart (1907–92), is that in easy cases there is a clear right answer, but in (many) hard cases, there may be no right answer, and judges may have discretion. Ronald Dworkin (1931–), the chief proponent of the view that there is always (or almost always) a right answer to legal questions, at first accepted the standard distinction between easy questions and hard questions, but later held that the process of judicial decision-making should be the same for both kinds of cases.

See **open texture; right answer thesis**

harm principle   The term originates from John Stuart Mill's (1806–73) pamphlet, *On Liberty* (1859), in which he wrote: 'The only purpose for which power can rightfully be exercised over any member of a civilised community against his will is to prevent harm to others.' Mill proffered this principle in the context of an argument for a limited role for government (and society) in the enforcement of morality, and an argument for a strong right of individual liberty. In this context, the justification of government regulation of private behaviour based on preventing harm to others is contrasted with justifications of regulation based either on the enforcement of morality or the protection of individuals from their own harmful choices (paternalism).

Various challenges to Mill's view have been raised, both at the time he was writing and more recently. One line of argument, sometimes labelled 'perfectionism', and associated with James Fitzjames Stephen (1829–94) in Mill's time and Robert P. George and Joseph Raz (1939–) more recently, asserts that it *is* part of the government's legitimate role to promote moral behaviour and deter immoral behaviour among its citizens.

A second line of argument, associated with Patrick Arthur Devlin (1905–92), urged that societies have a right to protect themselves by enforcing their existing conventional morality (what people *believe to be* morally correct, whether it be so or not), for that is a major cohesive force in keeping society together.

In recent decades, H. L. A. Hart (1907–92) and Joel Feinberg (1926–2004) have both argued for an extension of the harm principle to cover certain forms of offence: that it is legitimate for the government to restrict individual freedom for the purpose of preventing offence to others through public actions. This extension is meant to cover matters of public decency and public order, but not the regulation of private behaviour simply on the basis that some might be offended by the mere thought of what others are doing in the privacy of their own homes.

See **Devlin, Patrick; Mill, John Stuart; morality, critical v. conventional; morality, legal enforcement of; offence principle; Stephen, James Fitzjames**

Hart, H. L. A. Herbert Lionel Adolphus Hart (1907–92) was a central figure in the revival of legal positivism, and, more generally, of English-language analytical jurisprudence. H. L. A. Hart had a successful practice as a Chancery barrister, and worked for military intelligence before returning to Oxford as a philosophy tutor. In 1952, he was elected to the Chair in Jurisprudence at Oxford (which he held until 1968). Hart's 1958 exchange with Lon L. Fuller (1902–78) in *The Harvard Law Review* set the terms for the legal positivism–natural law theory debate for many years. Hart's most influential work, *The Concept of Law*, was published in 1961; a second edition, published after Hart's death, contained a Postscript that clarifies and modifies some of Hart's positions (largely through a response to Ronald Dworkin's (1931–) criticisms).

Along with his work on the nature of law, Hart also published important works on the nature of rights, theories of punishment, and causation in the law.

Theory of law, legal positivism

Hart's legal theory developed from John Austin's (1790–1859) more reductive command theory, by adding a hermeneutic turn (the internal point of view) and an emphasis on the different types of law (primary v. secondary, duty-imposing v. power-conferring). His portrait of legal systems centred on a 'rule of recognition', a set of criteria in existence (in force) because accepted by the system's officials, while all other rules within the system are valid because of their derivation from this rule.

Hart built his theory of law from simple distinctions, grounded in social practices and ordinary language regarding those practices: e.g. the difference between acting out of habit and acting according to a rule, and the difference between being obliged and having an obligation. From such distinctions, Hart emphasized that what is distinctive about rules is that they involve a critical attitude by those who accept them— a willingness to criticize others, or oneself, for deviation from the standard. Hart argued that Austin's command theory of law missed this 'internal aspect' of rules and of law: the importance of the rules being accepted as binding standards, at least by the officials of the system.

While Hart discouraged a focus on the question, 'What is law?' (considering such inquiries to be motivated by less metaphysical concerns: the relationship between law and morality, the extent to which law is a matter of rules, and the relationship between law and orders backed by threats), he did offer a view about the defining characteristics of a legal system: that there is general compliance with legal rules by the citizens combined with officials in the system taking an internal perspective towards the system's rule of recognition.

Hart emphasized the (conceptual or necessary) separation of law and morality as the key tenet of legal positivism. In his 1958 debate with Lon Fuller, he reversed a common criticism of legal positivism, and argued that positivism, with its separation of the questions 'is it law?' and 'is it moral?' is *more likely*, not less likely, than natural law theory to lead to clear moral evaluation of law, and resistance to unjust rules and evil regimes. While this probably overstates the case (legal theories probably have little effect on people's ability to discern or resist evil), it was a necessary corrective to those who had falsely equated legal positivism with amoral deference to power.

It is hard to overstate Hart's significance for English-language legal theory, particularly that part of legal theory focused on the nature of law. He added new life to the approach known as legal positivism. Before Hart, many people dismissed legal positivism as unpersuasive on its own terms, and as related in some way to the discredited view of legal reasoning known as legal formalism. Other people equated positivism with a kind of amorality which, it was asserted, made lawyers and citizens less likely to resist the rise of the Nazis and other evil regimes. Hart raised the sophistication and power of legal positivist theory by inserting ideas borrowed from ordinary language philosophy, the later works of Ludwig Wittgenstein (1889–1951), and hermeneutics. He also fought the equation of positivism with conservatism and with acquiescence to evil both by emphasizing the law reform credentials of such early legal positivists as Jeremy Bentham (1748–1832) and by arguing (not entirely persuasively) that positivism might be better able than natural law theory to allow judges and citizens to resist wicked legal regimes.

Hart did not deny that there is a significant overlap between law and morality—e.g. that morality has shaped the development of law, that it was properly considered in the interpretation of existing law, and that there is an ongoing need for the moral criticism of law. Additionally,

Hart put forward the idea of 'the minimum content of natural law': that taking into account current general circumstances (e.g. limited resources and human vulnerability), any society whose moral or legal norms did not offer certain minimal protections (e.g. protections against violence and some property rights), at least to a significant minority of the population, would not long survive.

Most contemporary English-language legal positivism derives from Hart's work, while legal positivist theories in other countries tend to derive from the work of Hans Kelsen (1881–1973). Some of the surface similarities of the theories of Hart and Kelsen operate only to disguise the sharp differences in their origin and methodology.

Other areas

Long before the publication of *The Concept of Law*, Hart offered two suggestive ideas about the nature of law that he later abandoned: (1) that the 'defeasibility' of legal concepts was central to understanding the nature of law; and (2) that legal concepts (e.g. 'valid contract') might be best understood as 'illocutionary acts'—not descriptions of what is the case, but speech acts (by judges) that change the legal or moral status.

Hart advocated the will theory as the best approach to understanding legal rights. Will theories emphasize the ability of right-holders to claim or waive another party's duty to act (or to demand or waive a remedy for failure to perform the duty in question). While noting that an interest theory of rights (equating rights with the legal protection of a party's interests) might better account for some aspects of our usage (e.g. using 'right' in contexts where the holder has no choice in the matter, as with inalienable rights and infants who lack legal capacity), Hart believed that a will theory better captured the way legal rights give their holders small realms of sovereignty.

On the enforcement of morality, Hart generally supported John Stuart Mill's (1806–73) view that the government should not use the criminal law to regulate actions that do not harm other people. Hart's views, published in *Law, Liberty, and Morality* (1962), were primarily a response to Lord Patrick Devlin's (1905–92) argument that a society has an interest, as a kind of self-defence, in defending the morality that undergirds that society. In the course of the critique, Hart emphasized the difference between conventional morality (what people happen to believe about how one ought to act) and critical morality (the truth about how one ought to act). Hart questioned what interest society could have in enforcing the current conventional morality.

Hart's social theory of rules—equating the existence of the rule with social practices referring to the rules as grounds for justification or criticism—has been subject to significant criticisms, criticisms Hart largely accepted in the Postscript to *The Concept of Law*.

> *See* acceptance; Austin, J. L.; Austin, John; defeasibility; Fuller, Lon L.; gunman situation writ large; harm principle; hermeneutics; interest theory (of rights); internal point of view; Kelsen, Hans; legal positivism; morality, critical v. conventional; morality, legal enforcement of; natural law, minimum content of; natural law theory; open texture; punishment; reductionist theories of law; rule of recognition; rules, practice theory of; *Verstehen* approach; will theory (of rights); Winch, Peter

Hart, Henry M., Jr. Henry M. Hart (1904–69) is best known within legal theory for his work on the casebook, *The Legal Process: Basic Problems in the Making and Application of Law* (tentative edn. 1958), co-authored with Albert M. Sacks (1920–91). *The Legal Process* was the basic text of the legal process school. Hart was also an influential figure in other areas of American law—in particular, in the study of federal court jurisdiction (where he wrote seminal articles and, with Herbert Wechsler (1909–2000), a widely used casebook), and also American constitutional law.

> *See* legal process; Sacks, Albert M.; Wechsler, Herbert

hate speech Expression whose primary content is derogatory references to a particular (oppressed) group, or a declaration that members of the group should be attacked, expelled, or otherwise ill-treated. The appropriate response to such speech has become one of the focal points of critical race theory. In America, the treatment of hate speech is particularly controversial because the First Amendment to the United States Constitution has been interpreted to offer a broad protection for expression, which might arguably extend even to speech of this kind.

Those critical race theorists arguing for legal prohibition of hate speech often offer an analysis similar to the one given by some feminists for greater regulation or prohibition of pornography, despite its purported constitutional protection: that hate speech, like pornography, should be treated as more of an action than an expression of ideas—an effort to exclude or degrade the object of the 'speech' (minority groups, in the case of hate speech; women, in the case of pornography).

> *See* critical race theory

Hayek, Friedrich A. von Friedrich August von Hayek (1899–1992) was one of the prominent members of the 'Austrian school' of economics. He received the 1974 Nobel Memorial Prize in Economic Science (with Gunnar Myrdal), for his work on business cycles, his analysis of monetary and credit policy, and his ideas about the advantages of decentralized economic systems over centralized planning. One of Hayek's two doctorates was in law (the other was in political science), and his work was influential in the understanding of the nature and value of the rule of law, in particular his *The Constitution of Liberty* (1960), and *Law, Legislation, and Liberty* (3 vols., 1973, 1977, 1979). Part of his argument was that well-defined and predictable legal rules are central to a well-functioning economic system.

See **rule of law**

Hegel, G. W. F. Georg Wilhelm Friedrich Hegel (1770–1831) was a German philosopher whose works, including *The Phenomenology of Mind* (1807) and *The Philosophy of Right* (1821), remain central to modern philosophy. His ideas on freedom, consciousness, society, and history were in part responses to Immanuel Kant's quite different approach; Hegel's work, in turn, was influential for much of what followed in continental European philosophy, especially the work of Karl Marx (1818–83). As Hegel has been slow to be received into English-language philosophy, so his influence on English-language *legal* philosophy has remained tangential, with some work applying his ideas to discussions of families, corporations, property law, and commercial law.

See **property law**

hegemony *See* **legitimation**

Heidegger, Martin A highly controversial German philosopher (1889–1976): some consider his work extremely valuable, while others dismiss it as worthless. Those who are critical sometimes raise Heidegger's apparent sympathies for Nazism as somehow reflecting on the nature and quality of his ideas. His most important work is *Being and Time* (1927).

The application of Heidegger's work to legal theory is far from obvious, but has been attempted from time to time. In particular, some commentators have tried, with varying levels of success, to suggest that Heidegger's metaphysical and existentialist ideas about 'authenticity' and the need to understand words and concepts within the larger context of practices can be helpful in discussions about legal interpretation, judicial decision-making, and other areas.

hermeneutics A theory or method of interpretation, often focusing on how the text in question was understood by contemporaries. This approach goes back at least to Friedrich Schleiermacher (1768–1834), is closely related to the *Verstehen* approach to the social sciences, and was strongly advocated in recent years by Hans-Georg Gadamer (1900–2002). Like other theories within or about interpretation, hermeneutics has been the occasional subject of discussion within legal theory. H. L. A. Hart's (1907–92) legal positivist theory has important hermeneutical elements.

Sometimes the term 'hermeneutic' is used more loosely and more generally to refer to any search for the meaning of some text.

See **Betti, Emilio; Gadamer, Hans-Georg; Hart, H. L. A.; interpretation;** *Verstehen* **approach**

hierarchy The division of society into levels of privilege or power (whether based on wealth, race, gender, ability, or some other criterion). The relevance to legal theory is that some critical theorists, in particular followers of critical legal studies, focused a great deal of attention on hierarchies within society, and the way in which practices and ideas helped to create and maintain them.

See **critical legal studies; legitimation**

historical jurisprudence An approach to understanding law in which history plays an important role. That legal systems may reflect the distinctive social character (and even climate) of their country is an idea that goes back at least to Montesquieu (1689–1755). The view that history has a significant role in explaining the current state of law, as well as its past development and likely future direction, is connected primarily with two figures: Friedrich Carl von Savigny (1779–1861) and Sir Henry Maine (1822–88).

Writers associated with historical jurisprudence have varied significantly in their beliefs and assertions, but many emphasized the importance of the customs and traditions of particular cultures as a way of explaining the way law did, and perhaps also the way it *should*, develop. Historical jurisprudence was seen to be in sharp contrast to natural law theory and other theories that emphasize a single right model for law everywhere. At the same time, the historical jurisprudence of both Savigny and Maine can be seen as responses to a certain kind of legal positivism—which saw law as no more and no less than whatever the sovereign commands. Writers such as Savigny opposed attempts to impose a rationalization or codification of a nation's laws. (Savigny appeared not so much to oppose codification as such, but only codification *at the wrong time*. Codification might be appropriate at the height of a culture's maturity, but at a time of development or decline it would be counterproductive.)

Maine (writing in response to the theories of Jeremy Bentham (1748–1832) and John Austin (1790–1859)) offered an evolutionary theory: claiming that predictable changes in society inevitably are reflected by changes in law. Maine famously argued in *Ancient Law* (1861), that both society and legal systems could be seen as moving '*from Status to Contract*'.

While there might seem to be a clear connection between historical jurisprudence and some of the justifications offered for common-law reasoning, historical jurisprudence—and its application to the common-law approach—was not often discussed by English-language legal theorists (the most prominent exception, Sir Henry Maine, did not apply his ideas about the connection between law and culture expressly to the common-law system).

See anthropology of law; Austin, John; Bentham, Jeremy; historicism; legal positivism; Maine, Henry; Montesquieu, Baron de; natural law theory; Savigny, Friedrich Carl von

historicism A term used in a variety of ways. One common usage is as a summary of the view that certain social or legal practices express the particular history of a particular culture—in contrast to a view that might see social or legal practices as expressing some eternal truth, as striving towards a single right way to respond to a functional problem or need, or as an arbitrary (or 'conventional') choice between alternatives. In the sense of seeing practices as reflecting historical events or developments, there is a rough overlap between historicism and historical jurisprudence.

Within general philosophy and social theory, 'historicism' sometimes refers to the position that ideas and claims must be understood in the context of the culture and time in which they were promulgated. The weaker version of this position is a fairly uncontroversial argument about needing to know the understandings and disputes in which claims are made in order to comprehend fully the assertions in question.

A stronger version of this position approaches, or reaches, relativism—that truth is relative to a culture or to a particular time.

See **historical jurisprudence**

Hobbes, Thomas An English political theorist (1588–1679), whose most famous work, *Leviathan* (1651), approached political theory through the pragmatic or realistic concern with self-interest and self-preservation. Hobbes portrays people entering civil society to avoid the state of nature, a 'war of every man against every man', and he sees people as endowing a sovereign with absolute power for the same reason.

While Hobbes purports to accept natural law, and discusses the matter at some length in *Leviathan*, in modern legal philosophy he is more often connected with legal positivism—primarily due to Hobbes's equation of law with the command of a sovereign (a view that was to be elaborated by the founder of legal positivism, John Austin (1790–1859)). In Hobbes's 'A Dialogue Between a Philosopher and a Student of the Common Laws of England' (1668), Hobbes has a character assert, against a prevailing understanding of the common law, that 'It is not Wisdom, but Authority that makes a Law.... [N]one can make a Law but he that hath the Legislative Power.'

See **Austin, John; Bodin, Jean; legal positivism; social contract; sovereign**

Hohfeld, Wesley N. Wesley Newcomb Hohfeld (1879–1918), an American legal theorist, wrote two influential articles for the *Yale Law Journal* in 1913 and 1917, which analysed legal concepts into ordered correlatives and opposites. Hohfeld was responding to the ambiguous way in which judges used the word 'right'. Hohfeld argued that the term 'right' was used in four different senses: to indicate 'claim-rights', liberties (which he called 'privileges'), powers, and immunities. In the more general analysis of legal concepts, Hohfeld posited two 'boxes' of legal connections:

(claim-)right	duty	power	liability
liberty	no-right	immunity	disability

In these boxes, the items across from one another (e.g. right/duty and immunity/disability) were correlatives: where one individual or entity had one, there must be someone else who has the other. The entries diagonal from one another were legal contradictories: e.g. liberty as the contradictory of duty, immunities as the contradictory of liability.

For Hohfeld, legal relationships inevitably had three variables: A has x against B: the notion that one might, e.g., speak of someone having a *right* without someone else having a correlative duty would, to Hohfeld, seem incomplete, and perhaps confused. Another part of this same approach is that legal relationships are understood at the atomistic level. For Hohfeld, broader or more complex claims (e.g., the *in rem* nature of property rights) were necessarily reducible to some combination of legal relationships between individual parties.

Hohfeld's work was intended as an analysis of *legal* rights, though most commentators consider it as valuable, with only some additional complications, when applied to discussions of *moral* rights.

According to one reading, it is central to understanding Hohfeld to see his analyses as *stipulations*: definitions offered to create clarity in thought and analysis. As stipulations, according to this view, these definitions are not subject to rebuttal by pointing to allegedly contrary facts. It can be shown that other people use these legal terms differently from the way that Hohfeld recommends, but that it is not a rebuttal. Under this approach, the only relevant question for Hohfeld's scheme is whether his stipulated definitions are *helpful* or not. Even by this approach, Hohfeld's scheme might be criticized to the extent that it does not fit the way judges and lawyers actually talk about 'rights' (and that this lack of fit reflects some important aspect of the way we view legal rights, and not just sloppiness in usage).

Among the criticisms sometimes raised against Hohfeld is that in the law, we do not always speak of correlates (it is unusual, e.g., to refer to the rights we have that would correlate to the duties imposed by the criminal law). Additionally, many theorists argue that certain rights are not best understood in terms of attachment to some correlative duty, but as the justification *for the creation* of certain additional rights and duties (one can make a similar argument for basic duties that justify the creation of other rights and duties). One might also challenge Hohfeld at a more basic level: challenging the extent to which rights are always analysable in terms of claims against identifiable parties (as contrasted to rights 'against the world'); or, contrasting Hohfeld with other theorists of rights, arguing that he misses the way that choice or protecting interests are the essence of rights.

See interest theory (of rights); legal rights; liberty; rights; will theory (of rights)

Holmes, Oliver Wendell, Jr. A judge and legal philosopher (1841–1935) who was central to both American legal practice and American

legal philosophy. While a member of the United States Supreme Court, he opposed the conservative approach to the United States Constitution that was then supported by a majority of the Court; a number of Holmes's dissenting opinions (especially relating to freedom of expression and the regulation of economic activity) were adopted by later Court majorities. Many consider Holmes to be the greatest judge in United States history.

Earlier in his life, as a state court judge (on the Massachusetts Supreme Judicial Court) and as a legal academic (at the Harvard Law School), Holmes helped to modernize legal thinking in many common law areas (e.g. moving American Contract Law from a subjective to an objective approach). His jurisprudential writings, especially *The Common Law* (1881) and 'The Path of the Law' (*Harvard Law Review*, 1897), presaged much of the American Legal Realist movement. In 'The Path of the Law', Holmes famously wrote that 'The life of the law has not been logic: it has been experience.' Holmes's work is sometimes seen as an important contribution in its own right to the philosophical pragmatism of his time; in any event, his pragmatism (whether innovative or derivative) was an important influence on the American legal realists: in particular, Holmes's view (shared with Roscoe Pound (1870–1964)) that law should be viewed according to the social purposes and social interests it serves, and should also be judged according to its efficacy in such service. Similarly, he generally saw common-law judicial decisions as reflecting not some transcendent truth, but rather a contingent and political decision, a choice between conflicting interests. (While Holmes sometimes indicated an opposition to active judicial reform of common-law rules, his analyses were used by other realists to justify such reforms.) In his judicial and non-judicial writing on doctrinal subjects, he tended to favour external or 'objective' standards—e.g. regarding when a contract had been formed, as against the subjective 'meeting of the minds' approach. This preference reflected both his view that external standards were better suited to social purposes (making contract validity predictable, and thus supporting the negotiability of commercial documents), and a more abstract view that the law, by its nature, regarded people's behaviour, not their inner being.

In 'The Path of the Law', Holmes recommends that when one thinks about law, one takes the perspective of 'the bad man', who wants to know only which activities will lead to sanctions and which will not. While this discussion is sometimes taken as introducing a predictive theory of law, it is probably better understood as simply arguing against an unduly moralistic or unduly metaphysical approach to law, while advocating a view of law more attuned to consequences and the day-to-day concerns of clients and citizens.

Through articles, judicial opinions, and a wide-ranging correspondence, Holmes wrote a vast amount over his long life, and partly for that reason it is not hard to find places where he has made contradictory remarks on various issues (and other places where his comments are not well thought through) but this does little to undermine the high regard in which he is generally held.

See American legal realism; bad man; Pound, Roscoe; pragmatism; predictive theory

human nature The notion of a common human nature underlies various theories within legal, moral, and political philosophy. Some early natural law theorists attempted to derive ethical conclusions from assertions about human nature. Writers in the Enlightenment and more recently have commonly attempted, with varying success, to derive claims for universal human rights from some common nature or value.

See natural law theory

Hume, David David Hume (1711–76) was a Scottish philosopher whose works, including *Treatise of Human Nature* (1739), *An Enquiry Concerning Human Understanding* (1748), and *An Enquiry Concerning the Principles of Morals* (1751), have been very influential in moral philosophy, philosophy of mind, and philosophy of religion. His effect on legal philosophy has primarily been indirect: deriving from his basic empiricism, or from his belief that reason is the slave of the passions rather than its natural master, two themes that have each appeared in various forms in both centrist and sceptical approaches to law. A more direct effect may come from the conclusion that 'ought' statements could never be derived from 'is' propositions—that is, that one could not derive a conclusion about how one should act if one's premises contained only assertions about how the world is. While it remains controversial both whether this view is fairly attributable to Hume (the usual source are some comments from his *Treatise of Human Nature*), and whether the claim is correct, belief in the 'is/ought divide' undermined natural law theory, at least those versions of it that derived ethical conclusions from claims about human nature or the nature of the world.

See human nature; natural law theory

hunches, legal and judicial reasoning as *See* Hutcheson, Joseph C., Jr.

Hutcheson, Joseph C., Jr. An American legal realist (1879–1973) best known for his 1929 *Cornell Law Quarterly* article, 'The Judgment Intuitive: The Function of the 'Hunch' in Judicial Decision', arguing that blind hunches were crucial to the decision-making process for judges. The idea can be traced to an earlier argument from John Dewey ('Logical Method and Law', in the 1924 *Cornell Law Quarterly*), asserting that legal reasoning, like all human reasoning, develops from hunches, not from systematic deliberation, however such reasoning might be presented after the fact. Hutcheson was a federal district judge for the Southern District of Texas when he wrote his most famous article.

Hutcheson was himself untroubled by the view of judicial decision-making grounded on hunches, for he thought that starting from a hunch would do no harm if it led to the right or just solution, and would equally do no harm if it led to a dead end, and the judge had to rethink his or her initial intuition. His only recommendation was that legal education should be changed to help students understand and refine the processes by which hunches were reached.

The idea of a judicial hunch is more troubling if one accepts the views of other American legal realists (and later critical theorists), that the legal materials can often or always justify more than one result. If more than one result can seem correct, then where the judge ends up depends a great deal on which way his or her hunch leads.

See **American legal realism; Dewey, John; legal reasoning**

I

ideal speech situation A concept connected with the work of German philosopher Jürgen Habermas (1929–), and his 'theory of communicative action', under which morality, values, and government structures are to be developed through free and uncoerced public deliberation and debate.

See **communicative rationality, theory of**

identity politics Usually a pejorative term used by critics of political or intellectual movements that are organized around an identifiable group of persons, though the term can sometimes be found used in a more neutral way. The group around which the movement is organized is usually a racial or ethnic group that considers itself oppressed within and by the larger society. (One also sometimes sees the term applied to feminist movements—women may be the numerical majority in many places, but many rightly still consider themselves oppressed, or at least discriminated against.)

Discussions of identity politics often occur within larger debates about 'multiculturalism' and group rights. The question is whether minority cultural, racial, and religious communities have a moral right to government recognition and support, or at least whether it is a recommended policy to protect and support such communities. These issues are also frequently raised in connection with communitarian theories of justice and society.

See **critical race theory; communitarianism**

ideology Within political theory (and political rhetoric), 'ideology' is a way of seeing the world. Political theorists differ on whether 'ideology' should be understood neutrally (*everyone* has a cluster of moral and political beliefs through which they perceive the world; *we all* have an ideology), or only pejoratively (that for some people, the moral and political beliefs through which they view the world—their ideology—have been systematically distorted while others perceive the world without distortion). The relevance of ideology to legal theory is primarily through the central role a pejorative idea of ideology plays within some critical theories about law, legal reasoning, and adjudication—in particular, theories from critical legal studies, but also from some of the more radical or sceptical adherents of other critical approaches (feminist legal theory, postmodern legal theory, etc.). Many of these critical theorists view law as itself a means of distortion and legitimation, causing institutions, rules, and processes that serve the interests of the powerful to appear natural or neutral.

See critical legal studies; legitimation; Marx, Karl

von Ihering, Rudolf *See* von Jhering, Rudolf

incapacitation The justification of punishment based on the removal of the offender from the general public, thus reducing the risk to the public, whatever else might (or might not) be accomplished by imprisonment. This approach to punishment might be best characterized as consequentialist, in that its surface justification is the consequences of the punishment for other members of society, but the approach also seems roughly compatible with retributive theories, for an incapacitation approach does not specify *the duration* of incapacity, and this term could be filled in as easily by retributive theory (what the crime, or the criminal, deserves) as by a utilitarian theory (the amount of imprisonment which will be optimal for the good of everyone).

See deterrence; punishment; retribution

inclusive legal positivism *See* legal positivism

incommensurability Narrowly understood, the term indicates that two (or more) actions or choices or values cannot be placed on the same scale. Sometimes the term is used more broadly to indicate that the actions, choices, or values cannot be meaningfully compared (that one cannot say that one is better than another *or* that the two are equally valuable). The two conclusions are sometimes conflated, especially by those who think that the first entails the second.

See incomparability

incomparability The claim that two alternatives (whether alternative actions, choices, or values) cannot sensibly be compared. The term is sometimes used interchangeably with 'incommensurability'. However, in a narrower usage, 'incommensurability' refers to the fact that two alternatives cannot be measured on the same metric; under this narrower usage, whether 'incommensurability' entails 'incomparability'—an inability sensibly to compare the two alternatives—is left for further argument (some commentators believe that incommensurability entails incomparability, while others disagree).

See **incommensurability**

indeterminacy The argument that legal questions do not have correct answers, or at least not unique correct answers. The issue is sometimes presented differently: whether the *legal materials* are collectively sufficient to determine a (single right) answer to the legal question. This second formulation is based on the argument that certain legal issues might have unique right answers when extra-legal materials (including moral principles or the background, training, or biases of the judges) are considered, but that the law itself is not determinate.

Those who argue that law is significantly indeterminate base that conclusion on a variety of grounds: on the general nature of rules, the nature of language (e.g. pervasive vagueness, or deconstruction); gaps or contradictions within the law; the availability of exceptions to legal rules; inconsistent rules and principles that overlap in particular cases; the indeterminacy of precedent; and the indeterminacy in applying general principles to particular cases.

Some commentators (e.g. Duncan Kennedy, in *A Critique of Adjudication* (1997)) have offered a 'phenomenological' view of indeterminacy, arguing that determinacy or indeterminacy is not a condition in or of the legal materials themselves, but rather an interaction between the legal materials and the 'work' an interpreter (an advocate or judge) is willing to do to reach a particular outcome. Under this approach, a legal issue that at first seems a clear case for one side can, with enough research or sufficiently creative interpretive argument, be shown to be unclear, or perhaps even a clear case for the other side (though these commentators also concede that some cases may 'resist' interpretive efforts, and not be able to be transformed through these strategies).

Many theorists who claim that law is indeterminate distinguish the question of whether the law, in action, is *predictable*. Some critical theorists have argued that many court cases have a predictable result, but this is based on the political or social biases of the judges, and it is those biases, and not the relevant legal materials, that determine the result.

The question of the determinacy of law has been central to at least three debates within Anglo-American legal theory: (1) the attacks of

American legal realist commentators on formalist legal and judicial reasoning; (2) the revival and modification of the realist critique by some members of the critical legal studies (CLS) movement, with some CLS theorists claiming that law was 'radically indeterminate'; and (3) Ronald Dworkin's (1931–) view that all, or nearly all legal questions have a unique right answer ('the right answer thesis').

See American legal realism; critical legal studies; deconstruction; objectivity; open texture; precedent; right answer thesis

individuation of laws A topic raised by Jeremy Bentham (1748–1832) (in *An Introduction to the Principles of Morals and Legislation* (1789), and elsewhere) and later in the earliest works of Joseph Raz (1939–): in Bentham's terms, 'Wherein consists the identity and completeness of a law?' The enquiry is based in part on the fact that however one attempts to separate out a single legal norm, it will often be the case that various aspects of the norm come from disparate sources. One statute might set out the basic definition of a criminal offence, certain key terms may have been defined through common-law decision-making, other decisions create certain defences, the suggested sanction is set forth in a different statute, etc. This point being made, however, one may be hard pressed to offer any further theoretical or practical interest to the topic (Raz himself stopped writing on the topic fairly early in his career.)

inevitable and derivative dependency These labels derive from the work of feminist legal theorist Martha Albertson Fineman (e.g. *The Neutered Mother* (1995)), as part of an argument that dependency is pervasive, and that harmful consequences follow from the implicit choice to leave care and support for such dependencies to families. Dependency is inevitable (and natural), in that everyone needs care when they are very young; also, many will need care when they are very old, or if they become ill or disabled. There is also 'derivative dependency', in that those who care for the dependant (usually women—mothers, wives, daughters, etc.) themselves need support because of the time needed for care. Fineman argues that it would be more equitable for the burdens of care to be distributed broadly rather than imposed on the family; and she criticizes the way the current approach to dependency tends to encourage traditional family forms and the inequality of women.

inner morality of law *See* internal morality of law

institutional competence   A phrase associated with the legal process school, and its primary text, Henry Hart and Albert Sacks, *The Legal Process: Basic Problems in the Making and Application of Law* (tentative edn., 1958). The basic idea of 'institutional competence' is that law (and, more generally, society) responds to different social problems through a variety of problem-solving institutions and procedures, with different institutions and procedures (e.g. legislation, administrative agency action, adjudication, mediation, etc.) having different strengths and weaknesses, and being appropriate to different sorts of problems. For example, adjudication might arguably be the best process when what one wants is a reasoned or principled decision, but legislation would arguably be a better choice when one is more concerned about democratic legitimacy or wide participation in the rulemaking process.

See **legal process**

institutional theories of law   Theories of law (exemplified by Neil MacCormick (1941–   ) and Ota Weinberger (1919–   ), *An Institutional Theory of Law* (1986)) that emphasize the importance of institutions to the understanding of law. At least in the case of MacCormick and Weinberger, the theory is connected with philosopher John Searle's (1932–   ) ideas about there being 'social facts' and 'institutional facts' (e.g. Searle, *The Construction of Social Reality* (1995)), and G. E. M. Anscombe's (1919–2001) earlier distinction ('On Brute Facts', *Analysis* (1958)) between 'brute facts' and 'facts in the context of our institutions'. Institutional theories of law can be seen as trying to take an intermediate position in terms of their ontology in discussing law: that law cannot be reduced merely to 'brute facts' (physical laws and other purely empirical observations), but denying, on the other hand, a richer normative universe in which legal norms might be said to exist as independent elements of the world. Rather, legal norms are seen as products of social or institutional action.

Integrity   Beyond its meaning as a moral virtue, the term is sometimes given a special usage, reflecting one prominent theory of law: in some of Ronald Dworkin's (1931–   ) later works, e.g. *Law's Empire* (1986), he argues that judges have an obligation to interpret past official actions (including statutes and judicial decisions) in a way that makes the society appear to speak with a single voice.

Dworkin's position, here, as elsewhere in *Law's Empire*, purports to be the best available interpretation of our actual practices, so the validity of his argument would depend on whether his theory is a tenable view of what actually occurs in (e.g. English or American) legal practice.

See coherence theory; interpretive theory of law

intention A belief or state of mind regarding a future action or the meaning or application of a standard. Questions relating to intention arise in criminal law (where it is an element of some crimes that the defendant must have had the requisite general or specific intention), in tort law (where it is sometimes relevant to the availability of punitive damages), and in the interpretation of texts.

In the context of the legal interpretation of texts, within a particular legal system, different kinds of texts (e.g. wills, contracts, trust documents, statutes, and constitutions) will often be held to be subject to quite different rules for interpretation. The extent to which discerning the drafters' intentions is central to the meaning and application of the text is especially likely to vary among various kinds of texts (and from one legal system to another).

In the context of using intention to help discern legal meaning, there are additional complications: for example, (1) intentions come at a variety of levels; e.g. lawmakers forbidding 'cruel punishment' can have intentions about whether they think capital punishment is cruel or not, intentions about whether future judges should apply contemporary or historical ideas about what is or is not cruel, and intentions about whether their own intentions should be consulted in applying the term to cases; (2) there is the problem of how to sum up intentions when actions are taken or legislation is written by a collective body rather than a single individual; and (3) there are questions of whether the lawmakers' counterfactual intentions are important (where no express statement is available on a matter, but it might be clear what they would have said had they been asked).

See interpretation

interest theory (of rights) The view (also sometimes known as the 'benefit theory') that 'rights' are best understood as interests sufficiently important to be legally or morally protected. The interest theory, championed by Jeremy Bentham (1748–1832) and Neil MacCormick (1941–   ), among many others, has usually been seen as an alternative to the 'will theory', as a conceptual theory of rights. (The interest theory was also put forward in continental Europe, by Rudolph von Jhering (1818–92)).

Among the arguments *for* the interest theory is that it does a better job of accounting for the full range of rights (in legal and common usage) than does the will theory, as the latter tends to exclude or downgrade inalienable rights, or rights given to children or others legally incompetent to make decisions on their own behalf.

Among the arguments raised *against* the interest theory is that it tends to reduce rights to mere shadows of duties, and that it arguably does less well than the will theory in bringing to light what is *distinctive* about rights.

See animal rights; Bentham, Jeremy; Hart, H. L. A.; Jhering, Rudolf von; legal rights; rights; will theory (of rights)

intergenerational justice The question of what duties, if any, people currently living have to those who lived in the past, or to those who might or will be alive in the future. Among the problems with coming to conclusions about intergenerational justice are (conceptual) questions as to whether the dead or the 'not yet born' (and the 'might never be born') can be said to have rights. In particular, conceptual questions arise from the fact that our actions now affect not only the conditions in which future people will live but also *which* future people will live.

See justice

internal morality of law The central argument of Lon Fuller's (1902–78) theory of law was that there were eight 'principles of legality' that were intrinsic to the process of 'subjecting human conduct to the governance of rules'. These principles Fuller called the 'internal morality' or 'inner morality' of law. The principles were that (1) laws should be general; (2) laws should be promulgated; (3) retroactive rulemaking and application should be minimized; (4) laws should be understandable; (5) laws should not be contradictory; (5) laws should not require the impossible; (7) laws should remain relatively constant through time; and (8) there should be a congruence between the laws as announced and as applied.

For some of these criteria, Fuller believed that a legal system must aspire to full compliance without expecting always to succeed whereas he considered other criteria to be minimal requirements for a legal system.

Critics of Fuller do not deny that these are worthy aspirations for a legal system (many commentators would discuss similar criteria under the rubric 'rule of law'), but rather tend to disagree that they should be considered 'moral'. H. L. A. Hart (1907–92) argued that these criteria are more about efficacy than morality, and one might as easily speak of the rules for efficient poisoning as 'an internal morality of poisoning'. While it is probably true that compliance with Fuller's criteria can be (and in some nations, has been) consistent with great injustice, this arguably need not be conclusive on the question of whether such 'procedural' requirements can be helpfully seen as elements of morality and justice (in other contexts, 'following the rules laid down' has been seen as an aspect of justice, even if certainly not all of justice).

See **Fuller, Lon L.; rule of law**

internal point of view H. L. A. Hart (1907–92) emphasized the importance of taking into account the internal perspective, the perspective of someone who accepts a rule or a legal system, for understanding fully rules and legal systems. 'Acceptance' in this context means treating the rule, or the rule system, as creating reasons for action. For Hart, someone who took an internal point of view on a rule used that rule as a justification for that person's own actions in compliance, and also as a basis for criticizing actions inconsistent with the rule.

The internal point of view is central to Hart's 'hermeneutic turn' in legal positivism, stressing the importance of the participants' perspectives in discussing the nature of law. The internal point of view summarizes the distinctions, first, between acting out of habit and acting according to a rule, and second, between feeling obliged (acting out of fear) and having an obligation (following a rule).

Neil MacCormick (1941–   ) has argued that the internal point of view is best understood as having both a cognitive aspect and a volitional aspect: cognitive, in understanding a standard or a congruence of practices *as a norm*; and volitional, in a willingness to enforce that norm (e.g. through the criticism of those who deviate from it).

See **acceptance; Hart, H. L. A.; rules, practice theory of;** *Verstehen* **approach**

internal scepticism In Ronald Dworkin's (1931–   ) work, in particular in *Law's Empire* (1986), a key part of his argument turns on the distinction between 'internal scepticism' and 'external scepticism'. The difference is whether a sceptical challenge is being brought 'within' the practice, challenging the claims of the practice on its own terms. Dworkin's particular focus was on challenges to truth-value claims within law and morality (as in the sceptical challenges to morality by the logical positivists or by John Mackie (1917–81)).

The difference between the two is that one accepts the basic premises of the practice in question (the internal sceptic), and the other challenges the basis of the practice in general (the external sceptic). The external sceptic is making a global claim often grounded in metaphysics: e.g. that there are no moral entities that could make moral claims true or false. One argument in favour of internal or non-global attacks over external or global scepticism offered by some commentators is that internal scepticism meets the requirements of substantive disagreement—that the criticism and the proposition being criticized are actually disagreeing about some matter, rather than talking past one another.

See **external scepticism**

international law There are a variety of interesting, if largely tangential, connections between international law and legal theory: e.g. (1) international law has one of its historical groundings in the natural law theory of Hugo Grotius (1583–1645) (who sought basic moral-legal principles that could be applied to commercial disputes between merchants who did not share the same sovereign or the same religious views); (2) the legal positivist Hans Kelsen (1881–1973) was a significant figure in international law theory, though Kelsen's work in that area arguably has only modest connections with his legal positivism; and (3) legal theorists occasionally argue over whether international law is 'law' in the fullest sense of the term; e.g. John Austin (1790–1859) treated international law as not 'law strictly so called' because there was no overall sovereign.

See **Austin, John; Grotius, Hugo; Kelsen, Hans**

interpretation An explanation or characterization of a text whose meaning or significance is not self-evident. As the interpretation and application of legal texts (statutes, constitutional provisions, contracts, wills, trusts, prior judicial decisions, etc.) is central to legal practice, it is not surprising that legal philosophy has frequently ventured onto the question of the proper approach to legal interpretation.

For most purposes, commentators tend to follow Ludwig Wittgenstein's (1889–1951) comment (in the *Philosophical Investigations* (1953)) that there is a kind of understanding that is *not* an interpretation—that is, that the term and the practice 'interpretation' should be seen as being confined to difficult texts or to certain important contexts. A minority of commentators view interpretation as a pervasive activity (and some tend to view the 'texts' that need to be interpreted quite broadly as well).

As interpretation occurs in other fields with texts—most obviously with literature—there are questions regarding the extent to which legal interpretation is similar to, or can learn from interpretation in other fields. Some commentators, such as Ronald Dworkin (1931–), have argued that legal interpretation and literary/artistic interpretation are essentially the same, both examples of 'constructive interpretation': making of the object the best it can be within its genre. (Dworkin has made interpretation central to his approach to legal theory, arguing that both determinations of what the law is on a certain issue and the proper understanding of law in general are interpretative.) Other commentators (e.g. Richard Posner (1939–)) have insisted that legal interpretation is far different from literary/artistic interpretation: for example, in the need for finality, the need for a single correct answer, and the deference to the intentions of the authors/lawmakers.

The debate regarding the connection, or lack thereof, between literary/artistic and legal interpretation raises general issues about interpretation that have applications to interpretation in the legal context: can one speak of 'true' and 'false' with interpretations, or only 'better' and 'worse'? and what constraints, if any, are there on acceptable or tenable interpretations of a text? On the last point, Dworkin, for example, argues that if an interpretation does not sufficiently fit the data it means to explain, then it does not even qualify as an interpretation, however attractive the interpretation might be on other grounds.

See authority; constructive interpretation; hermeneutics; intention; interpretive community; law and literature

interpretive community A concept introduced by the American literary critic Stanley Fish (1938–) as part of a distinctive approach to literary or textual interpretation. The 'interpretive community' is the community of readers or practitioners that collectively determines which interpretations are acceptable. Fish had rejected the notion that the meaning of a text is 'in' the text, while the interpreter is completely constrained by the words in the document. At least as a description of actual interpretive practices (e.g. in literature and in law), this view of full constraint by the text fails to take into account the fact of substantial disagreement. However, a contrary view, that interpreters are fully free to impose whatever meaning they chose, would be contrary to the fact of significant agreement. Fish's compromise is to say that interpreters are constrained by the group to which an interpreter belongs—a group that could be defined by styles of interpretation (e.g. new criticism) or by profession affiliation (Member of the Bar of a particular state or country). The idea was that if interpretive communities play a significant role in deciding which interpretations were correct and which incorrect, it would be easier to explain the phenomena of agreement, disagreement, and change in interpretive practices.

See interpretation

interpretive theory of law An approach to legal theory and the nature of law associated with Ronald Dworkin (1931–   ), in particular with his later jurisprudential writings (especially *Law's Empire* (1986)). Under this approach, both understanding the nature of law and determining what the law requires in a particular legal system on a certain question involve constructive interpretation. Constructive interpretation is a reflection on past practices, (re-)interpreting them in the light of their purposes. For Dworkin, the purpose of law is the justification or constraint of state coercion, and an additional factor is that the community should be seen, in its laws, to be speaking with a single, principled voice (what Dworkin calls the value of 'Integrity'). One determines what the law requires by offering theories that adequately fit past official actions, and choosing the one that is morally best.

Dworkin's theory was developed in response to, and criticism of the legal positivist theory of H. L. A. Hart (1907–92); it is a 'natural law theory' (a term Dworkin rarely adopted for his own work) in the broad sense that it asserts that there is no sharp conceptual separation between what law is and what it ought to be; rather, moral evaluation is an integral part of the process Dworkin proposes for determining what the law requires.

The advantages of the interpretive theory of law include that it seems better to explain why and how there can be pervasive disagreements in an ongoing legal practice (which more conventionalist theories have trouble accounting for); and that it explains why judges and lawyers often speak of there being 'right answers' even in difficult cases. Its disadvantages include that it arguably understates the role of authority in the concept of law, and seems to confuse a theory of adjudication with a theory about the nature of law.

See constructive interpretation; fit; integrity; natural law theory

intersectionality A concept raised most often within critical race theory (by Kimberlé W. Crenshaw (1959–   ), among others), pointing out that some individuals may be subject to a series of converging or overlapping forms of exploitation (e.g. based on race, gender, class, religion, etc.). Under such circumstances, arguments based on only one form of exploitation may be inadequate to understanding the situation. For example, it has sometimes been argued that a feminist analysis that looks only to what is shared by all women may be of little help in understanding the situation of African-American and Latina women.

See essentialism

is/ought *See* David Hume

J

Jhering, Rudolf von Rudolf von Jhering (1818–92) was a German legal philosopher whose important works in legal history and theory included *The Spirit of Roman Law* (*Der Geist des römischen Rechts*) (1852–8) and *The Struggle for Law* (*Der Kampf uns Recht*) (1872). His influence on English-language legal theory came primarily through his efforts to incorporate utilitarian ideas into his approach to law—that law should serve, and is best understood as serving individual and community interests. This seemingly obvious point none the less had critical force in response to formalist approaches to law that viewed law as primarily being about the correct analyses of abstract legal properties. Von Jhering's critique of such thinking, presented through his satire of 'The Heaven of Legal Concepts' (1884), was endorsed and adopted by a number of American legal realists, including Felix Cohen (1907–53).

Von Jhering also offered an early version of an interest theory of rights (in opposition to Friedrich Carl von Savigny's (1779–1861) early version of a will theory of rights).

See **American legal realism; free law movement; interest theory (of rights)**

judicial legislation The term applied to when judges, in the course of deciding the disputes before them, make new law, rather than simply declaring and applying existing law. The difficulty is that the line distinguishing the declaration of existing law and the creation of new law is rarely clear. (This difficulty may be confined largely to common-law countries, where the courts have the power to change the law. In civil-law countries, the courts' power to change the law may be limited, and later courts may be free, in principle, to decide contrary to the decisions rendered in prior cases.)

The discussions of judicial legislation are often complicated—certainly in England and the United States—by the fact that judges rendering decisions, and the advocates who appear before judges, almost always speak in terms of declaring what the law is, however much commentators after the fact might claim that the decision is a change or addition to the law.

There are numerous debates within legal philosophy regarding the value of judicial legislation (e.g., Jeremy Bentham (1748–1832) was a strong opponent, while his friend and protégé John Austin (1790–1859) thought it an acceptable and healthy practice) and also regarding its possible inevitability.

See **countermajoritarian difficulty**

jurisprudence The philosophical study of law. Some people use the term more loosely to mean any theoretical study of law—or even any study, regardless of how theoretical, of legal topics (the word derives from the Latin, *jurisprudentia*, meaning 'knowledge of law'). At the other extreme, some commentators try to offer distinctions between 'jurisprudence', 'philosophy of law', and 'legal theory'—for example, that 'jurisprudence' is a broader category than 'philosophy of law', as the former includes work that originates from non-philosophical disciplines, like historical jurisprudence and sociological jurisprudence, or that it includes any theoretical and general discussion of legal matters. However, in general these terms are used interchangeably, and even among those commentators who try to distinguish among the terms, there is little consistency as to which term has what reference.

justice The set of moral and political constraints on human interactions. Discussions of justice usually centre on one or more of the sub-categories of justice: corrective justice, distributive justice, retributive justice ('retribution'), and procedural justice ('legal justice').

There are significant debates regarding the general nature and source of the standards we call 'justice'. Some sceptical thinkers (going back at least to some of the interlocutors in Plato's *Republic*) argue that standards of justice can be grounded only in the conventional views of society, or in a community's traditions. Other theorists (including John Rawls (1921–2002), in his view of 'justice as fairness') have viewed the principles of justice as connected with what people would agree to under certain ideal conditions. A traditional view of justice sees it as describing standards that are eternal and unchangeable, established by God, the nature of the universe, human nature, or some combination of these.

The relationship of justice to morality or ethics generally has frequently been in dispute. Some utilitarian theorists argued that justice, like other values and virtues, could be reduced to the foundational principle of maximizing social utility. Other theorists (e.g. Rawls, in his later works, such as *Political Liberalism* (1993)) have argued for justice as the political structure within which people with different moral ideas and ideals could coexist and co-operate.

See Aristotle; corrective justice; desert; distributive justice; intergenerational justice; justice as fairness; procedural justice; Rawls, John; retribution; utilitarianism

justice as fairness A phrase John Rawls (1921–2002) has used to summarize his approach to justice (e.g. in his *A Theory of Justice* (1971)). Under Rawls's approach, the principles required by justice are those principles people would choose who were ignorant of their natural assets, their place in society, and their conceptions of the good (what Rawls calls 'the original position', with people behind a 'veil of ignorance'). Rawls explains that the phrase 'justice as fairness' does not reflect an equation of the two terms, but rather the fact (or claim) that under his approach 'the principles of justice are agreed to in an initial situation that is fair'. The fairness of the original situation is that the bargainers do not have any information that would bias their decision to favour their particular conditions.

See fairness; justice; original position; Rawls, John; veil of ignorance

justification In discussing legal practice, or an aspect of legal practice (e.g. American constitutional law or English tort law), some theorists would distinguish the 'justification' for the practice as a whole, or some part of the practice, and the 'legitimacy' of a particular argument or conclusion *within* the practice. Those making this distinction usually see 'justification' as an 'external' moral evaluation of the practice, while seeing 'legitimacy' as an 'internal' analysis of whether the argument or conclusion in question is consistent with the usual accepted standards of the practice.

See legitimacy

K

Kaldor-Hicks analysis A form of analysis that was developed within economics, as an alternative or supplement to Pareto analysis. Under Pareto analysis, the change from one state of affairs to another was Pareto superior if at least one person preferred the second state of affairs and everyone else was at worse indifferent, no one preferring the original state of affairs. In the real world, there will be few actions that lead to Pareto superior situations, as usually some will be made worse off by any action significant enough to leave others better off. The Kaldor-Hicks analysis (named after the Cambridge economists J. R. [John Richard] Hicks (1904–89) and Nicholas Kaldor (1908–86)) tries to find an analysis that could allow comparison in situations where some are better off while others are worse off, without having to make significant interpersonal comparisons (e.g. that A's gain is *worth more* than B's loss).

A situation is 'Kaldor-Hicks superior' when those who have been made better off *could* fully compensate those made worse off, and still themselves remain better off—that is, if a transfer could be made among the affected individuals to create a Pareto superior situation (some better off, no one made worse off). The key here is that compensation *could* be made, with the point being that in fact it is not. If the compensation were to be made, we would be back in simple Pareto analysis (and it explains why 'Kaldor-Hicks superior' is sometimes labelled 'potential Pareto superior'). Rather it is a way of claiming that situation X is *better than* situation Y if a transfer could be made within situation X that would make it Pareto superior to Y. The fact remains, however, that *without* this transfer (which, by definition, does not occur in a Kaldor-Hicks analysis) some have gained and some have lost, and a potentially controversial moral analysis is required before concluding that the loss of some is justified by the gain of others.

Tibor Scitovsky (1910–2002) proved that in some circumstances, it can be the case that two states of affairs are Kaldor-Hicks efficient (superior) to one another ('A Note on Welfare Propositions in Economics', *Review of Economic Studies* (1941)). This became known as the 'Scitovsky paradox'.

Though the purpose of Kaldor-Hicks is to find an analysis as uncontroversial as Pareto analysis, in practice Kaldor-Hicks tends to reduce to a kind of utility or wealth maximization, with all the controversial trade-offs among individuals that those analyses entail.

See efficiency; Pareto efficiency; utilitarianism; wealth maximization

Kant, Immanuel A German writer (1724–1804) who may be the most influential philosopher since Aristotle, with important works in moral philosophy, epistemology, and aesthetics. His direct influence on legal philosophy has not been great. Indirectly, however, Kant's importance may be hard to overstate. For example, much of the emphasis in current moral, legal, and political thought on individual autonomy— honouring people's choices and holding them responsible for them— can be traced to Kant's work.

One place of direct influence is punishment theory, in which Kant is often offered as a strong advocate of retributism (particularly in *The Metaphysics of Morals* (1797)): that those who violate the criminal law should be punished according to the culpability of their offence (as contrasted to more utilitarian justifications of punishment according to deterrence or rehabilitation objectives). Consistent with this approach, he argued that only those proved guilty of crimes should be punished, that it was important to hold those proved guilty responsible through punishment, and that punishment should be proportional to the seriousness of the crimes. Kant appeared to argue that any approach to punishment other than retribution would be a deviation from the strict requirements of justice, and would be immoral because it treated the subject of punishment solely as a means, rather than as an end in himself or herself. He argued that *every* criminal must be punished, and proportionately, even if deviation might serve a great social purpose or even if society were about to disband. (Some Kant scholars, most prominently Thomas E. Hill, Jr., argue that Kant's approach to punishment is better understood as a mixture of deterrence and retribution.)

Additionally, (1) Kant's argument that moral culpability is based on the actors' will (intentions) rather than on the outcomes of their actions (a view later reworked into the idea of 'moral luck') remains a powerful argument within criminal law and tort law, even if the rules in those areas often deviate from that principle; (2) some commentators trace the modern 'will theory of rights' to Kant's writing on political theory; and (3) neo-Kantian theory, which builds on a variation of Kant's theory of knowledge (in particular, using arguments analogous to Kant's 'transcendental argument', which supported conclusions by purporting to show that if they were not true experience would not be possible), was important for Hans Kelsen's (1881–1973) theory of law.

See deontological; Kelsen, Hans; moral luck; neo-Kantian analysis; punishment; retribution; will theory (of rights)

Kelsen, Hans An Austrian legal scholar (1881–1973) who spent much of his adult life in the United States, Hans Kelsen produced work on legal theory and international law that has had lasting influence, though probably more so within continental European countries and in South America than in either Britain or the United States. While Kelsen published literally hundreds of publications during his six decades of writing, he is perhaps best known within legal theory for his text, *Reine Rechtslehre* (1934, 2nd edn. 1960, translated and revised as *Pure Theory of Law* (1967)).

Kelsen sought to create an approach to law free of sociological, historical, political or moral claims—thus a *'pure* theory of law' (*reine Rechtslehre*). His approach to law can be understood broadly as being in the legal positivist school, in that it avoids assuming any moral content or moral criteria for law; however, Kelsen's approach differs significantly from either John Austin's (1790–1859) command theory, or H. L. A. Hart's (1907–92) more hermeneutic approach.

Kelsen's work has certain external similarities to Hart's theory, but it is built from a distinctly different theoretical foundation: a neo-Kantian derivation, rather than (in Hart's case) the combination of social facts, hermeneutic analysis, and ordinary language philosophy. Kelsen tries to apply something similar to Immanuel Kant's (1724–1804) 'Transcendental Argument' to law: Kelsen's work can be best understood as trying to determine what follows from the fact that people sometimes treat the actions and words of other people (legal officials) as valid norms. His work can be seen as drawing on the logic of normative thought. Every normative conclusion (e.g. 'one should not drive faster than 55 miles per hour' or 'one should not commit adultery') derives from a more general or more basic normative premise. This more basic premise may be in terms of a general proposition (e.g. 'do not harm other human beings needlessly' or 'do not use other human beings merely as means to an end') or it may be in terms of establishing an authority ('do whatever God commands' or 'act according to the rules set down by a majority in Parliament'). Thus, the mere fact that someone asserts or assumes the validity of an individual legal norm ('one cannot drive faster than

55 miles per hour') is implicitly to affirm the validity of the foundational link of this particular normative chain ('one ought to do whatever is authorized by the historically first constitution of this society').

Like Austin but unlike Hart, Kelsen is a 'reductionist', in the sense of trying to understand all legal norms as variations of one kind of statement (Austin may also have been a reductionist in a different sense of the term, in arguably trying to reduce normative phenomena to empirical propositions; Kelsen was certainly not a reductionist in that sense). In Austin's case, all legal norms are to be understood in terms of commands (of the sovereign); in Kelsen's case, all legal norms are to be understood in terms of an authorization to an official to impose sanctions (if the prescribed standard is not met).

Some of Kelsen's work in international law follows from his core work in legal theory: e.g. in trying to discuss international law in a 'scientific' way, free from political ideology; in focusing on the extent to which there are effective sanctions to the norms of international law; and in arguing that international law and a country's domestic law must in some way form a single normative system.

(Kelsen's ideas developed and changed over the course of six decades of writing; the claims made about his work here apply to most of what he wrote, but will generally not apply to his last works, when he mysteriously rejected much of the theory he had constructed during the prior decades.)

See **Basic Norm; deontic logic; Hart, H. L. A.; international law; Kant, Immanuel; legal positivism; neo-Kantian analysis; pure theory of law; reductionist theories of law**

L

LatCrit theory *See* critical race theory

law and economics The application to various legal questions of the forms of analysis found in economics—'economics' here understood broadly as including neo-classical economics, public choice theory, and game theory. Economic analysis can be used to predict what effects legal rules will have, to argue for legal reform in favour of more economically 'efficient' rules, and to predict how legal rules will change in the future. Economic analysis has also been used as an *explanation* of existing rules, describing in economic terms why these rules were chosen (or have developed) rather than alternative rules.

One foundation of law and economics is the Coase theorem, that shows that in a world without transaction costs, the initial distribution of legal entitlements would not affect the eventual distribution of rights and activities, because parties would enter into voluntary agreements until rights ended up with the parties who valued them the most. In a sense, the Coase theorem showed how the market would usually triumph over the law, with entitlements ending up with those who were willing to pay the most for them. The Coase theorem also noted that this result would not occur if the transaction costs were too high. Some theorists have used this aspect of the Coase theorem to argue for legal rules and decisions (e.g. in tort cases) that would either minimize transaction costs or mimic what the market would have done had there not been significant transaction costs.

Particularly at its earliest stages of development, there was also a 'descriptive' or 'positive' side to law and economics, in which some theorists tried to argue that most common-law rules were efficient (in different terms, that they maximized social wealth). Economic efficiency was proposed as the conscious or unconscious goal of the judges who developed the common law doctrines in various private law areas. Few theorists still support this line of argument: claims of whether doctrines were or were not efficient were highly controverted, and it was never easy to explain how or why nineteenth-century judges could have been the unknowing agents of wealth maximization (which is not to deny that sometimes judges decided the way they did in a conscious or unconscious way to try to help businesses and capitalism).

Also at the earliest stages of the law and economics movement, some theorists urged a strong normative role for wealth maximization, arguing that it was the appropriate standard of justice. This strong claim has all but disappeared from most recent writings. The more common approach to wealth maximization (and its near-cognate, efficiency) is that it is, at best, one value among many, or, sometimes, a useful proxy for other values and objectives.

Discussions of wealth maximization and efficiency are often tied with views about the market: that voluntary transactions generally increase the well-being of the transactors, and generally work for the common good, while respecting the parties' autonomy. For this reason, reinforced by the argument of the Coase theorem (above), law and economics theorists, at least in the early years of the movement, tended to support minimal government regulation of (market) transactions.

The applications of and variations on the 'rational actor' model—e.g. public choice theory, game theory, and behavioural economics—have also found analogues in legal scholarship. Public choice theory regards political and legal outcomes as the product of a kind of market within which all participants act for their self-interest; individuals and interest groups seek advantage indirectly through government action, and officials are interested in their own benefit (generally, power or influence). There is an overlap and tension between a public-choice view of common-law decision-making and some traditional law and economics views of common-law decision-making. As mentioned, some theorists see judicial decisions as moving towards efficient (wealth-maximizing) laws. By contrast, public-choice theorists would be more likely to note how organized interests can deflect decisions away from efficient outcomes.

Game theory looks at individuals' strategic interaction, when each person's actions and choices turn at least in part on what that person expects others to do. Game theoretical models show promise in analysing social problems—both in understanding why co-operation happens or fails to happen in the absence of law, and in determining which legal rule or standard might best increase the chance of obtaining social goals. One advantage of game theory over traditional economic analysis is that it is well suited to discuss situations of imperfect information and significant transaction costs. The strategic behaviours that have already been subject to game theoretical analysis range from contract negotiation (and renegotiation after breach or change of circumstances) to negotiations within marriage and the proper standard of tort liability to cause individuals to exercise due care.

Behavioural law and economics modifies some of the assumptions of 'rational choice' behaviour in the light of what has been learned about actual decision-making. It is hoped that a better model of decision-making will result in more accurate predictions. Some theorists have argued that certain apparently paternalistic legal rules are best explained as reflecting or responding to these 'irrational' elements of most people's decision-making process. However, there remains a problem in constructing an alternative model of decision-making sufficiently simple to make a quantity and range of predictions comparable to that given by the neoclassical 'rational choice' model.

See behavioral law and economics; Coase theorem; efficiency; *ex ante* v. *ex post*; Hand formula; Levi, Edward H.; liability rules; market failure; neoclassical economics; opportunity costs; Pareto efficiency; public choice theory; rationality; risk aversion; Smith, Adam; tort law; utilitarianism; wealth maximization; welfare economics

law and literature   An approach to law or subject of study that loosely collects a variety of ways in which law and literature can be said to overlap or where one area might 'learn' from the other. This usually includes theories of interpretation (in which legal interpretation is normally borrowing from, or distinguishing itself from, literary interpretation), the way that legal practice can be understood as narrative, narrative legal scholarship ('storytelling'), the analysis of rhetoric in judicial opinions, the portrayal of lawyers in fiction, etc. Many commentators trace the modern law and literature movement to James Boyd White's book, *The Legal Imagination* (1973), though discussions of the connections of law and literature go much further back.

One matter of continuing discussion and dispute is the extent to which law can draw on literary theory in matters of understanding texts (only occasionally is the contrary direction, literary theory learning from law, suggested). Those who affirm the value of literary theory note the centrality of interpreting language (usually in texts written long before) to both pursuits, and how similar methods are used by literary theorists, lawyers, and judges. Those denying the connection have emphasized the different purposes and structures of the two activities: arguing, for example, that authority and certainty of meaning have an importance in law that they do not have in literature. It may also be that some of the opposition to the borrowing from literary theory comes from suspicion of or opposition to some of the sceptical or questioning movements within the literary theory of recent decades (e.g. deconstruction, post-modernism).

The possible connections between law and literature have also been raised in discussions of judicial reasoning. Ronald Dworkin (1931–   ) equated judicial decision-making with the writing of a 'chain novel', with each judge (especially in common-law decisions) adding to a 'story' already begun by other judges, thus leaving the judge partly constrained by what has already been written, but with some freedom, and, Dworkin argues, with a general obligation to make the 'story' the best it can be. (Dworkin has also argued that both legal and literary interpretation should be understood as forms of 'constructive interpretation', finding the interpretation that both fits the text adequately and makes the text the best it can be of its kind.)

As mentioned, some commentators in the law and literature move-ment focus on the way that legal advocacy and judicial opinions can be seen as 'storytelling' or 'translation', or can be analysed using standard teachings of rhetoric.

Some commentators in the law and literature movement have argued that reading great works of literature could increase the empathy, or the general moral sensibilities, of judges and lawyers. This is a highly controversial claim (its initial plausibility undermined by the fact that one can find more than a few well-read people, including some literature professors, who are far from moral paragons). Other theorists have used the possible connection between stories and empathy to justify or advocate the use of fiction, fable, autobiography, and personal anecdote ('narrative scholarship') to portray the perspectives of minority and oppressed groups to a majority-group audience.

See **constructive interpretation; deconstruction; interpretation; narrative scholarship; postmodernism**

law and society 'Law and society', also known as 'socio-legal studies', involves the study of law through the social sciences, in particular sociology and empirical political science. It is a broad group or move-ment, but tends towards the study of 'law in action', in contrast to the conceptual study of law one finds in analytical jurisprudence.

Much of the work in the field fits the label 'law in action': investi-gations of the effectiveness, or just the general effects, of certain legal rules. The empirical study of law's effects goes back at least to the American legal realists, and before them to the sociological approach to law of theorists such as Roscoe Pound (1870–1964). Once law is seen not (solely) as the elaboration of intricate concepts or the discovery of universal eternal standards, but rather as a human product meant to achieve human goals, the natural follow-up inquiry involves the extent to which current legal rules succeed at their purposes (and the extent to which certain legal reforms might be an improvement).

See anthropology of law; Montesquieu, Baron de; Pound, Roscoe; sociological jurisprudence

legal determinacy *See* indeterminacy

legal enforcement of morality *See* morality, legal enforcement of

legal gaps Legal gaps refers to a purported failure of legal rules and standards to cover or to resolve all actual or possible issues or all possible disputes. Sometimes the claim of a 'gap in the law' refers to there (allegedly) being no legally authorized standard available, and sometimes the claim entails only that there is no conclusive answer based on a legal source, even though there may be relevant legally authorized standards (e.g. that there are two equally weighty legal rules, or that there is an applicable external norm that the law permits, but does not require, the judge to apply). Discussions of legal gaps cover issues ranging from the relatively abstract question of whether legal systems are necessarily 'closed' normative systems to the more concrete question of how judges should decide cases where there is not (or does not seem to be) applicable law.

Writers such as François Gény (1861–1959) and the members of the German free law movement argued, in the context of codified law in civil law countries, that there were inevitably gaps in the law, and that judges did and should have significant discretion in deciding disputes that fall into such gaps.

H. L. A. Hart's (1907–92) discussion of 'open texture' (e.g. in *The Concept of Law* (1961)) was a claim that due to the nature of language or of rules, most laws would have a core of clear application, but also a fringe area where the legal standard would be uncertain. Hart argued that in those areas of 'open texture' judges would have discretion to make new law.

See discretion; free law movement; Gény, François; Hart, H. L. A.; indeterminacy; open texture; right answer thesis

legal norms *See* norms

legal philosophy *See* jurisprudence

legal pluralism The extent to which a single nation or community is subject to entirely separate sets of norms. Sometimes the term is used to apply to situations where, for example, colonial rulers had recognized or incorporated in part local customary law, along with the rules that the colonial powers had brought with them. Other theorists use the term more loosely, to indicate the way that *most* societies are subject to multiple law or law-like orders.

legal positivism Legal positivism asserts (or assumes) that it is both possible and valuable to have a morally neutral descriptive or conceptual theory of law. (Legal positivism is *not* related to Auguste Comte's (1798–1857) sociological positivism or the logical positivism put forward by the Vienna Circle philosophers in the 1920s.)

In one sense, legal positivism is best understood as the belief that positive law is a subject worthy of separate study. ('Positive law' is law that is created by human officials and institutions, as contrasted with 'natural-law' moral principles, which are asserted to be timeless and, according to some natural-law theorists, of divine origin). This contrasts with earlier approaches to law, which focused more on the prescriptive task of arguing what laws should be enacted, rather than on the descriptive or conceptual study of law ('as it is'). In this limited sense of focusing on positive law, or bringing a purely descriptive or conceptual approach to law, legal positivism can probably be traced back to Thomas Hobbes (1588–1679). Some have even nominated Thomas Aquinas (1225–74), the great natural-law theorist, as the originator of the idea that positive law is a subject worthy of separate analysis. However, modern legal positivism is more conventionally traced to the work of Jeremy Bentham (1748–1832) and John Austin (1790–1859). While Bentham may have been the more powerful theorist, the text most consider his best work on legal theory, *Of Laws in General*, completed in 1782, was not published until long after Bentham's death. Therefore, positivism is usually seen as beginning with Austin's *The Province of Jurisprudence Determined* (1832), where he wrote what is sometimes considered the summary of legal positivism: 'The existence of law is one thing; its merit or demerit is another.'

Legal positivism was traditionally contrasted with natural law theory or at least some of the more 'naive' forms of traditional natural law theory that equated legal validity with not being unjust. By contrast, legal positivism purports to separate the question of whether some norm is 'law' within a particular system, and whether the system as a whole deserves the title 'law', from the question of the merits of that norm or that system.

Varieties of legal positivism

If the dominant strand of English-language legal positivism clearly follows the work of H. L. A. Hart (1907–92) (subdividing into 'inclusive legal positivism' and 'exclusive legal positivism', based on contrary interpretations of law's conceptual separation from morality, as will be discussed below), there remain other strands in legal positivism that deserve mention. Historically, the first strand is the command theory that both Austin and Bentham offered. This approach reduced law to a basic picture of a sovereign (someone others are in a habit of obeying, but who is not in the habit of obeying anyone else) offering a command (an order backed by a threat). Though the command theory (in particular, Austin's version of it) was subjected to a series of serious criticisms by Hart and others, this approach continues to attract adherents. Its potential advantages compared to the mainstream Hartian theories are: (1) it carries the power of a simple model of law (if, like other simple models of human behaviour, it sometimes suffers a stiff cost in distortion); (2) its focus on sanctions, which seems, to some, to properly emphasize the importance of power and coercion to law; and (3) because it does not purport to reflect the perspective of a sympathetic participant in the legal system, it does not risk sliding towards moral endorsement of the law.

The second strand is that of Hart and his followers. Hart's approach (e.g. in *The Concept of Law* (1961)) can be summarized under its two large themes: (1) the focus on social facts and conventions, and (2) the use of a hermeneutic approach, emphasizing the participant's perspective on legal practice. Both themes, and other important aspects of Hart's work, are displayed in the way his theory grew from a critique of its most important predecessor. Hart built his theory in contrast with Austin's command theory, and justified the key points of his theory as improvements on points where Austin's theory had fallen short. Where Austin's theory reduced all of law to commands (by the sovereign), Hart insisted on the variety of law: that legal systems contained both rules that were directed at citizens ('primary rules') and rules that told officials how to identify, modify, or apply the primary rules ('secondary rules'); and legal systems contained both rules that imposed duties and rules that conferred powers—conferring powers not only on officials, but also on citizens, as with the legal powers conferred in the ability to create legally binding contracts and wills.

Austin's work can be seen as trying to find a 'scientific' approach to the study of law, and this scientific approach included trying to explain law in empirical terms: an empirically observable tendency of some to obey the commands of others, and the ability of those others to impose sanctions for disobedience. Hart criticized Austin's efforts to reduce law to empirical terms of tendencies and predictions, for to show only that part of law that is externally observable is to miss a basic part of legal practice: the acceptance of those legal norms, by officials and citizens, as giving reasons for action. The *attitude* of those who accept the law cannot be captured easily by a more empirical or scientific approach, and the advantage of including that aspect of legal practice is what pushed Hart towards a more 'hermeneutic' approach. The possibility of popular acceptance (whether morally justified or not) is also what distinguishes a legal system from the mere imposition of rules by force by gangsters or tyrants.

The third strand is that of Hans Kelsen (1881–1973), who published much of his work in German, and remains better known and more influential on continental Europe than he is in England and the United States. Kelsen's work has certain external similarities to Hart's theory, but it is built from a distinctly different theoretical foundation: a neo-Kantian derivation, rather than (in Hart's case) the combination of social facts, hermeneutic analysis, and ordinary language philosophy. Kelsen tries to apply something like Kant's Transcendental Argument to law: his work can be best understood as trying to determine what follows from the fact that people sometimes treat the actions and words of other people (legal officials) as valid norms. Kelsen's work can be seen as drawing on the logic of normative thought. Every normative conclusion (e.g. 'one should not drive more than 55 miles per hour' or 'one should not commit adultery') derives from a more general or more basic normative premise. This more basic premise may be in terms of a general proposition (e.g. 'do not harm other human beings needlessly' or 'do not use other human beings merely as means to an end') or it may be in terms of establishing an authority ('do whatever God commands' or 'act according to the rules set down by a majority in Parliament'). Thus, the mere fact that someone asserts or assumes the validity of an individual legal norm ('one cannot drive faster than 55 miles per hour') is implicitly to affirm the validity of the foundational link of this particular normative chain ('one ought to do whatever is authorized by the historically first constitution of this society').

Inclusive v. exclusive positivism

The debate between 'inclusive legal positivism' (also sometimes called 'soft legal positivism' or 'incorporationism') and 'exclusive legal positivism' (also sometimes known as 'hard legal positivism') is a difference in elaborating one detail of legal positivist belief: that there is no *necessary* or 'conceptual' connection between law and morality. Exclusive legal positivism (whose most prominent advocate has been Joseph Raz (1939–)) interprets or elaborates this assertion to mean that moral criteria can be neither sufficient nor necessary conditions for the legal status of a norm. In Raz's terms: exclusive legal positivism states that 'the existence and content of every law is fully determined by social sources'.

The most common argument for exclusive legal positivism is one based on the relationship between law and authority. Legal systems, by their nature (the argument goes) purport to be authoritative, and to be capable of being authoritative legal norms must be ascertainable without recourse to the (moral and other) reasons the norms were meant to resolve. Under this argument (and in Raz's phrasing), those subject to an authority 'can benefit by its decisions only if they can establish their existence and content in ways which do not depend on raising the very same issues which the authority is there to settle' (*Ethics in the Public Domain* (1994)).

Inclusive legal positivism (whose advocates have included Jules Coleman, Wilfrid Waluchow, Philip Soper, and David Lyons) interprets the view differently, arguing that though there is no *necessary* moral content to a legal rule (or a legal system), a particular legal system may, by conventional rule, make moral criteria necessary or sufficient for validity *in that system*. The strongest argument for inclusive legal positivism seems to be its fit with the way both legal officials and legal texts talk about the law. Additionally, the inclusive view allows theorists to accept many of Ronald Dworkin's (1931–) criticisms of legal positivism without abandoning what these same theorists consider the core tenets of legal positivism (its conventional or social facts grounding). It is sometimes convenient to distinguish situations when moral criteria are said to be *necessary* conditions for legal validity (the common situation of moral criteria as part of constitutional judicial review) and when they are said to be *sufficient* conditions for legal validity (the way some commentators view the operation of common-law decision-making, and a possible explanation for the operation of legal principles in other forms of decision-making).

Ethical positivism

The term 'ethical positivism' (or 'normative positivism') describes a position (associated with Tom Campbell and others) that sees the separation of law and morality *not* as a necessary or conceptual truth about the nature of law, but as a good thing, something to be sought for various political or moral reasons.

See acceptance; Austin, John; authority; custom and customary law; Hart, H. L. A.; Kelsen, Hans; natural law; rule of recognition; separability thesis; sources thesis

legal process The legal process school is an approach to law emphasizing institutional competence. The school centred on a law-school casebook, *The Legal Process: Basic Problems in the Making and Application of Law,* that had been distributed widely among American academics in the middle and late 1950s, even though it was not formally published at the time (the common citation is to the 1958 'tentative edition'; that edition was finally published formally in 1994). The casebook authors were Henry M. Hart, Jr. (1904–69) and Albert M. Sacks (1920–91), both at that time professors at the Harvard Law School.

The legal process school is often seen as a response to the critiques raised by the American legal realists of the prior generation. Legal process conceded that there might not always be clear right answers in law, and that lawyers and judges had no particular expertise on the type of moral or policy judgements that might be central to deciding legal cases. However, lawyers and judges could be characterized as having some expertise in procedures: in finding the structure and style of decision-making that would be most apt to come to the right decision in various kinds of disputes.

Henry Hart was strongly influenced by his Harvard Law School colleague, Lon Fuller (1902–78), and the legal process school can be seen as a kind of embodiment of the 'internal morality' view of law Fuller put forward.

The criticisms of legal process have tended to be that its notion of a neutral, technocratic approach to decision-making was simultaneously too optimistic and too naive. Additionally, some thought that too great a focus on procedure led to an indifference to the justice or the results obtained.

See American legal realism; Fuller, Lon L.; Hart, Henry M., Jr.; institutional competence; internal morality of law; neutral principles; Sacks, Albert M.; Wechsler, Herbert

legal reasoning Some commentators use this term broadly, to cover all forms of analysis done by those involved in the process of applying the law to facts (judges, and derivatively, the advocates trying to influence judicial opinions and legal scholars evaluating judicial decisions). Other commentators use the term more narrowly, to refer to what is entailed by the legal materials. Granting that judges can or should look to extra-legal materials, such thinkers would distinguish 'what the law is' or 'what the law requires' from 'how the judge will/should decide this case'. Legal reasoning, in this interpretation, is analysis from the legal materials, 'legal materials' narrowly understood, while 'judicial reasoning' would have a different or broader referent.

A large part of the American legal realism movement involved criticisms relating to legal reasoning, both a correction in the understanding of current practices and suggested reforms of those practices.

See **American legal realism; analogical reasoning; coherence theory; Hutcheson, Joseph C., Jr.; Levi, Edward H.**

legal rights Legal rights are strong claims of a certain kind that arise within and/or derive from legal sources. 'Right' is a basic concept within both legal and moral discourse, and there are ongoing debates about the best understanding of the nature of legal rights, the connection between legal rights and other legal concepts, and the connection between legal rights and moral rights. On the relationship between legal rights and moral rights, the question is whether they are of a similar nature, divided only by the context of the claims being made, or whether the two kinds of rights actually have quite different natures.

Certain kinds of questions regarding rights are probably equally applicable to legal and moral rights: e.g. whether rights are best understood in terms of choice or in terms of protected interests; and to whom rights can be ascribed (can one speak of infants having rights? what about foetuses? animals? the dead? trees?). The connection or overlap between legal and moral rights becomes especially complicated in the areas of constitutional rights (legal rights arising from a foundational legal text, where such rights often refer to general moral concepts such as 'equality', 'dignity', and 'due process') and human rights (rights purportedly deriving from human nature; a type of analysis familiar to the natural law and natural rights tradition, but which in modern times often also has textual and institutional grounds, e.g. in international treaties and declarations).

Debates about the nature of legal rights are frequently characterized as arguments between 'will theories', which locate the nature of rights in powers and choices given to a right-holder, and 'interest (or benefit) theories' which locate the nature of rights in the legal protection of an interest.

Wesley Hohfeld (1879–1918) offered a well-known stipulative definition of 'right', as that term was used in judicial decisions, in four kinds: (1) claim rights, (2) liberties (Hohfeld used the term 'privilege'), (3) powers, and (4) immunities.

See **Hohfeld, Wesley N.; interest theory (of rights); rights; will theory (of rights).**

legal validity In discussions within and about law, the term 'valid' has a number of distinct meanings, though these meanings are frequently related or overlapping. The description 'valid' or its opposite 'invalid' is usually ascribed to individual rules or norms, relative to a particular legal system. A rule or norm may be described as 'valid' if it is consistent with the other rules or norms of the legal system (including being authorized by some 'higher' or 'more basic' rule or norm); or if it is generally accepted by legal officials or generally followed by the citizens ('efficacy').

There are occasional references to 'valid' legal systems, where 'valid' means something like 'legitimate' or 'just', but this usage is rare.

legitimacy A term referring to the moral value of a practice, institution, or entire system. The term is used primarily for discussing political actors, actions, and institutions, and some would use the term exclusively in that context. Others apply the term more broadly, to all (or almost all) rule-bound practices.

Some theorists have suggested a (controversial) distinction between 'legitimacy' and 'justification', with the first applying to whether an action is consistent with the rules accepted within a practice, and the second to evaluate (morally) the practice as a whole.

Similarly, some theorists have suggested that 'legitimate' should be distinguished from 'just': in that it may be sufficient for legitimacy that a government work hard to achieve justice, even if it is ultimately unsuccessful.

See justification

legitimation Critical theorists, in particular theorists associated with critical legal studies, often emphasized the extent to which law could make oppressed groups erroneously perceive their society as just, by the way that law portrays society's rules as neutral and fair, and legal officials as representing the interests of all.

Discussion of legitimation within legal theory can be traced to the works of earlier theorists from other fields, Antonio Gramsci (1891–1937), Louis Althusser (1918–90), and, to a lesser extent, Max Weber (1864–1920). (Within Marxist theory, the same concept sometimes goes under the label 'hegemony'.)

The emphasis on legitimation can be seen as a way of viewing and explaining law, more subtle than a 'naive Marxist' view that law directly serves the interests of the powerful. Such a view runs up against apparent counterexamples, where court decisions or legislative rules seem to favour the less powerful. A theory of legitimation allows critical theorists to argue that such occasional victories for the less powerful only increase the usefulness of the law for the interests of the powerful: by giving the less powerful some basis for believing that the government is *generally just*, the system, which in fact (under this argument) predominantly serves the interest of the powerful, can go forward with little or no organized resistance.

See **critical legal studies; Gramsci, Antonio; ideology; Marx, Karl**

Levi, Edward H. Edward Hirsch Levi (1911–2000) was at various times the Attorney General of the United States (under President Gerald R. Ford) and president of the University of Chicago, but within legal theory he may be best known for a small text, *An Introduction to Legal Reasoning* (1949), a concise introduction to the vagaries and paradoxes of legal reasoning in general, and common-law reasoning in particular. Less well known, but perhaps equally important, was Levi's decision, as a law professor teaching antitrust law, to team up with an economist. Many commentators trace the development of the 'law and economics' school to that decision, and also credit it for encouraging the growth of interdisciplinary work in law (in later years Levi was to add a statistician and a sociologist to team-teach courses with law professors). Levi founded the *Journal of Law and Economics* in 1958, which remains a prominent journal in law and economics.

See **common law; law and economics; legal reasoning**

lex iniusta non est lex 'An unjust law is not law.' The phrase, in Latin or English, is usually associated with traditional natural law theory. One can find similar statements in the works of St Thomas Aquinas (1224–74), and also in the works of Plato, Aristotle, Cicero, and Augustine.

The meaning or significance of the phrase is contested. Many critics of natural law theory understand the phrase as indicating that unjust laws do not have the status of 'law' in any sense, and one can find texts by writers sympathetic to natural law theory that seem to support that reading (e.g. Sir William Blackstone (1723–80), early in his *Commentaries on the Laws of England* (1765–9)). However, the more common reading of Aquinas and most other significant natural law theorists is that an unjust law is not law *in the fullest sense*: that is, that one can speak of unjust enactments as 'law', but they lack part of what just laws have. In Aquinas's phrase, unjust laws do not 'bind in conscience'; citizens have no obligation, generally speaking, to obey them.

See **Aquinas, Thomas; natural law theory, obligation to obey the law**

lex talionis *See* **retribution**

liability rules Though the term often refers simply to whatever the standards are for imposing legal liability on a party, within legal theory there is a specialized meaning of the term. In a famous 1972 *Harvard Law Review* article, Guido Calabresi (1932–   ) and A. Douglas Melamed suggested that entitlements could be analyzed as either 'liability rules' or 'property rules'. When an entitlement is protected by a liability rule, an infringement only leads to money damages. When an entitlement is protected by a property rule, infringements can be enjoined. Sometimes people have the right to infringe an entitlement as long as they pay for the infringement (liability rules), while on other occasions no infringement would be allowed without the consent of the right-holder (property rules). Calabresi and Melamed argued that which type of rule would or should be chosen to protect the interest in question would usually turn on transaction costs: using property rules (injunctions) where the parties could feasibly negotiate, but liability rules (damages) where transaction costs make negotiations towards agreement impractical.

See **law and economics; transaction costs**

liberalism In the context of discussions of political theory and legal policy, the term 'liberal' and 'liberalism' can take on a wide range of meanings. Sometimes the term is used broadly to refer to any approach to government and social policy that emphasizes individual rights—in contrast with the type of conservatism that emphasizes the importance of tradition, custom, and authority, or contrasted with communitarian approaches; both traditional conservative approaches and communitarian approaches frequently focus on society and social good, as against the 'liberal' focus on the individual.

At other times, the term is used more narrowly to refer to a particular kind of leftist or progressive political view (usually entailing support for egalitarianism, government responsibility to help the poor, redistribution of income, and like policies). This use of the term 'liberal' may derive from 'liberality' as meaning generosity.

'Classical liberalism', focused on individual liberty, is often associated with John Stuart Mill (1806–73), and Mill's 'harm principle' (that government interference with individual liberty is only justified by prevention of harm to others). Strong advocates of such positions (e.g. Richard Epstein (1943–) and Robert Nozick (1938–2002)) often go by the name 'libertarians'.

See communitarianism; Mill, John Stuart

liberty Usually understood as the absence of constraints on action, in particular the lack of legal constraints. Isaiah Berlin (1909–97) distinguished between two concepts of liberty in his 1958 Inaugural Lecture of that title. Negative liberty (or 'negative freedom') reflects the conventional understanding of liberty as the absence of external constraints. Positive liberty, or 'positive freedom', involves having the *ability* to do the action in question, and thus, arguably, the right to be enabled or supported by the state or by society in the matter in question.

Within Wesley Hohfeld's (1879–1918) analysis of rights, 'liberties' (Hohfeld preferred the term 'privileges') were one category of legal protections that often go under the name 'right', loosely understood (the other categories were 'claim rights', 'powers', and 'immunities').

See Berlin, Isaiah; Hohfeld, Wesley

Llewellyn, Karl N. Karl Nickerson Llewellyn (1893–1962) was arguably the most prominent and most articulate American legal realist, and also perhaps the one with the greatest practical influence, which came primarily from his role in drafting Article Two of the Uniform Commercial Code (UCC), a law which (in revised form) governs the sale of goods in the United States to this day. His most important jurisprudential works included *The Cheyenne Way* (with E. Adamson Hoebel) (1941); *The Bramble Bush* (1951); *The Common Law Tradition— Deciding Appeals* (1960); 'A Realistic Jurisprudence—The Next Step' (*Columbia Law Review*, 1930); and 'Some Realism About Realism— Responding to Dean Pound' (*Harvard Law Review*, 1931).

Like many of the American legal realists, Llewellyn developed a 'sociological' or 'functional' approach to law: that legal rules should serve social purposes, and to the extent that they failed to serve those purposes, those rules should be changed. Additionally (and again like many other legal realists), Llewellyn argued that a formalistic understanding of legal concepts and legal reasoning does not match what judges actually do in deciding cases and developing law.

Llewellyn offered a moderate scepticism about rules (distinguishing between 'real rules' and 'paper rules'), arguing *not* that rules had no importance in legal practice or in understanding law, but that their importance was often and easily overstated: that the legal rules as stated in the books *might or might not* be a good description of how judges decide cases; and *might or might not* be a good prediction of how future cases would be resolved.

In *The Common Law Tradition*, Llewellyn developed some of these ideas into advice for judges to use their 'situation sense' (taking into account political and economic considerations as well as more conventional legal reasoning) and a 'grand style' of decision-making (a less formalistic approach, willing to develop the law to adapt to changing circumstances).

Llewellyn's work on the UCC put many legal realist ideas into action: in particular, that judges should focus more on the perceptions and needs of citizens subject to law and less on formalistic understandings or technical applications of legal concepts.

See **American legal realism; Pound, Roscoe**

Locke, John An English theorist (1632–1704), and towering figure in political philosophy and epistemology, Locke's major works included *Two Treatises of Government* (1690) and *Essay Concerning Human Understanding* (1690). His impact on legal theory was mostly through three ideas: (1) that human beings have inalienable rights to life, liberty, and property (it is a version of Locke's natural rights ideas that appears in the American Declaration of Independence (1776)); (2) related to the natural rights view, Locke argued that government is based on a social contract, which binds current citizens through their express or tacit consent; and (3) that ownership of property is legitimate where someone mixes his or her labour with the land, as long as the person leaves 'as much and as good' for others (though Locke thought this last proviso, though applicable in the 'State of Nature', might no longer be applicable after the introduction of money).

Locke's *Essays on the Law of Nature* (*c.*1660), unpublished in his lifetime, is considered by some to be an important work in early 'modern natural law theory'. The work offers a voluntarist view of natural law theory similar to that of Samuel Pufendorf (1632–94), who published his early work on natural law theory, *The Elements of Universal Jurisprudence*, in 1660.

See consent; natural law theory; property law; Pufendorf, Samuel; social contract

Luhmann, Niklas A German sociologist (1927–98), whose work on social systems theory has had a large impact in Germany and parts of continental Europe, but has received far less attention in English-speaking countries. Luhmann's version of systems theory, autopoiesis, views social systems as entities that reproduce themselves by appropriating elements of their environment. Within Luhmann's theory, social systems are seen as basically systems of communication, which process meaning. Luhmann, Gunther Teubner (1944–), and others have tried to apply autopoiesis to law, discussing the ways in which and the extent to which law defines and controls its own meanings (e.g. the way that the question of whether something is 'legal' or 'illegal' is determined entirely by and within the legal system).

See autopoiesis

M

Maine, Henry Sir Henry James Sumner Maine (1822–88) was an English writer influential within the historical jurisprudence school. Based upon a detailed consideration of legal practices in various times and places, Maine developed theories of legal evolution, under which law changes to reflect and facilitate social and cultural change. One such change is the basis of Maine's best-known comment: in *Ancient Law* (1861), he stated that 'we may say that the movement of the progressive societies has hitherto been a movement *from Status to Contract*'. Maine's arguments were in large part a response to the legal positivism of Jeremy Bentham (1748–1832) and John Austin (1790–1859), viewing those theorists as overestimating the importance of legislation, and underestimating the importance of history or evolutionary social change to explaining law. Maine also argued that legal change often occurs through a set progression: from legal fiction (covering the change in the rule) to established exceptions (e.g. in equity) to fully recognized changes codified by statute or judicial legislation.

See Austin, John; Bentham, Jeremy; historical jurisprudence; Savigny, Friedrich Carl von

market failure A phrase from economics, deriving from the presumptive preference for problems to be dealt with through voluntary market transactions or other 'private ordering'. The argument is that under ideal conditions (fully competitive, parties having full information, etc.), the markets will allocate resources in an optimal way. Under this approach, government regulation of transactions is warranted (only) where some circumstance, a 'market failure', prevents the market from functioning normally. Among the circumstances usually subsumed under 'market failure' are monopolies, 'externalities' (where the costs or benefits of a transaction spill over onto entities who are not parties to the transaction), high transaction costs, and a severe absence of information.

The extent to which taxes, subsidies, tort liability, or the reassignment of rights can cure certain kinds of market failures is tied up in the debates regarding the Coase theorem, a theorem that indicates that government intervention is often both unnecessary and ineffective in responding to certain kinds of market failures.

See **Coase theorem; externalities; law and economics**

Marx, Karl Karl Heinrich Marx (1818–83) was a German-born political theorist, economist, and philosopher whose work helped to define modern communism. His relevance to legal philosophy is through those theorists who try to apply Marx's ideas to legal history or legal doctrine. There have been some significant Marxist legal philosophers (e.g. Evgeny B. Pashukanis (1891–1937)), but mostly Marx's work has been adopted only in part, or in a modified form—as was frequently the case with the critical legal studies theorists.

Among Marx's ideas that have been influential among legal theorists are: (1) his materialism, his focus on the economic and social conditions, and argument that human character and motivation derive largely from the modes of production and people's position within them; (2) a related idea, 'ideology'—that the ideas of the dominant class and their ways of perceiving the world are distorted to reflect the interests of that class; and (3) from Marx's earlier works, Marx's discussion of the 'alienation' of human beings caused by capitalism in general and modern production techniques in particular.

See **base and superstructure; critical legal studies; ideology; legitimation; Marxist theories of law; Pashukanis, Evgeny B.**

Marxist theories of law 'Marxist' is applied to a large category of theories of law, as Marxism itself contains a wide variety of ideas and doctrines which potentially apply to theories about the nature of law. There can be contrast, and even conflict within the category. For example, some Marxist legal historians take a traditional (or 'naive') Marxist line that law is merely 'superstructural', a reflection of the economic base of the society and the interests of the ruling class. Such historians will always look for how doctrinal changes reflected the interests of owners (and went against the interests of workers and other oppressed peoples). Other Marxist legal historians may follow later Marxist thinkers such as Antonio Gramsci (1891–1937), and see how changing legal doctrines, even when not directly supporting the interests of the ruling class, help that class *indirectly* by *legitimating* a generally unjust, generally oppressive system.

See **base and superstructure; Gramsci, Antonio; legitimation; Marx, Karl; Pashukanis, Evgeny B.**

maximin principle A rule for choice under uncertainty, according to which one ranks alternatives by their worst possible outcomes. Arguably that rule of decision makes most sense when knowledge of the likelihood of different outcomes is highly uncertain, when what can be lost in the worst cases is much more substantial or important than what could be gained in the best cases, and/or where the worst cases would not be acceptable.

The maximin principle plays a key role in John Rawls's (1921–2002) theory of justice: in the hypothetical negotiation he describes (the 'original position'), the principle justifies the participant's relatively cautious choice of a fairly egalitarian principles of distributing goods within society ('the difference principle'), over, for example, the less risk-averse choice of utilitarian principles.

See **difference principle; original position; Rawls, John; risk aversion**

mechanical jurisprudence *See* formalism

metaphysical realism *See* realism

metaphysics A general term in philosophy, usually used to name any inquiry beyond the empirical—reaching the most basic and abstract questions of thought and existence. Sometimes the phrase is used more narrowly to refer to ontological questions—questions of what types of things exist. The relevance of metaphysical inquiries to legal philosophy remains controversial; some theorists (e.g. Michael Moore (1943–)) have built elaborate and controversial theories grounded on particular metaphysical (and epistemological) claims, while others (e.g. Ronald Dworkin (1931–)) have forcefully argued for the irrelevance of onto-logical claims to the truth or value of the theories they have proposed.

See **moral realism; realism**

Mill, John Stuart An English philosopher and political theorist (1806–73), Mill's most important works, *On Liberty* (1859) and *Utili-tarianism* (1861), both have importance for legal theory. Mill's work was also important in political philosophy, economics, philosophy of science, logic, and women's rights.

On Liberty put forward 'the harm principle', which contended that state interference with individual liberty is justified only to prevent harm to third parties, thus rejecting both the enforcement of morality and paternalism as justifications for state regulation. The same text also argued for significant freedom of thought, belief, and expression, on the basis that a free marketplace of ideas would be more likely to result in truth, and would carry other social benefits. *Utilitarianism* propounded the view that morality and justice were best thought of in terms of the maximization of the happiness of all persons. Here Mill was developing ideas first promulgated by Jeremy Bentham (1748–1832), though Mill's version of utilitarianism deviated from Bentham's on a number of points (e.g. Mill was willing to speak of some pleasures being more valuable than others, while Bentham avoided such judgements).

Mill argued, with varying levels of persuasiveness, that a utilitarian approach to moral questions was consistent with most of our moral intuitions, and could explain our conventional notions of what justice requires.

See Bentham, Jeremy; Devlin, Patrick; harm principle; liberalism; morality, legal enforcement of; Stephen, James Fitzjames; utilitarianism

minimum content of natural law *See* natural law, minimum content of

Montesquieu, Baron de Charles-Louis de Secondat, Baron de La Brède et de Montesquieu (1689–1755) was a French writer best known today for his work, *The Spirit of the Laws* (1748). In that text, Montesquieu argues for the separation of powers within government, and it is Montesquieu who was often invoked by the Founding Fathers of the United States to justify the governmental structure set forth in the US Constitution.

For legal theorists, *The Spirit of the Laws* has an additional interest: its efforts to explain the variety of laws and legal systems as reflecting the different circumstances of the various countries, with explanatory factors extending not only to the form of government and religious beliefs, but also to the climate and quality of the soil. Because of this claim, Montesquieu has been seen as a forerunner both to historical jurisprudence and to modern sociology.

See historical jurisprudence; law and society

moral hazard A term from economic analysis, which historically was sometimes confined to the discussion of insurance policy provisions—that the fact of insurance coverage may increase the likelihood of an accident, because the insured has less incentive to take precautions. In modern usage, the phrase is generally applied to any circumstance where an actor maximizes his or her own utility, and where this may cause harm to the interests of others, but the actor does not bear the costs. For example, corporate officials often have the responsibility for other people's funds, without carrying full liability should they manage those funds negligently.

Moral hazards are often analysed in terms of high monitoring costs (e.g. the difficulty or expense for insurance companies to observe the level of care of the person covered by the insurance policy, or for shareholders to monitor the actions of a corporate executive) or in terms of information asymmetries (that the insurance policy holders and the corporate executives have information about their plans and tendencies that the other parties do not have).

Sometimes the problems of moral hazard can be overcome by more comprehensive contracts or legal rules which succeed at imposing ('internalizing') all the costs of negligent action on the actor.

See **principal–agent problem**

moral luck The idea that our moral situation or status is determined to a significant extent by factors beyond our control. Though the term was introduced by Bernard Williams (1929–2003) in 1976 (in *The Proceedings of the Aristotelian Society, Supplementary Vol. 50*), and elaborated by Thomas Nagel (1937–) in the same year (and the same volume), the concept is often thought to derive from, or at least be connected to, the work of Immanuel Kant (1724–1804) (particularly the *Groundwork of the Metaphysics of Morals* (1785)), who had argued that one is morally responsible only for *chosen* actions. Within criminal law, the question arises whether it is just to judge more culpable the person who murders than one who attempts murder but fails; or to judge more culpable the person who drives recklessly or when intoxicated and causes injury, and another person, equally reckless or intoxicated, who does not cause injury.

See **consequentialism; Kant, Immanuel; responsibility**

moral realism Taking a realist position about moral terms—'realism' here in the philosophical sense (grounded in the nature of things, not simply reflecting subjective human reactions or social conventions) rather than in the conventional or artistic sense of 'realism' (showing things as they 'really are', unadorned by sentiment or idealization). Moral realism entails an objectivity in moral judgement, in contrast to more relativist or nihilistic approaches. The relevance to legal theory is that when many theories of legal reasoning and judicial reasoning make truths of legal claims turn on moral reasoning, it becomes important to know something about the latter. For example, if a theory of legal/ judicial reasoning incorporates moral reasoning, the possibility of unique *legal* right answers will often depend on whether there are unique *moral* right answers.

See morality, critical v. conventional

morality, critical v. conventional In brief, the difference between 'conventional morality' and 'critical morality' is the difference between what people in a community *believe to be* morally correct, and what *is in fact* morally correct. The distinction was discussed by H. L. A. Hart (1907–92) (in *Law, Liberty and Morality* (1963)), using slightly different terminology ('positive morality' instead of 'conventional morality'), in the course of criticizing Patrick Devlin's (1905–92) argument for the general legal enforcement of morality. Devlin's argument had been that a shared morality is crucial to a society, and societies have a right to defend themselves against those who would undermine the society by subverting its shared morality. Hart responded that there was little empirical support for the view that changes in shared moral beliefs 'undermined' society, as contrasted with simply changing the society in normal ways. Hart added that a society's interest in defending conventional beliefs about morality must, necessarily, be far weaker than its interest in reinforcing what is actually morally correct.

The difference between what one *thinks is right* regarding moral matters and what *is right* will be a valid distinction for all but those who are sceptical about morality and who believe that there is no moral truth beyond the majority or consensus view of a given community. (Though a belief in ascribing truth and falsehood to moral propositions is often associated with a metaphysically realist position about morality, the two are not equivalent. However, the major alternative to realism for grounding the truth of moral propositions is conventionalism. For the purposes of discussing 'critical morality' and 'conventional morality', it might be possible to assert that the truth or falsehood of moral propositions *neither* derives from their correspondence, or lack thereof, with some human-independent aspect of reality, *nor* from their agreement, or disagreement, with conventional beliefs about what morality requires, but this might be a difficult position to make out.)

Of course, just because an official claims to be acting in the name of critical morality rather than conventional morality is no guarantee that the official is in fact acting consistently with what morality requires. No one has privileged or irrefutable access to moral truth, and history seems to be full of examples of both societal majorities and the elite in a given era making egregious errors on some moral issues. What most people, after considered reflection, believe about some moral issue may be good, if far from conclusive, evidence regarding what morality *in fact* requires.

See Devlin, Patrick; harm principle; Hart, H. L. A.; moral realism; morality, legal enforcement of

morality, legal enforcement of   The phrase usually refers to the enforcement of *certain kinds* of moral obligations. No one seriously argues that the law should *never* sanction activities prohibited under moral codes. Most of criminal law, tort law, contract law, property law, etc., involves the legal codification of moral standards. Instead, the phrase usually refers to the legal regulation of activities that do not, in any obvious way, affect the public order or the smooth functioning of commercial life. The targeted objects for regulation are usually activities that arguably affect only the actor, and the regulation of which could probably be justified only in terms of either paternalism or adherence to a moral code.

The view most often associated with debates about the legal enforcement of morality is John Stuart Mill's (1806–73) harm principle. Mill wrote in his pamphlet, *On Liberty* (1859): 'The only purpose for which power can rightfully be exercised over any member of a civilised community against his will is to prevent harm to others.' This view has been criticized by 'perfectionist' theorists, such as James Fitzjames Stephen (1829–94), who argue that governments do and should have a role in encouraging virtue and discouraging vice; by Sir Patrick Devlin's (1905–92) argument that societies have a type of 'self-defence' right to enforce conventional morality; and by those who argue for paternalistic legislation.

See autonomy; Devlin, Patrick; harm principle; Hart, H. L. A.; Mill, John Stuart; morality, critical v. conventional; paternalism; pornography; Stephen, James Fitzjames

morality, separation of law and   *See* separability thesis

N

narrative scholarship An approach to legal scholarship that diverges sharply from traditional case and doctrinal analysis, to tell stories. Sometimes these are autobiographical stories exploring the author's own experiences; sometimes stories of other people's experiences; and sometimes fictional stories or fables with no claims to historical truth, but with ambitions to reveal some deeper truth. Narrative scholarship is most frequent within, and associated with, critical race theory, though it has also been common within feminist legal theory, and used by scholars of a wide variety of other perspectives.

Some critics have attacked narrative scholarship as not being 'real scholarship' (a charge that can have significant consequences, where hiring, tenure, and promotion decisions often turn in part on an assessment of an individual's scholarship). The critics emphasize the difficulty of verifying the facts and causal connections alleged in the stories. The stories are also said frequently to imply a connection (what happened to one person happens to all, most, or many members of an oppressed group) which is rarely substantiated.

See **critical race theory; law and literature**

Nash equilibrium A term from game theory, named after the theorist John F. Nash, Jr. (1928–), though the basic idea might be traceable to the writings of Antoine Augustin Cournot (1801–77). Nash equilibrium describes a stable point in a 'non-cooperative game', a situation, resulting from a combination of players' strategies, under which no player could improve its position by changing its strategy. While a Nash equilibrium is sometimes referred to as the 'solution' to the game in question, (1) not all games have a Nash equilibrium, and many games have more than one; and (2) there is no assumption that a Nash equilibrium is desirable (for the parties involved or for interested others). The best-known example of this last point is the way that the stable Nash equilibrium for the prisoner's dilemma is where both parties have 'defected', a result far from the optimal one for the parties.

John Nash was the co-recipient of the Nobel Memorial Prize in Economic Science in 1994 (with John Harsanyi and Reinhard Selten).

See **game theory, prisoner's dilemma**

natural kinds analysis An idea from philosophy of language, originating largely from the works of Hilary Putnam (1926–) and Saul Kripke (1940–). The argument is that for many objects, the meaning of a term describing the object is not set by our beliefs about it, but rather by our best scientific theory about the nature of the object. The idea is sometimes summarized by saying that the meaning is not in our minds; rather, the meaning is determined in part, or entirely, by the world. For natural kinds, extension determines meaning rather than the other way around. This sort of analysis makes most sense for physical objects whose existence does not depend upon us, as contrasted with objects and categories that are entirely our invention.

The relevance to legal theory is that a number of theorists (e.g. Michael Moore (1943–), Nicos Stavropoulos) have tried to use natural kinds analysis, or a variation, as the proper approach to legal concepts or to interpreting non-legal concepts when they appear in legal texts. A natural kinds approach has also been the basis for arguing for greater objectivity in law. The argument of such theorists is that lawmakers have, or should be held to have, the intention that their references to legal and moral concepts (e.g. 'cruel and unusual punishment' or 'malice') are to the objective entity or category named by the term, rather than to the (imperfect) beliefs that the lawmakers might have regarding those categories.

natural law, minimum content of The 'minimum content of natural law' derives from an analysis offered by H. L. A. Hart (1907–92) in ch. 9 of *The Concept of Law* (1961). The book offered a view of legal positivism, the position that denies that the criteria of legal validity must make reference to morality or justice. In the context of a general overview of the various ways in which law and morality can be said to overlap or to influence one another, Hart offers that the notion that legal systems (*and* conventional morality) *must* have some minimum of moral content could be seen to be correct *in the sense that* given certain truths about human nature (our vulnerability, limited resources, and the like) and the current state of technology, no society could survive long without offering to at least a significant portion of the population at least some protection against physical attack and some variation on the institution of property.

It should be noted, first, that this is more a prediction (under what circumstances a society could and could not survive) than a conceptual analysis. Second, to whatever extent it is a 'concession' to natural law theory, it still leaves substantial room for disagreement with traditional natural law theory. The most evil regimes (whether one thinks of Nazi Germany, Stalin's Soviet Union, or Apartheid South Africa) have all easily met the 'test' of the minimum content of natural law.

See Hart, H. L. A.; natural law theory

natural law theory Natural law theory is a mode of thinking systematically about the connections between the cosmic order, morality, and law. This approach has been around, in one form or another, for thousands of years. Different natural law theories can have quite disparate objectives: e.g. offering claims generally about correct action and choice (morality, moral theory); offering claims about how one comes to correct moral knowledge (epistemology, moral meta-theory); and offering claims about the proper understanding of law and legal institutions (legal theory). Additionally, natural law has played a central role in the development of modern political theory (regarding the role and limits of government and regarding natural rights) and international law.

Important aspects of the natural law approach can be found in Plato (*c.*429–347 BC), Aristotle (384–322 BC), and Cicero (106–43 BC); it was given systematic form by Thomas Aquinas (1224–74). Early natural law thinking can also be seen as deriving in part from the *ius gentium* ('law of [all] peoples') of ancient Roman Law (mentioned by Gaius, *Institutes* 1.1) which was thought to derive from general principles of reason, and thus be legitimately applicable to dealings of Romans with foreigners (though Gaius distinguishes *ius gentium* from 'natural law', *ius naturale* (*Institutes* 2.65)).

In the medieval period and through the Renaissance, with the work of writers such as Francisco Suárez (1548–1617), Hugo Grotius (1583–1645), Samuel Pufendorf (1632–94), John Locke (1632–1704), and Jean-Jacques Rousseau (1712–78), natural law and natural rights theories were integral parts of theological, moral, legal, and political thought. The role natural law has played in broader religious, moral, and political debates has varied considerably. Sometimes it has been identified with a particular established religion, or more generally with the status quo, while at other times it has been used as a support by those advocating radical change. Similarly, at times those writing in the natural law tradition have seemed most concerned with the individual-based question, how is one to live a good ('moral', 'virtuous') life?; at other times, the concern has been broader—social or international: what norms can we find under which we can all get along, given our different values and ideas about the good?

Some of the modern legal theorists who identify themselves with the natural law tradition seem to have objectives and approaches distinctly different from those classically associated with natural law, most of whom were basically moral or political theorists, asking: How does one act morally? or, more specifically, What are one's moral obligations *as* a citizen within a state, or as a state official? and, what are the limits of legitimate (that is, moral) governmental action? By contrast, some modern theorists working within the tradition are social or legal theorists, narrowly understood. Their primary dispute is with other approaches to explaining or understanding society and law. In fact, much of modern natural law theory has developed in reaction to legal positivism, an alternative approach to theorizing about law. The two different types of natural law—natural law as moral/political theory and natural law as legal/social theory—can be seen as connected at a basic level: as both exemplifying a view of (civil) law not merely as governing, but also as being governed.

Many of the modern legal theorists identified (or self-identified) as 'natural law theorists' are working within the tradition established by the work of Aquinas (the most prominent example may be John Finnis (1940–)). However, there are also theorists identified to varying degrees with 'natural law' who offer quite different approaches: e.g. the 'procedural natural law' theory of Lon Fuller (1902–78) and the 'interpretive theory' of Ronald Dworkin (1931–).

See **Aquinas, Thomas; Aristotle; Cicero; Fuller, Lon L.; Grotius, Hugo; Hart, H. L. A.; human nature; legal positivism;** *lex iniusta non est lex*; **Locke, John; natural law, minimum content of; Pufendorf, Samuel; Radbruch, Gustav; Stammler, Rudolf; Suárez, Francisco; teleology; voluntarism**

naturalism Within philosophy, naturalism is a school of thought under which even traditionally metaphysical topics and issues are approached in the manner of the natural sciences. For example, W. V. O. Quine (1908–2000) advocated a naturalized approach to epistemology ('Two Dogmas of Empiricism', *Philosophical Review* (1951)). Within legal philosophy, some theorists, most prominently Brian Leiter (1963–), have argued that jurisprudence should stop approaching such questions as 'What is law?' with the tools of conceptual analysis, but should rather use empirical inquiries.

Occasionally, the term 'naturalism' will be used to identify a follower of natural law theory, but this usage is relatively rare.

See **necessity**

necessary and sufficient conditions Within logic and philosophy 'necessary condition(s)' and 'sufficient condition(s)' are basic terms of analysis, often described under the rubric of 'if–then' statements. If A is a necessary condition for B, then B cannot be the case unless A is the case (e.g. 'it is a necessary condition for that object to be my hat that it be brown'); here, 'if B, then A'. If A is a sufficient condition for B, then if A is the case, B is also the case (e.g. 'it is sufficient that the object has three sides for it to be a triangle'); 'if A, then B'.

Necessary and sufficient conditions sometimes describe different aspects of causation, where, for example, a purported 'cause' of an accident (e.g. the driver's inattention) might have been a necessary condition, but not a sufficient one for the accident to occur. Certain doctrinal consequences (e.g. reduced liability) might flow from a cause being only necessary, and not sufficient.

Discussions of necessary and sufficient conditions also arise in general legal theory, particularly in discussions of whether 'law' itself, or particular legal concepts, can be analysed in terms of necessary and sufficient conditions. Some commentators have argued that these concepts must be understood in a different way: e.g. as 'defeasible' terms, or as 'family resemblance' concepts or under a paradigm-based approach.

See **causation; defeasibility**

necessity Within philosophy generally, some assertions are considered 'necessary truths' if they could not have been otherwise. Here 'necessity' is contrasted with 'contingent truths', matters that could have been otherwise. Within general philosophy, the question of whether there are in fact any 'necessary truths' has become highly contested, owing to the challenges of W. V. O. Quine (1908–2000) and other naturalist philosophers. Legal philosophers from John Austin (1790–1859) to Joseph Raz (1939–   ) have regularly made claims that expressly or implicitly involve assertions of necessary truths about the nature of law, though they have only sporadically reflected on whether assertions of necessary truths are appropriate within jurisprudence.

See **conceptual analysis, naturalism**

neoclassical economics Another name for the mainstream of economic analysis. Under this approach, commercial and non-commercial behaviour is modelled through the use of various simplifying assumptions: that individuals seek to maximize the satisfaction of their preferences, individuals are rational, there are no transactions costs, and all actors are fully informed of all relevant facts (or can obtain such information without cost). This model has proved to be extremely powerful in both analysis and prediction, but the unrealistic assumptions grounding the neoclassical modelling has motivated the development of rival economic approaches that build on somewhat different assumptions.

See behavioural law and economics; new institutional economics

neo-Kantian analysis 'Neo-Kantianism' was a movement in German philosophy during the late decades of the nineteenth century and the early decades of the twentieth century, with work seeking to apply the ideas of Immanuel Kant (1724–1804) to a wide variety of areas. The relevance to legal theory is that the Marburg School of neo-Kantianism, through such writers as Hermann Cohen (1842–1918), was very influential on the work of the legal positivist Hans Kelsen (1881–1973). Like Cohen, Kelsen applied a version of Kant's 'transcendental argument' (derived from the theory of knowledge in Kant's *Critique of Pure Reason* (1781)): using experience as data to be explained, and working backwards to some presupposed category or principle. While for Cohen the focus was ethics (and the result a kind of Kantian socialism), for Kelsen, the data to be explained is our normative experience of law. Kelsen draws the connection with Kantian and neo-Kantian thought as follows (*Pure Theory of Law* (1960)): 'Kant asks, "How, without appealing to metaphysics, can the facts perceived by our senses be interpreted in the laws of nature, as these are formulated by natural science?" In the same way, [my] Pure Theory of Law asks, "How, without appealing to meta-legal authorities like God or nature, can the subjective sense of certain material facts be interpreted as a system of objectively valid legal norms that are describable in legal propositions?"'

For Kelsen, the result is the 'category' of the Basic Norm (*Grundnorm*), which we are said to presuppose when we view the law normatively.

See **Basic Norm; Kant, Immanuel; Kelsen, Hans; pure theory of law; Radbruch, Gustav**

neutral principles The term comes from Herbert Wechsler's (1909–2000) article in the *Harvard Law Review* (1959), in which he argued that in developing American constitutional law, the United States Supreme Court is constrained by the requirements that cases be decided 'on grounds of adequate neutrality and generality' and that the Court develop constitutional principles in a way that 'transcend[ed] the immediate result that is achieved'.

The idea of 'neutral principles' is a core view of the 'legal process school', an approach to law influential in the United States in the 1950s and early 1960s. This was an approach that accepted much of the American legal realist critique (thus the view implicit in Wechsler's argument that the Supreme Court had significant discretion in how it developed constitutional doctrine), but argued for constraints based on institutional design and relative institutional competence.

Attacks on the possibility of neutrality in decision-making were central to the arguments of the American legal realists, and to later critics (e.g. critical legal studies).

See **American legal realism; critical legal studies; legal process; Wechsler, Herbert**

new institutional economics An approach to economics that is offered as a rival to neoclassical economics ('transaction cost economics' either is identical, or at least strongly overlaps). Advocates of this approach (e.g. Oliver Williamson (1932–)) tend to emphasize the importance of transaction costs to understanding economic institutions (a point that was central to Ronald Coase's (1910–) work), the problem of bounded rationality, and the problem of asymmetric information (the way in which transactions often occur in contexts in which one party has significantly superior information regarding key matters). The extent to which these points require rejection of neoclassical economics, or only slight modifications of its model, or whether the simpler model of neoclassical economics is still to be preferred despite its imperfections, are highly controversial issues.

See **neoclassical economics**

Nietzsche, Friedrich A German philosopher (1844–1900) whose contrarian views were influential in moral philosophy, psychology, and aesthetics. It is mostly his later work and some of his unpublished work that has had influence in legal philosophy. Nietzsche's ideas of the 'will to power' and 'perspectivalism' have been discussed in the context of views of legal interpretation that downplay the constraint of the text or emphasize the political nature of interpretation: in the context of such discussions, there are occasional references to 'Nietzschean judges' who impose their will on the texts. In a similar way, some postmodern theorists refer to Nietzsche's scepticism about truth (in an unpublished work, Nietzsche wrote of truth as a 'mobile army of metaphors, metonyms, and anthropomorphisms'—fixed conventions whose origins as mere metaphors have been forgotten) as justification for a postmodern approach to legal interpretation.

Nietzsche's challenges to conventional morality—e.g. that it basically denies life (in favour of what Nietzsche denounces as a non-existent life to come), and that it derives historically from the interests and resentments of weaker groups ('slave morality')—have occasional resonance in various theorists' works on the nature of morality and its proper role within law.

See **Foucault, Michel**

nihilism A total rejection of beliefs in religion or morals. Some adherents of critical legal studies were accused of being nihilists, and a few accepted that label. In the debates within and about critical legal studies, the term was often being used (imprecisely) to indicate scepticism or relativism about moral truth.

See **critical legal studies**

Nino, Carlos S. Carlos Santiago Nino (1943–93) was a highly regarded Argentinian philosopher and public intellectual. His activities ranged from abstract analytical discussions of the nature of legal validity and legal rights to work for political and constitutional reform in his home country. He was an internationally known and respected theorist and activist on human rights issues. Nino was also an important figure in the introduction of analytical legal philosophy to the Spanish-speaking countries of Central and South America.

normative What *ought* to be done. The normative aspect of a discussion or a set of facts is its implications for how people should act, how rules should be changed, or even how theories should be constructed.

While references to 'normative' frequently refer to the moral analysis, 'ought' statements are not confined to moral evaluations. There are also purely self-interested or 'prudential' reasons for action, and one can also have a reason for action relative to some larger project (e.g. becoming a lawyer, building a boat, or robbing a bank)—though this project may be immoral or contrary to one's short-term or long-term interests.

normative legal positivism *See* legal positivism

norms Standards for how one ought to act. In discussion of laws and legal systems, the term 'norm' is sometimes used interchangeably with 'rule'. In the terms of practical reasoning, norms are standards that give reasons for action.

One question that has been raised by some legal philosophers is whether norms have their own distinctive logic (a question that could be applied either only to *legal* norms or to normative systems generally). This question has some practical applications in considering, for example, the proper treatment of legal norms within a single system that appear to be contradictory (whether two contradictory legal norms can both be valid, or whether one of the norms voids or modifies the other by some rule of inference derived either from the particular legal system or from the essential nature of normative thought, etc.).

While it is usual to connect norms with moral and legal *duties* (as in the beginning of this entry), it is important to note that statements of legal and moral claim-rights, immunities, powers, and liberties are also frequently classified as 'norms'.

See rules

Nozick, Robert An American philosopher and political theorist (1938–2002) whose first book, *Anarchy, State, and Utopia* (1974), had a lasting impact on thinking about justice and government. He also did significant work on Newcomb's Problem (an important problem or paradox within decision theory), and the philosophical problems relating to identity, knowledge, and rationality.

In large part a response to John Rawls's (1921–2002) *A Theory of Justice* (1971), *Anarchy, State, and Utopia* argued against the vision of an interventionist state redistributing property in the name of justice. Instead, Nozick advocated a minimalist 'night-watchman' state, arguing that it was unjust to take property (for redistribution) from someone who rightfully owned it (that is, who acquired it by just means from someone else who had acquired it by just means, etc., going back to someone who had initially created or acquired the property in a just way). Nozick summarized this analysis by saying that natural rights (of property) act as 'side constraints' on action.

Nozick's work was also significant for debates about justice in that he pointed out the practical difficulties with any distributive goal that depended on a particular pattern of distribution—egalitarian distributions being an obvious example, but even a Marxist distribution of 'to each according to his need' would be in the same category. Once the desired distribution was obtained (e.g. by redistributive taxation and government payments), it was vulnerable to being immediately and continually undermined by the voluntary choices of individual citizens, choosing to buy the goods and services other citizens offer. For Nozick, this was part of the reason for arguing in terms of 'justice in holdings' (that property was being held by those who obtained it in just transactions going back to the person who justly first created or obtained the object as property) rather than viewing justice as requiring a particular pattern of distribution.

See **Rawls, John**

O

objectivity The distinction between objective and subjective judgements frequently turns on whether the judgements relate to an external object, or only to people's perceptions of or beliefs about the object. In a looser sense, the terms are sometimes used to refer to a level of agreement (a judgement is objective in this sense if everyone, or all competent participants, agree on it, while judgements that evoke ineradicable disagreement are subjective), without concern for the metaphysical or epistemological grounds of that agreement or disagreement.

Within law, as in morality and aesthetics, there is substantial controversy over whether statements within or about the practice are, or can be, objective.

Some commentators have distinguished questions of *metaphysical* objectivity (which usually relate to the possibility of right answers in the law) from questions of *epistemic* objectivity (inquiries regarding biases within the legal system's method of reaching its conclusions).

Issues of objectivity in law are frequently related to, but not identical to, questions of legal determinacy—whether there are always, frequently, sometimes, or never right answers to legal questions.

Questions of legal objectivity often overlap questions about legal truth: what is it that makes statements within a legal practice (e.g. 'X and Y have a valid contract', 'Z has a right to keep that book') true? To the extent that the truth of legal propositions is thought to be determined by their correspondence with some (legal) reality that is independent of individual beliefs, it is more likely that law will be objective. To the extent that legal truth is determined by the future actions of officials or by the shifting beliefs of legal actors, law will be seen as less objective (and some have argued that legal truth is determined one way for 'easy cases' and a different way for 'hard cases').

A more mundane aspect of 'objectivity' is the sense that judges should come to disputes with an open mind and without bias.

See **indeterminacy; right answer thesis; subjective**

obligation *See* **duty**

obligation to obey the law An important and recurrent issue within jurisprudence is whether or to what extent there is an obligation to obey the law. By an 'obligation to obey', the usual reference is to a *moral* obligation, a *legal* obligation to obey the law being a near-tautology. Secondly, the obligation is usually assumed to be at most a prima-facie obligation, one that could be overcome if there is a stronger moral reason for acting contrary to the law's prescription. Third, among those commentators who believe that there is a moral obligation to obey the law, the conclusion is usually held to apply only to those legal systems that are generally just.

Those who argue that there is no obligation to obey the law, first, usually mean that there is no *general* obligation to obey the law. They are not asserting that there *never* is a moral obligation to obey *particular* laws, only that no moral obligation applies broadly to *all* legal norms, just because they are *legal* norms. Second, those arguing against the moral obligation to obey the law try to distinguish such a moral obligation from the fact that one has independent moral obligations that the law happens to echo. For example, one has a moral obligation not to murder, but one has that obligation independent of the legal prohibition of murder, and many opponents of a general obligation to obey the law would argue that the legal prohibition in no way adds to or increases the moral obligation.

There are a few standard types of arguments for a moral obligation to obey:

1. *Consent.* Through some significant act or omission (voting, accepting government benefits (e.g. police protection) or by not moving to another country), one has expressly or tacitly consented to abide by the rules set down by the government;

2. *Fairness, reciprocity,* or *fair play.* Civil society is seen as a kind of beneficial joint enterprise in which each person restricts his or her liberty with the expectation that others will do so as well, and in reasonable reliance upon that like restriction (here the obligation to obey the law is an obligation owed to one's fellow citizens, not to the government).

3. *Gratitude.* As citizens receive benefits from the state, they have a gratitude-based obligation to obey the state's laws.

4. *Moral duty to support just institutions* (an argument that obviously applies only if the legal system in question is just).

See **evil regimes;** *lex iniusta non est lex*

offence principle Thought by some to be a needed supplement to 'the harm principle', which asserts that state criminal prohibition is justified (only) when one person's actions will harm another person. The offence principle asserts that certain forms of offence can also justify the state's intervention, through criminal sanctions, to prevent certain behaviours.

The view, forcefully presented by Joel Feinberg (1926–2004), among others, is that certain forms of public offence to the sensibilities of others suffice to justify state intervention—though offence caused merely by the knowledge of what other people may be doing in the privacy of their homes may not justify such intervention.

See harm principle

Olivecrona, Karl *See* Scandinavian legal realism

ontology The study of 'what is', usually a study of what kinds of entities exist, and how to describe those entities. Ontological questions in law include questions about in what sense 'legal rules' exist. Another example would be Scandinavian legal realism, which was built around a deep scepticism regarding the existence of certain legal objects, e.g. 'rights', that could not be easily recharacterized in empirical terms.

See rights; Scandinavian legal realism

open texture Within legal philosophy, H. L. A. Hart (1907–92) used 'open texture' to refer to vagueness in the boundaries of a term's application. The concept derives from a related but distinct concept of the same name (*Porosität der Begriffe*) that Friedrich Waismann (1896–1959) had introduced to the theory of meaning and verification (not vagueness, but the possibility of vagueness, when some unforeseen factor or circumstance arose relating to some category or concept).

For Hart, the inevitable uncertainty in the application of terms and rules to borderline cases—what he was describing by 'open texture'— was a justification for legal indeterminacy and judicial legislation, at least for 'hard cases'.

See hard cases; Hart, H. L. A.; indeterminacy; paradigm; Waismann, Friedrich; Wittgenstein, Ludwig

opportunity costs A term from economics that emphasizes how the 'costs' associated with an option should include the choices that had to be foregone. Thus the costs of an afternoon reading for pleasure would include the money one could have made if the same time had been spent working. Similarly, the value of resources can be calculated by determining how much would have been paid by others for some alternative use. Usually 'opportunity cost' will refer to the most highly valued of the opportunities or alternatives *not* chosen. As James M. Buchanan, Jr. (1919–) and others have explained, opportunity costs should be understood as the alternatives that affect the process of making a choice, not to be confused with choices already made (e.g. 'sunk costs') that, rationally, should not affect the choices still to be made.

See law and economics; sunk costs

original position The structure for a thought experiment developed in John Rawls's (1921–2002) *A Theory of Justice* (1971), for determining what justice requires. We are to imagine individuals who are behind a 'veil of ignorance': unaware of their strengths, weaknesses, position in society, or comprehensive theory of the Good. Such individuals, Rawls contends, would not be tempted to argue for principles that would favour their own interests, and any principles such negotiators could agree upon would be presumptively fair (he therefore calls his approach, 'justice as fairness').

As a number of commentators have pointed out, and Rawls basically confirms, the original position is as much itself reflecting a moral position as it is a mechanism for deriving moral conclusions. It affirms the importance of some elements of human beings while discounting others, in particular discounting, at least temporarily, individual character, preferences, and achievements.

Rawls argues that those choosing in the original position would be relatively risk-averse: following a 'maximin' policy of maximizing the worst possible outcome, based on a chooser's fear that he or she might end up in that position. This assumption of risk-aversion is controversial, and the original position would probably result in quite different principles of justice and society if that assumption were modified.

See difference principle; justice as fairness; maximin principle; Rawls, John; risk aversion; veil of ignorance

overlapping consensus In John Rawls's (1921–2002) later work (e.g. *Political Liberalism* (1993)), he portrayed his theory of justice as primarily political not metaphysical—that is, one responding to the practical problem of building and maintaining a just society in the context of a population having quite varied comprehensive theories of the good. Rawls argues for principles of justice being seen as principles that the different reasonable theories of the Good can independently support—principles where the different theories of the Good converge or overlap.

See **Rawls, John**

P

paradigm It is part of some approaches to the philosophy of language that the meaning of terms is understood or taught on the basis of paradigm cases, central cases in which the application of a term is at its clearest. The question is then what the paradigm cases tell us about the application of the term to borderline cases. Discussions of paradigms in this sense appear in the work of both H. L. A. Hart (1907–92) (his notion of 'open texture', that judges have discretion in the application of statutes to borderline cases) and Ronald Dworkin (1931–   ) (the construction of a theory of law may be founded on paradigmatic applications of 'law', though these paradigmatic cases might themselves, in principle, be subject to challenge in the completed theory).

A different sense of 'paradigm' derives from Thomas S. Kuhn's (1922–96) *Structure of Scientific Revolutions* (1962), in which he argued that science develops within a 'paradigm', a framework of concepts, and that when data accumulate that cannot be accounted for within the existing 'paradigm', a new paradigm will eventually be offered that will take over as the framework within which work is done. 'Paradigms' of this sort are sometimes mentioned within legal philosophy as part of an argument that the basic assumptions or world-view within some area had shifted radically during some period.

See **open texture**

parentalism *See* **paternalism**

Pareto efficiency A view of efficiency grounded in the work of Italian economist and sociologist, Vilfredo Pareto (1848–1923), and reflecting the extent to which one situation or distribution is clearly better than another because everyone either prefers the second situation or is indifferent between the two. Where an altered state of affairs (e.g. affected by some transaction) would be preferred by at least one person, and everyone else either also preferred the second state of affairs or was indifferent between the second state of affairs and the original, the second state of affairs is considered 'Pareto superior' to the first. As a necessary corollary, the first state of affairs is characterized as being 'Pareto inferior' to the second (altered) state of affairs. A situation is 'Pareto optimal' if there is no move or transaction that would be 'Pareto superior' to it—and this is the understanding of 'efficiency' that is associated with Pareto analysis.

Being Pareto optimal should not be confused with being 'optimal' in any conventional sense of that term. Given a potential distribution of goods, there will probably be a number of Pareto optimal distributions, some of which will have little to be said in their favour (for example, a distribution in which one person had *all* the goods would be Pareto optimal).

Pareto analysis is often discussed together with Kaldor-Hicks analysis—'Kaldor-Hicks superior' sometimes carries the confusing label 'potential Pareto superior'. 'Kaldor-Hicks superior' occurs where the parties who are better off *could*—could, *but do not*—compensate those left worse off, in such a way that the resulting distribution would be Pareto superior. However, while it is hard to understand how anyone could object to a transaction that leads to a Pareto superior situation (everyone is left at least indifferent between the second state of affairs and the original), it is easy to discern possible objections to transactions that are only Kaldor-Hicks superior, as some people are left worse off, and are not compensated for their losses.

Even in its traditional form, Pareto analysis has been subject to criticism as a guide to moral or social choice. For example, Amartya Sen (1933–   ) has argued that Pareto analysis may be inconsistent with core liberty rights.

See efficiency; Kaldor-Hicks analysis; law and economics

Pareto optimal *See* Pareto efficiency

Pashukanis, Evgeny B. Evgeny Bronislavovich Pashukanis (1891–1937) was the leading Soviet legal theorist in the early years of that country. However, under Stalin's reign, his work was 'denounced', and he was eventually arrested, tried, and shot. Pashukanis's *The General Theory of Law and Marxism* (1924) was very influential upon publication, and was 'rediscovered' by a number of Marxist theorists in the late 1970s. Pashukanis applies traditional Marxist theory to law (for example, that both the State and law will wither away with the move to communism), but adds some original ideas of his own. He emphasized the extent to which law reflects (and facilitates) commercial transactions, how legal form expresses commodity form. While Pashukanis rejected the view of law as merely ideological, he pointed out the legitimating effects of law's treatment of all citizens equally as right holders, as (potential) owners of commodities.

See **Marx, Karl; Marxist theories of law**

paternalism Also known as 'parentalism', this refers to situations where the government treats its citizens protectively, broadly analogous to the way parents act for children too immature to care for themselves. The issue comes up in legal theory within the debate about the legal enforcement of morality. One alternative, or supplement, to John Stuart Mill's (1806–73) minimalist 'harm theory' (government coercion is justified only to prevent harm to others) is paternalism, in which government action would be justified on the basis that the government is sometimes better at protecting individuals than those individuals acting on their own behalf. Paternalist justifications have been offered for mandatory seatbelt use in motor cars and helmets for cyclists and motorcyclists; limits on rates of interest for loans; restrictions on gambling; etc.

See **harm principle; morality, legal enforcement of**

path dependency A term that derives in part from economic analysis, and that covers all the ways in which prior decisions affect current decisions. The general idea is that earlier actions can have significant effects later. Sometimes the claim focuses on choices that seemed reasonable and efficient when made, but turn out not to have been so; and sometimes on decisions or circumstances that seemed unimportant, but turn out over long periods of time to have significant effects.

The term 'path dependency' is often associated with purported examples of how less-efficient machines and processes appeared to prevail over more efficient alternatives (e.g. in typewriter keyboards, videotape technology, or software) because of being first, or some other relatively arbitrary circumstance. (The extent to which there are such examples, in which inferior technologies won out by historical circumstance, is sharply contested.)

The term is also associated with some of the work of Herbert A. Simon (1916–2001), whose work on bounded rationality included assertions that the way most people decide matters makes it likely that decisions may turn on the order in which alternatives are presented.

See **bounded rationality; sunk costs**

patriarchy Some feminist legal theorists have argued that the law—not just the substantive legal rules, but also the way people reason within and about the law—helps to create or maintain a patriarchal society, one run primarily by and for men, with the intention or effect of subjugating women.

See feminist legal theory

penalty default *See* default rule or term

perfectionism A belief that the State should be in the business of promoting virtue. It contrasts with the classical liberal position of theorists such as John Stuart Mill (1806–73) and John Rawls (1921–2002), that the State should be 'neutral' between different theories of the Good. Its prominent advocates have included theorists as diverse as James Fitzjames Stephen (1829–94), a contemporary of Mill, and present-day theorists Joseph Raz (1939–   ) and Robert P. George.

See Stephen, James Fitzjames

Plato Plato was an early Greek philosopher (*c.*429–347 BC), who along with his pupil Aristotle, set the foundation for all Western philosophy. His influence on all theory has been both wide and diffuse. Within *legal* theory, Plato's effect might be most directly seen (1) in his metaphysically realist beliefs, which, in their application to both language and morality, are important for theories of adjudication and legal interpretation; and (2) in his theories of politics and justice—in his dialogue, *The Republic*, the well-ordered society is analogized to the well-ordered soul, and each is said to require individual parts properly performing their own tasks.

Plato has also had an indirect effect on law: his portrayal of Socrates' method of trying to instil knowledge through persistent and challenging questions has 'inspired' (if that is the right word) the 'Socratic Method' of teaching law that is prevalent in American law schools.

See realism

policies (v. principles) Within Ronald Dworkin's (1931–   ) early works on legal theory (especially *Taking Rights Seriously* (1977)), policies are contrasted with principles as the basis for making governmental decisions. Legislatures are said to be forums where policy, the greatest good for the greatest number, etc., is a legitimate basis for decision. By contrast, courts are to be 'forums of principle', deciding for one party over another, *not* on the basis of the consequences, but on the basis of which party has *a right* to prevail. This ties in to Dworkin's theory that there is a unique right answer for every legal question.

See **Hart, H. L. A.; principles; right answer thesis**

pornography Conventionally defined as any sexually explicit text, picture, or film. The extent to which law should regulate pornography has been central to discussions both of the legal regulation of morality and feminist legal theory—though it is important to note that the relevant definition of 'pornography' often varies between the two debates. Within debates about the legal regulation of morality, the issue is access to any (or almost any) explicit depiction of sexuality, as the argument is that such materials are immoral, or lead to immoral behaviour. (Within American free speech doctrine, there has been a defence against finding a text 'constitutionally unprotected' because pornographic, if the text otherwise has 'redeeming social value'.)

Within feminist legal theory—in particular, in the writings and legal proposals of Catharine MacKinnon (1946–) and Andrea Dworkin (1946–)—the focus is on sexually explicit materials (whatever their alleged 'redeeming social value') which depict women as enjoying subordination, humiliation, or rape. MacKinnon and Dworkin are less concerned with the morality of sexually explicit texts and images, than with the way certain forms of such material 'sexualizes' the subordination of women within society, and works, indirectly, to silence women's speech.

See **feminist legal theory; morality, legal enforcement of**

positive discrimination *See* **affirmative action**

positive political theory *See* **public choice theory**

postmodernism In painting and architecture, 'postmodernism' was a reaction against 'modernism'. In legal philosophy, there never really was a 'modernist' movement, so 'postmodernism' in this context can gain its meaning only by analogy to its use in other areas. Discussions of postmodernism among legal theorists primarily tends to invoke the use of that term among literary theorists.

While there is no consensus view of what is meant by legal postmodernism, there are some themes that regularly appear: rejection of the idea of foundational or transcendent truth; rejection of 'grand narratives'; belief that many basic concepts (including gender and race) are socially constructed; a general denial of certainty and constancy; and an emphasis on the irrational and unconscious influences on our actions and beliefs.

See deconstruction; feminist legal theory; law and literature; scepticism

post-structuralism *See* postmodernism

Pound, Roscoe Roscoe Pound (1870–1964) was an important figure in early twentieth-century American jurisprudence. In the early part of his career he was a strong advocate for a (more) sociological approach to law, arguing, for example, that the focus should be on the objectives legal rules were supposed to serve, seeing how well the rules were serving those objectives, and modifying the rules that were not serving their purposes well. This seems an obvious point to modern readers, but appeared radical against the more formalistic or conceptualistic reasoning of that time. Pound served as Dean of the Harvard Law School, and in his later years came to oppose, or at least urge caution on those who sought a more 'realistic jurisprudence' inspired by his work and the work of Oliver Wendell Holmes, Jr. (1841–1935), Pound's caution about legal realism was most famously displayed in a 1931 exchange with Karl Llewellyn (1893–1962) in the *Harvard Law Review.*

See American legal realism; Holmes, Oliver Wendell, Jr.; law and society; Llewellyn, Karl N.

practical reasoning An approach to morality and ethics that focuses on the reasons we have for and against particular actions and choices. The term often refers to or derives from Aristotle's distinction between practical and speculative reasoning, with practical reasoning being tied to (eventual) action. Within the philosophy of law, Joseph Raz (1939–) has been prominent in analysing rules and 'law' in terms of reasons for action (e.g. *Practical Reason and Norms* (1975)). Within philosophy generally, practical reasoning (reasons for action) is often contrasted with theoretical reasoning (reasons for belief).

Some commentators (e.g. when arguing that legal reasoning should be understood as simply another form of 'practical reasoning') use the term more loosely or colloquially to mean something like 'common sense'.

practice theory of rules *See* rules, practice theory of

pragmatism Pragmatism refers generally to a philosophical movement in the early decades of the twentieth century, whose main figures included John Dewey (1859–1952), William James (1842–1910), and Charles Sanders Peirce (1839–1914), and to more recent theories and theorists (such as Richard Rorty (1931–) and Hilary Putnam (1926–)) whose positions are similar. While the theorists who share the label 'pragmatist' differ significantly in the details of their views, they generally preferred that the grand concepts of philosophy—such as 'truth' and 'justification'—be thought of instead in the more mundane terms of 'what works'. The pragmatists opposed 'foundationalism' in philosophy and absolutism generally. In analysing terms and concepts, the pragmatists tended to focus on how they were used in life.

The early twentieth-century pragmatists strongly influenced the American legal realists, with the philosopher Dewey writing influential articles on legal topics, and the judge and legal theorist Oliver Wendell Holmes, Jr., (1841–1935) being considered by some to be a significant force within philosophical pragmatism.

More recently, a number of legal theorists have labelled their approach to law as 'pragmatist', but there seems to be a wide variety of views that fall under that label.

See **American legal realism; Dewey, John; Holmes, Oliver Wendell, Jr.**

precedent 'Precedent' refers to prior decisions, in particular prior decisions on the issue currently before the court. A core aspect of common-law reasoning is the way that prior decisions bind later courts, that authoritative status usually being confined to higher courts (and, sometimes, also courts of the same level) within that legal system. In most civil law systems, courts are not similarly bound by prior decisions.

What keeps the process flexible in most common-law systems are the following characteristics: (1) courts are generally bound only by the decision of the prior court, and by the reasoning *necessary* for that decision (*ratio decidendi*); they are not bound by other statements of the prior court (*obiter dictum*); and (2) later courts usually have significant discretion in how they characterize the prior court's ruling and reasoning; they need not defer to that court's characterization of its own decision. The combination of these two allows courts a great deal of freedom to 'distinguish' prior decisions as not being truly on point for an issue currently before the court.

See coherence theory; common law; indeterminacy; *stare decisis*

predictive theory Scattered comments among the American and Scandinavian legal realists (e.g. in O. W. Holmes, Jr.'s (1841–1935) 'The Path of the Law' (1897) and some of Alf Ross's (1899–1979) work) that suggest an equation of 'what the law is' with a prediction of how judges will decide future cases. Such approaches have value as a corrective for theorists otherwise inclined to a too-abstract or too-metaphysical view of the law and they may also be good advice to legal counsel regarding what the client most wants to know (Holmes's quotation comes in the context of the 'bad man', who 'care[s] a good deal to avoid being made to pay money, and will want to keep out of jail if he can').

However, as theories about the nature of law, predictive theories have well-known weaknesses. Most obviously, they cannot explain the behaviour of judges (at least the judges of the highest court, who need not fear reversal on appeal), who could hardly be said to be predicting their own conduct.

See **bad man; Holmes, Oliver Wendell, Jr.**

preferences Economic analysis, especially in neoclassical economics (which is the foundation of modern law-and-economics analysis), starts from an assumption that individuals are rational maximizers of their preferences. However, the concept of 'preferences' remains an unexplored core concept in this model. Some theorists have suggested that the idea of 'preferences' is more complex or problematic than economic analysis allows, and that further work needs to be done on that topic.

A key assertion or assumption of neoclassical economics is that our preferences can be derived from our choices ('revealed preferences'). However, for a given set of choices, there will often be more than one possible set of preferences that would explain them.

Also, neoclassical economic analysis and law and economics are faulted for their unconcern with *how* we come to have the preferences we do, and unwillingness to judge the wisdom, justice, or morality of those preferences.

See **revealed preferences**

prima-facie obligation An obligation that exists, unless there is a special countervailing reason; the idea of a prima-facie obligation is often attributed to W. D. Ross (1877–1971), in *The Right and the Good* (1930). Commentators view prima-facie obligations differently (a difference that might merely be one of stipulative usage, though it is usually portrayed as a substantive moral point). The question is one of the status of such obligations if and when one determines that there is a stronger countervailing reason. Does the moral reason still exist (which seems to have been Ross's position), or has it been 'nullified' by the countervailing reason? (No one doubts that one should *not* keep one's promise to meet a friend for lunch when one comes across an emergency situation where one might save a life; the only question is whether one would say that the moral reason to keep the promise was 'cancelled' or whether it continued, but was overridden.)

The term often occurs in legal philosophy as part of the debate over the moral binding status of legal rules. Much of the debate is about whether a generally just legal system creates a prima-facie obligation to obey. Within the debate, positions range from those who argue that legal systems and legal rules, even at their most just, *never* create a prima-facie obligation of obedience, to those (like Thomas Hobbes (1588–1679)) who argue that *any* legal system, even an unjust one, creates an obligation of obedience that is almost never defeated.

principal–agent problem A common topic in the economic analysis of commercial and legal relationships, regarding the difficulty of regulating relationships where one party is supposed to be acting in the interests of another (e.g. not just when employees act as an agents for their employers, but also tenants who occupy the landlord's property, managers controlling the property of corporate shareholders, and so on). In these sorts of situations, the principal is usually unable to supervise the agent's actions constantly or effectively, and seeks some structure of incentives that will encourage the agent to continue to act in the principal's interests. To the extent that the contract, statutes, or by-laws connecting the parties fail to overcome the principal–agent problem, and the agents have an incentive to act in their own interest and contrary to the interests of their principals, there is sometimes said to be a 'moral hazard'.

See **agency costs; moral hazard**

principles Within Ronald Dworkin's (1931–) earlier work (in particular, *Taking Rights Seriously* (1977)), principles play two important roles in the theory of law and the theory of adjudication presented. First, principles are contrasted with rules, where 'principles' refers to moral standards that do not apply in a conclusive and all-or-nothing fashion. There can be principles supporting both sides of a legal dispute, while it is arguably the case that wherever a rule properly applies (without being overruled, or an exception found), it is conclusive as to the result. Also in contrast with rules, principles can vary in the weight they have, for or against a particular result in a particular case. (Some later commentators have remained sceptical that legal rules and principles can be so sharply divided along the lines Dworkin indicated.)

The distinction between rules and principles relates to Dworkin's critique of H. L. A. Hart's (1907–92) discussion of judicial discretion. Hart had stated that legal rules run out in hard or borderline cases, and in such cases the judge must legislate anew. Dworkin argued that the law—in the sense of the standards that judges have an obligation to apply—consists of principles as well as rules. The existence of principles *as well as* rules within a legal system meant that it would be harder to argue that the law 'runs out' in many cases (which principles were part of the law was to be determined by considering which standards had received express or implicit support in past statutes, judicial decisions, and other official actions). If law did contain numerous principles as well as rules, Dworkin was in a stronger position to claim that there were unique right answers to every legal question, though the right answer thesis would still not be proven.

The second role for principle in Dworkin's early work was in contrast to policy—here, principle being understood as decision on the basis of legal or moral right, while policy is decision on the basis of consequences. According to Dworkin, legislatures frequently made decisions on policy grounds, deciding which regulations would create the greatest overall benefit for society, and that such considerations were appropriate for a legislature. Courts, however, were to be 'forums of principle', deciding only on the basis of rights (according to Dworkin, rights, by their nature, trump utilitarian considerations). This part of Dworkin's analysis, like the distinction between principles and rules, is also tied to his right answer thesis, for it is part of his argument that, for any case before the court, one party or the other could be said to have 'a right to prevail' (the law, properly understood, supports that party).

See **Hart, H. L. A.; policies; right answer thesis; rules**

prisoner's dilemma The simplest and most basic 'game' in game theory, it is also the standard example showing how and why the social good may not always be furthered by individuals acting in their own self-interest, and why some external means of coordinating behaviour may be needed to maximize social welfare. The idea is conventionally attributed to Melvin Drescher and Merrill Flood (1908–   ) from work they did in 1950, as part of the Rand Corporation's output on game theory, while its name originated in an article formalizing the concept written by the Princeton mathematician, Albert W. Tucker (1905–95). (Tucker also supervised the doctoral dissertation that eventually won John Nash (1928–   ) the 1994 Nobel Memorial Prize in Economic Science.)

Two persons are being charged with committing a crime together, but they are being held and questioned separately. Each understands that if one confesses while the other does not, the confessor will testify against the silent prisoner and go free, while the silent prisoner will be convicted and serve a high sentence. If both stay silent, they will both be convicted of only a minor crime, and will serve only a minor sentence. If both confess, both will serve long sentences (though not as long as if they had been convicted without having confessed). These alternatives are usually presented in a two-by-two box (Fig. 1).

Though each prisoner knows that co-operation (that is, neither confessing) would lead to the outcome that would be best for them together (a total of 2 years of combined prison time, as contrasted with 12 and 16 years for alternative outcomes), 'not confessing' never seems to be the individually rational decision to make. For example, from A's perspective: A thinks, 'if B confesses, I am better off to confess (8 years in prison is better than 12 years); and if B does *not* confess, then I am still better off to confess (0 years is better than 1 year).' B's perspective is identical. Thus, by individual rational decision-making the two prisoners are led from the *best* joint outcome (2 years total prison time) to the *worst* joint outcome (16 years total prison time).

The prisoner's dilemma is often given as a proof (or at least a metaphorical suggestion) that self-interest will lead to 'cheating' and 'defection' even when ongoing co-operation would be to the individuals'

	A (confess)	A (not confess)
B (confess)	(A—8 years) (B—8 years)	(A—12 years) (B—0 years)
B (not confess)	(A—0 years) (B—12 years)	(A—1 year) (B—1 year)

Fig. 1.   Prisoner's dilemma

longer-term interest, as well as the social interest. (Of course, in the standard prisoner's dilemma example, the prisoners are assumed to be guilty, so though their confessions are not in *their* best interests, they would seem to be in the interest of their society.)

A different dynamic can develop when the question of defection versus co-operation occurs in a repeated ('iterated') game. Where the same players are involved in a repeated interaction, various forms of co-operation (including a kind of tit-for-tat game, in which one party co-operates, but responds to a defection with a defection of its own) can become rational. This dynamic has its own complications (e.g. what happens when a repeat prisoner's dilemma game seems as though it is about to end?), about which there is a substantial literature.

The 'tragedy of the commons' can be seen as a variation or generalization of the prisoner's dilemma, involving many players. If there is a common ('open access') grazing or fishing area, the long-term interests of the grazers and fishermen is for modest restraint by all to maintain the long-term viability of the common area. However, each individual has an incentive *not* to co-operate, but rather to get as much benefit as possible from the commons, while hoping that others show restraint. With everyone having that incentive, no one shows restraint and the commons are soon overgrazed or overfished.

David Lewis (1941–2001) proved (*Philosophy and Public Affairs* (1979)) that the prisoner's dilemma is in fact a version of a less well-known paradox of rationality, Newcomb's Problem. In Newcomb's Problem, there are two boxes—one contains either a million dollars or nothing, and the second contains a thousand dollars. You are free to take the first box alone, or to take both boxes. The content of the first box depends on another person's earlier reliable prediction of your action, such that it will contain a million dollars if the prediction is that you will take only the first box, but nothing if the prediction is that you will take both boxes. What should you do? The paradox is that there seem to be good reasons for either strategy (taking only one, because then the reliable predictor will have sensed that, and put in the million dollars; or take both, because the prediction has already occurred, and one can only end up with the same or more by taking both boxes, whatever the content of the first box). The relation between the box-chooser and the predictor can be seen as structurally similar to that between the two prisoners.

See **collective action problem; co-ordination games; game theory; Nash equilibrium; social norms; tragedy of the anti-commons; tragedy of the commons**

procedural justice The procedural aspects of justice (sometimes referred to as 'legal justice' or 'justice according to law') that involve following the rules laid down previously, giving sufficient notice to individuals of the rules that will apply to them, and allowing the affected parties the opportunity and right to participate in the process that will lead to the rules and decisions that bind them (indirect participation—voting—for legislation, and direct participation in adjudicative proceedings). Procedural aspects of justice are frequently contrasted with more substantive aspects. The two can easily clash: consistent application of a wicked law can be, in that sense, procedurally fair, even when requiring a substantively unjust result in a particular case. However, there are reasons to think that systems that are more procedurally just will tend also to be more substantively just (because of the underlying goodness of the officials, or because it may be more difficult—though certainly far from impossible—to reach substantively unjust ends using just procedures).

Lon Fuller's (1902–78) procedural natural law theory was largely an elaboration of the procedural aspects of justice, and their role within a good legal order.

One question for legal ethics, and for morality generally, is what moral force, if any, comes from following the rules laid down when those rules are immoral (in general, or as applied to particular facts)?

See justice; Fuller, Lon L.; procedural natural law

procedural natural law The phrase usually refers to Lon Fuller's (1902–78) legal theory, one similar to traditional natural law theory in positing a significant moral test that must be passed before a rule or a system of rules can be called 'legal' (or 'legal in its fullest sense'), but different from traditional natural law theory in that the criteria relate primarily to the *procedures* by which the rules are promulgated and applied, rather than the *content* of those rules.

See Fuller, Lon L.; internal morality of law; procedural justice

promise-keeping (and contracts) A basic and recurring question for contract law theory is the extent to which contract law is merely an institutional form of the moral obligation to keep promises. Given that most contract law systems leave many types of promises and bargains legally unenforceable (e.g. in the English and American systems, agreements that lack 'consideration' are usually unenforceable), the discussion of the moral justification of contractual liability will be more complicated than the simple enforcement of promises. It also complicates the analysis for legal systems (like the English and American systems) that generally do not take into account the culpability of the failure to keep one's promise (treating most 'innocent' breaches of agreements comparably with 'intentional' breaches). The fact that the moral justification of promise-keeping is itself controversial adds another level of difficulty to the theoretical analysis of contract law.

property law The philosophical foundations of property law have traditionally been seen as tied up with questions of political theory and political legitimacy in a way that other aspects of private law (e.g. contract law and tort law) rarely are. However, the arguments at the grand level between the likes of John Locke (1632–1704) (a natural right to property, and a legitimate claim to resources with which one has 'mixed one's labour', as long as one leaves 'as much and as good' for others), G. W. F. Hegel (1770–1831) (private property as one of the intermediate institutions that must be present if individual freedom is to be possible); and Karl Marx (1818–83) (private property within a capitalist system is inherently exploitative and must be abolished), do not often trickle down to the arguments over more specific property law doctrines, though it does occur from time to time.

This mixture most often occurs when the courts are forced to face novel or foundational questions: e.g. what kind of things can be treated like property (commodification issues—e.g. whether one should be allowed to sell an extra kidney, blood plasma, surrogacy services, and sexual services—and intellectual property issues—whether one should be able to gain a right over a genetic code or a computer code); and the relative claims of colonizers and native peoples (e.g. the United States Supreme Court's famous, or notorious, decision in *Johnson* v. *M'Intosh* (1823)).

At the conceptual level, questions about property include whether property rights have certain essential attributes (e.g. to what extent must property rights equate with the right to possess, use, alienate, and sell the good in question), or whether property is just a grouping of legal claims ('bundle of sticks') that societies may alter for property in general or for particular kinds of property, according to what seems best for the social good. Also, questions are frequently raised about whether people can be said to have property rights in their bodies, and, if so, what follows from that (a variation of this argument having once been used to justify slavery).

Questions have been raised by economic analysts regarding the social benefits and costs of property rights in the context of the Coase theorem (initial distribution of entitlements frequently not crucial, because, at least in a world without transaction costs, entitlements will end up with the parties who value them the most); 'the tragedy of the commons' (common ownership leads to inefficient overuse of resources); and 'the tragedy of the anti-commons' (where resources are divided between too many individual property owners, transaction costs can prevent the efficient use of those resources).

Finally, there are numerous issues within property law theory that are philosophical only in the sense of raising questions of moral philosophy (and policy science): e.g. what should be the scope of the government's power to take property for public use (and when must the government compensate for such takings, or for regulatory restrictions on property that could be characterized as 'takings'); when government should be allowed to restrict the use of property through zoning, mandatory terms of leases (e.g. 'rent control' or tenant rights), or mandatory housing or building codes; and whether there should be restrictions on the enforcement of discriminatory covenants that run with the land.

See Coase theorem; commodification; Hegel, G. W. F.; Locke, John; tragedy of the anti-commons; tragedy of the commons

property rules   *See* liability rules

proximate cause   *See* causation

prudence   Within moral philosophy and practical reasoning, 'prudence', in the sense of moderate self-regard and self-protection, is often contrasted with 'moral' or 'altruistic' ways of thinking. While this use of 'prudence', as innocent self-interest, is narrower and less rich than the conventional use of the term ('prudence' as a virtue), it is none the less fairly common in the literature. Within legal philosophy discussions, 'prudence' (narrowly understood in the way described) is considered in the context of the questions of the extent to which our right or duty to protect our own interests (and the interests of those close to us—family and friends) can or must be balanced against our duties to others. There is also a long tradition, in both moral philosophy and economics, of trying to equate self-interest and moral action, either to urge people to act morally or to explain the development of moral norms from what some theorists assume to be our exclusively self-interested nature.

public choice theory Public choice theory is the application of rational choice theory (the basic approach, and the basic assumption, of economic analysis) to the behaviour of those acting on public affairs, including voters, public officials, and bureaucrats. More precisely, the theory is built on the view that public officials, like business people, should usually be understood as trying to further their own interests (which could include, for politicians, being re-elected, gaining more power, gaining prestige, or obtaining more campaign contributions; for judges the interests might include not having decisions overturned on review, and being appointed to a position on a higher court).

Public choice does not claim that public officials never act selflessly to promote the public welfare (any more than economists deny that business people sometimes do), but only that such actions will usually be rare compared to actions done for the officials' self-interest.

Some theorists have tried to argue, grounded in public choice theory, for reforms of the way law is understood and practised: e.g. that legislation should be understood as 'bargains' between different interest groups, and that judges, in interpreting legislation, should strive to enforce those bargains.

Public choice theory can be traced back to the work of earlier mathematicians such as Marie Jean Antoine Nicolas de Caritat, the Marquis de Condorcet (1743–94), who discovered certain paradoxes relating to voting. (In a broader sense, public choice can also be traced to the view of leaders given by Niccolò Machiavelli (1469–1527) in *The Prince* (1513).) Important modern public choice texts include Duncan Black (1908–), *The Theory of Committees and Elections* (1958); and Gordon Tullock (1922–) and James M. Buchanan, Jr. (1919–), *The Calculus of Consent* (1962). To the extent that public choice focuses on the analysis of voting, it tends to overlap social choice theory.

Some commentators use the label 'positive political theory' to refer to a category of theories related to public choice theory; however, since the use of 'positive political theory' varies widely (and public choice theory has its own variations in use), it is difficult to be precise about the relationship. Generally, 'positive political theory' seems (in most usages) to assume a rational actor model approach to political action, to focus more on the role of institutions, and not always to assume self-interested preferences.

See **Arrow's theorem**; **Condorcet jury theorem**; **Condorcet voting paradox**; **law and economics**; **rent-seeking**; **social choice theory**

public goods A term from economic analysis, which refers to goods where consumption by one person does not leave less for others, and where exclusion of other people from enjoyment of the benefit is costly or impossible. Examples include clean air and national defence. Because it is difficult for such goods to distinguish those who have paid from those who have not, giving the benefit only to the former, these goods cannot normally be left to market mechanisms, and are usually supplied by the government (who can ensure, through taxation, that everyone pays for the benefits they receive). The problem of people benefiting from a public good without contributing to pay for it is a paradigm example of free riding.

The idea of 'public goods' goes back at least as far as David Hume (1711–76), in his *A Treatise of Human Nature* (1739). In determining the appropriate or optimal level of public financing for public goods, the work of Paul Anthony Samuelson (1915–   ), in particular, 'The Pure Theory of Public Expenditure' (*Review of Economics and Statistics* (1954)), has been central.

See **free rider**

public–private distinction Modern legal and political thought often distinguishes the public and the private in two quite different ways: (1) the private marketplace of goods and labour versus the political regulation of certain limited matters of public interest; and (2) market (public) versus home/family (private). These public–private distinctions usually turn on notions of freedom and voluntary action in one area, with state intervention and state coercion present in the other sphere, in order to protect private interests or the public good.

Some of the American legal realists, most notably Robert Hale (1884–1969), criticized the first sort of public–private distinction, that resting on the alleged voluntariness of market and labour transactions. The realists pointed out that though the state may be nominally absent from such transactions, it sets the background conditions against which the transactions occur (e.g. what type of persuasion, collective action, force, or deception will be allowed in transactions, and under what circumstances property claims and rights of exclusion will be upheld). These background conditions establish the relative power of individuals and groups, and the conditions are enforced (when tested) through state power. This realist critique was later taken up and elaborated by various critical legal studies theorists.

The second public–private distinction, between market and home/ family, has been the target of feminist legal theorists and critical legal studies theorists. One point is that when the state treats the family as a place beyond public regulation, it implicitly reinforces the domination of whichever party is stronger physically or economically (in both cases, usually the husband/father). While people might once have responded to allegations of domestic abuse or child neglect within a household that it was 'no one else's business' or that it was 'not the state's business', this is (in most countries) no longer an accepted response, which indicates a partial removal, or adjustment, of this public–private distinction.

As a number of commentators have pointed out, the attack on the public–private distinction is often overstated. While it is appropriate to focus attention on the baseline against which 'private' action occurs, and to subject that baseline to criticism where appropriate, it is an error not to acknowledge that the setting-up of the baseline should be subject to a different standard of analysis and evaluation than the government's actions where it regulates directly.

See **American legal realism; critical legal studies; Hale, Robert L.**

public reason An idea (and ideal) with a long history, going back at least to Immanuel Kant (1724–1804), but given its most forceful modern form by John Rawls (1921–2002), arguing that discussions regarding the good of society should be grounded on political values, justifiable on the basis of reasoning or truths widely accepted or available to all citizens. This is in contrast to justifying positions or policies on the basis of religious or philosophical doctrines which are highly contested or whose persuasiveness is tied to personal inspiration or divine revelation. Particularly controversial is the extent to which such arguments seem to exclude political arguments grounded on religiously based ideas that certain practices (e.g. slavery, segregation, or abortion) are unjust. Rawls later modified his own views on the question, becoming more accepting of religion-based arguments, at least in some circumstances.

Pufendorf, Samuel A German legal theorist and theologian (1632–94), who was teaching at the University of Lund in Sweden when he published his most important works, *On the Law of Nature and of Nations* (1672) and *On the Duty of Man and Citizen According to Natural Law* (1673). Pufendorf was a natural law theorist greatly influenced by Hugo Grotius (1583–1645), and like Grotius he argued that certain moral standards apply to all persons and all nations. However, he disagreed with Grotius about the basis of our moral obligation: he argued that all obligation is grounded on the commands of superiors to inferiors, and moral obligations are similarly reflections of divine command. Some commentators name Pufendorf (and his early text, *The Elements of Universal Jurisprudence* (1660)) as the beginning of modern natural law theory. Like Grotius, Pufendorf is also considered an important figure in the early development of international law.

See **Grotius, Hugo; natural law theory; voluntarism**

punishment Sanctions imposed on someone, usually by the State, for a misdeed. Within philosophy of law, there is substantial discussion of the justifications for punishment (retribution, rehabilitation, deterrence, shame, incapacitation, or community expression), and connected debates over the limits of punishment (e.g. is it ever justified to impose criminal liability regardless of fault—'strict liability'? What excuses or justifications must the criminal law include? When must a defence of insanity be recognized?).

There are a variety of justifications and goals offered for punishment. Backward-looking objectives such as retribution and expression (denunciation) focus on the crime that occurred; forward-looking objectives such as deterrence, incapacitation, and rehabilitation look to the consequences of the punishment on the wrongdoer and on society. (The lines between forward-looking and backward-looking actions are not always clear here. For example, the commentators who speak of an 'expressive theory of punishment' sometimes refer not merely to the (backward-looking) denunciation of what occurred, but also to the (forward-looking) function the punishment might have of morally educating citizens regarding society's views.)

There are also moral questions raised regarding whether some punishments are too cruel or barbaric to be imposed, even if they would otherwise be justifiable. (This moral question can also be a legal question where a country has a relevant constitutional guarantee or has signed a human rights treaty that constrains punishment in this way.)

See **Beccaria, Cesare Bonesana; criminal law; deterrence; Hart, H. L. A.; incapacitation; Kant, Immanuel; rehabilitation; responsibility; retribution; utilitarianism**

pure theory of law This is the name Hans Kelsen (1881–1973) gave to his own approach to legal theory. By 'pure', Kelsen meant that the theory should be, in his terms, focused 'on the law alone', not 'entangled', as other theories of law had been, 'in psychology and biology, in ethics and theology'. He wanted to separate the analysis of law from the issues of policy that concerned the direction of law rather than its nature. By creating a 'human science' of law, he hoped to achieve the objectives of all scientific pursuits, 'objectivity and exactitude' (one must keep in mind that Kelsen is writing in a German tradition in which the term 'science' (*Wissenschaft*) is used far more broadly than it is in English).

In substance, Kelsen's Pure Theory is a neo-Kantian account of what follows from the fact that people treat the acts of legal officials normatively. The argument is that certain further matters are implied by looking at facts normatively—in particular, assuming a foundational normative premise that is the ultimate ground of a normative conclusion. For example, someone who argues that one ought not to do something because it is proscribed by a holy text is implicitly accepting the premise that one ought to act as the sacred text states (or that one ought to do what a particular supernatural being has ordered).

There appeared to be some limits to the 'purity' of Kelsen's pure theory. His theory was not entirely abstracted from all empirical matters. For example, for Kelsen, the existence of a legal system (and the change from one Basic Norm to another in a revolution), turned in part on the efficacy of the system—though Kelsen, like other legal theorists, was quick to insist that he was not equating validity with efficacy or power.

See **Basic Norm; Kelsen, Hans; neo-Kantian analysis**

Q

quasi-rent A term from economic analysis and law and economics that indicates the value of a good above its next best available use. This concept can be applied to objects (a certain stack of wood may be worth £10 more when used to construct furniture compared to the next best use, as firewood), and even to personal choices (how much happier is Lisa married to Rob than she would be unmarried, or married to her second choice, Bill?). The conventional distinction between 'quasi-rents' and 'conventional rents' is that quasi-rents refer to temporary situations—the time during which resources are unresponsive to a change in price. The term was probably first used by the British economist, Alfred Marshall (1842–1924), in his piece, 'On Rent' (*Economic Journal* (1893)).

See economic rent; rent-seeking

queer theory Like feminism, critical race theory, and some of the offshoots of both, queer legal theory asserts that it is useful to treat as a category some or much of the work done by homosexuals, bisexuals, and 'trans-gendered' individuals about the place and treatment of those groups within law and society. Queer theory generally makes a point of not being 'essentialist' about sexuality, and it tends to assume or insist that homosexuality, as a status, is, at least to some extent, socially constructed. However, like other identity-based movements, such as critical race theory and feminist legal theory, there is a tension between, on the one hand, arguing against 'essentialism' and for 'social construction', and, on the other hand, asserting that members of this (socially constructed) group have a distinct perspective to offer. (A middle position is to assert that one's distinct perspective comes not from a distinct essentialist nature, but from the experience of being oppressed, discriminated against, and stereotyped by society.) In general, queer theorists tend to view nearly all forms of sexuality as liberating, putting those theorists in tension with some feminist legal theorists who view some forms of sexuality as exploitative or degrading.

See critical race theory; essentialism; feminist legal theory

R

race In conventional thinking in many countries, people are categorized according to 'race'—general groupings based on some combination of skin colour, other physical features, and country of ancestry. These groupings frequently have significant implications for social status and legal treatment. It is a commonplace among biologists, geneticists, and social theorists that racial categories are almost entirely socially constructed, with little or no biological/genetic basis.

A focus on the nature and implications of racial and ethnic categories is central to critical race theory and affiliated approaches to law. It is central to these theorists that law operates to promote the interests of the dominant racial group (whites) and to facilitate the subordination of other racial groups.

Like other theoretical movements grounded on difference, there are tensions within critical race theory writings between those who would treat the group in question as defined by some 'nature' or 'essence' distinct from the majority group(s). Thus, while most critical race theorists treat race as socially constructed, some also assert or imply that members of minority or oppressed racial groups, because of their unique nature or experiences, have different ways of perceiving and of thinking than members of majority groups. Most critical race theorists take a less radical view, arguing 'merely' that the experience of pervasive racism and discrimination that members of minority groups face necessarily affects their experience of and within society (and gives them an understanding of oppression that members of majority groups will probably never obtain).

See **critical race theory; discrimination; social construction**

Radbruch, Gustav A German legal theorist (1878–1949) who may be best known to English-language legal theorists as the commentator whose ideas where the centre of discussion in H. L. A. Hart's debate with Lon Fuller (1902–78) in the 1958 *Harvard Law Review*. While Radbruch's earlier work (e.g. *Rechtsphilosophie* (1932)) was within the legal positivist tradition, with some neo-Kantian elements, his later work was influenced by the rise of the Nazi regime. Radbruch believed that the legal positivist views of German lawyers and legal academics was a factor in their failure to resist the Nazis, and the willingness of German judges to apply Nazi law without complaint or attempt at reinterpretation. After the war, Radbruch advocated a kind of natural law theory, under which laws that were clearly unjust should have no legal status.

See **Fuller, Lon L.; Hart, H. L. A.; natural law theory; neo-Kantian analysis**

rational choice theory A form of analysis that is sometimes seen roughly to overlap traditional ('neoclassical' or 'Chicago School') economic analysis, and to be a subfield of economics, in which individual behaviour is modelled and analysed under an assumption that people make choices 'rationally', that is, that they seek to maximize the fulfilment of their desires or goals under the circumstances as they perceive them.

A frequent criticism of rational choice theory is that it does not accurately reflect human decision-making (the deviations of actual decision-making from the assumptions of 'rationality' are sometimes summarized under the term 'bounded rationality'). One response is that if rational choice falls short as a description, that is no different from most models of human behaviour: the only question is the extent to which the rational choice model (1) is successful in predicting or explaining human behaviour; and (2) is *more* successful than alternative models.

Another line of criticism of economists' ideas of rationality, associated with Amartya Sen (1933–   ), is that it cannot account for personal commitment—whether seen in terms of long-term goals or moral obligations—though such commitments are both integral parts of most people's decision-making, and important aspects of individual and collective long-term welfare.

See **behavioural law and economics; bounded rationality; rationality; social norms**

rationality Within economic analysis, and approaches connected to economic analysis, the rationality of actors is a key assumption (or assertion) in the models used to analyse and predict behaviour. Within economic analysis, rationality is usually equated with the pursuit of self-interest (broadly construed). This model of human behaviour has been subject to frequent criticism—that it is not an accurate picture of how people actually make decisions, and thus creates distortions in economists' analyses and predictions. Many of these criticisms are summarized by the idea of 'bounded rationality'.

The extent to which economic analysis of 'rationality' purports to be descriptive is not always clear. For example, John Harsanyi (1920–2000) argued that the rational behaviour assumed in game theory was meant to show how each player *should* act to maximize that player's interests, not to predict how individuals *will in fact* act. There is significant experimental data that individuals in various situations deviate from what would be predicted under the economists' model of rationality. One response to these deviations is to complicate the model (either by noting problems of asymmetric information, or by modifying the rationality model in ways summarized by the topics, 'bounded rationality' and 'social norms'); another response is to concede that the model is not perfect, but that it retains significant explanatory and predictive power, while a more complicated model might fail in those respects.

Outside economic analyses, 'rationality' usually means something different and more substantial: not merely the maximization of chosen ends, but also a certain insight in evaluating both means to an end and ultimate objectives.

The 'rational' and the 'reasonable' are sometimes the focus of discussion elsewhere in legal philosophy: e.g. to the extent that 'objective' standards in the law are asserted to be less neutral than advertised, and in fact express a male bias or perspective. Or the extent to which legal analysis overly values reason at the expense of emotion (again, this argument is usually raised by feminist critics). While the two terms, 'rational' and 'reasonable' are frequently used together, or seen as interchangeable, they have occasionally been distinguished. First, some commentators (e.g. W. M. Sibley, 'The Rational Versus the Reasonable', *Philosophical Review* (1953)) view 'rationality' narrowly as means–end thinking while 'reasonableness' is viewed more broadly to include a sense of concern for other people's well-being. A related distinction appears in John Rawls's (1921–2002) work (e.g. *Political Liberalism* (1993)), where he argues that the parties in his 'original position' are rational, but not reasonable—because, by the terms of that thought experiment, these parties have the ability to pursue their interests instrumentally (i.e., 'rationally') but they lack any conception of the Good, and are ignorant of many of the other reasons that would normally ground moral and political action (including due regard for the interests of others).

See bounded rationality; law and economics; original position; rational choice theory; Rawls, John; social norms

Rawls, John John Bordley Rawls was an American political philosopher (1921–2002) whose book, *A Theory of Justice* (1971), was arguably the most important English-language work on justice, and perhaps in political philosophy, of the twentieth century. Beyond his theory of justice, Rawls also made significant contributions to debates about the obligation to obey the law, the role of religion in public debate, and international human rights.

His work on justice was grounded on Kantian moral philosophy and social contract theories of political legitimacy. The Kantian moral philosophy is exemplified by a strong critique of utilitarian theories of justice and morality.

His theory of justice, sometimes labelled 'justice as fairness', equated justice with those principles people would agree upon for the governance of their society. Because people's knowledge of their actual circumstances (and thus what principles would work to their benefit or their detriment) would make actual agreement on such principles unlikely, Rawls created a thought experiment, 'the original position', where hypothetical bargainers have been stripped of all knowledge of their circumstances in life and of their comprehensive views about the Good. This condition Rawls labelled the 'veil of ignorance'. Rawls argued that what justice requires can be determined by figuring out what principles would be agreed upon by bargainers in the original position.

Rawls concluded, in *A Theory of Justice*, that bargainers in the original position would agree to these principles: (1) 'Each person is to have an equal right to the most extensive system of equal basic liberties compatible with a similar system of liberty for all'; and (2) 'Social and economic inequalities are to be arranged so that they are both: (*a*) to the greater benefit of the least advantaged... and (*b*) attached to offices and positions open to all under conditions of fair equality and opportunity' ('The Difference Principle'). The first principle was to have lexical priority over the second: that is, he believed that the negotiators in the original position would not be willing to trade equal claims for liberty for some possible economic benefit.

In subsequent publications (e.g. *Political Liberalism* (1993)), Rawls modified and clarified his ideas about justice—for example, emphasizing that his was a *political* theory, not a metaphysical claim about human nature (a metaphysical reading of *A Theory of Justice* had been common).

Rawls's theory can be seen in the long tradition of liberal theory, and the effort to show how the state must act in order to be considered legitimate. Rawls's theory has also been described as showing what the wealthy must do in order to justify their gains to those who have much less.

Rawls's theory has had numerous critics—prominent examples include the libertarian Robert Nozick (1938–2002), and the communitarian Michael J. Sandel. Some economically minded theorists have argued that the original position is built on inappropriate assumptions about the position negotiators would take (or should take) towards risk. And some feminist critics have argued that Rawls's theory of justice does not pay sufficient attention to justice within families, and the importance of families to societal justice.

See justice; justice as fairness; maximin principle; Nozick, Robert; original position; overlapping consensus; reflective equilibrium; social contract; veil of ignorance

reasonableness versus rationality *See* rationality

realism The term 'realism' can have quite different, almost contradictory meanings in legal theory discussions. The more common usage derives from the way the term is used both in common parlance and in literature and painting: 'realism' referring to a more *realistic*, less idealized portrayal of the world. In this sense, both the American and Scandinavian legal realism movements attempted to eliminate the mystifying and legitimating layers of rhetoric in discussions within and about law.

The other meaning of 'realism' derives from the philosophical use of the term, which involves an assertion that terms of a certain kind of discourse pick out something that really exists in the world. As the term is commonly used in philosophy to discuss the debate about moral terms, a realist of this sort might believe in the existence of Platonic 'Ideas' or 'Forms' that have a kind of other-worldly existence, but are the referents, in this approach, to terms such as 'good'.

(Even within the philosophical discussion, the use of 'realist' and 'realism' is under dispute, with some theorists characterizing views of areas of discourse as 'realist' whenever one can assign truth values to propositions in the area—even without the further ('Platonist') ontological claims about what exists in the world.)

See American legal realism; Plato; Scandinavian legal realism

reasons for action The terminology used by theorists who analyse ethical questions or social institutions in terms of practical reasoning.

'Reasons for action' are to be contrasted primarily with 'reasons for belief'. Theorists such as Joseph Raz (1939–   ) who analyse in terms of reasons for actions have developed a selection of different sorts of reasons. The main distinction is between first-order reasons (reasons for acting or not acting) and second-order reasons (reasons affecting whether one acts on certain first-order reasons). Raz introduced the controversial idea of 'exclusionary reasons', that there might sometimes be reasons *not* to act on other (otherwise valid) reasons. Raz argued that legal (and moral) rules work as exclusionary reasons, in that those subject to these rules were to exclude most of the reasons they would normally consider in determining whether to act in a particular way.

See **practical reasoning**

reductionist theories of law Reductionist theories are theories that portray legal systems or legal rules as being reducible to basically one type of proposition. Examples of reductionist theories include those of John Austin (1790–1859) (law equated with commands of the sovereign) and Hans Kelsen (1881–1973) (legal rules are reducible to authorization of officials to impose sanctions).

The strengths and weaknesses of reductionist theories reflect the general strengths and weaknesses of simple models and theories: on one hand, they can be seen to show a basic insight; but on the other hand, the simplifying process might involve too much distortion (and thus, any alleged 'insights' do not in fact relate to the real object(s) being studied).

H. L. A. Hart (1907–92) argued against reductionism (in particular, John Austin's form of reductionist theory) in developing his own approach to legal theory. Hart emphasized the multiplicity of forms and functions of legal rules. Hart's own theory emphasized different categories of legal rules (primary v. secondary, power-conferring v. duty-imposing) and avoided any reduction of law to one basic normative form.

The term 'reductionist' when applied to legal theory sometimes refers to something quite different: the effort to 'reduce' normative phenomena to empirical terms. In this sense of reductionism, Austin is (again) a reductionist, but Kelsen is emphatically not one (the separation of the normative and the empirical, the 'ought' and the 'is', being central to his theory of law).

See **Austin, John; Hart, H. L. A.; Kelsen, Hans; rules**

reflective equilibrium An approach to moral reasoning John Rawls (1921–2002) discussed (e.g. in *A Theory of Justice* (1971)), in which settled, specific moral judgements are reconsidered in the light of proposed moral principles. In general, the idea is one of testing judgements and intuitions by theory, and testing theories against judgements and intuitions, until a view is reached that is coherent and contains no troubling elements. Rawls developed this idea from a similar notion Nelson Goodman (1906–   ) used in *Fact, Fiction and Forecast* (1965), where Goodman spoke of a 'virtuous circle' of testing rules of deductive inference against our deductive practices.

See equilibrium; Rawls, John

rehabilitation An approach to punishment where the purpose is to make the subject fit to be a full participant in civil society. It is often contrasted with the objectives of retribution and deterrence. Like deterrence, and unlike retribution, rehabilitation is a forward-looking policy, centered on affecting future behaviour rather than responding to past behaviour. Thus, rehabilitation is often considered a 'utilitarian' or 'consequentialist' approach to punishment (though it could also be seen as a moral goal separate from, and frequently in conflict with, the objectives of punishment).

See also deterrence; incapacitation; punishment; retribution

reification To treat a concept or an idea as if it were a physical entity. Some of the legal realists (e.g. Felix Cohen (1907–53)) argued that the prevalent form of judicial reasoning at the time they were writing (the early decades of the twentieth century), a form of reasoning to which they gave the derogatory title 'formalism', involved a great deal of reification (Cohen himself used the neologism, 'thingification'): treating humanly created concepts, such as 'contract' and 'due process' as if they were objects whose nature could be discovered through abstract inquiry.

relational feminism *See* cultural feminism

rent *See* economic rent

rent-seeking A term used in economic analysis to describe actions taken by individuals and groups to alter public policy in order to gain advantage or profit at the expense of others. (Within economic analysis, 'rents' are a resource's profits above its value in a competitive market or its 'opportunity cost', which should turn out to be the same thing.) This can occur, for example, when a company persuades the government to create a monopoly in its favour. Monopolies create inefficiencies in the market; the concept of 'rent-seeking' notes that there are costs in the initial creation of the monopolies. In general, there are a number of 'inefficiencies' that can be created by government intervention (including subsidies and protective tariffs); economic theory predicts additional inefficiencies as different entities compete to get the potential benefits of government action (e.g. different corporations each paying lobbyists £800,000 to try to persuade legislators to change the law in a way that could benefit one of them by £1,000,000).

The term was probably introduced by Ann O. Krueger, in 'The Political Economy of the Rent-Seeking Society' (*American Economic Review* (1974)), though the basic idea can probably also be found in earlier economic works on government action.

See economic rent; public choice theory; quasi-rents

republicanism *See* civic republicanism

responsibility Much of the law, especially the criminal law and tort law (accident law), turns on questions of moral responsibility for action. The difficulty is that this invites lawyers and legal scholars into philosophical debates that may be intractable, beyond the competence of the legal actors, and difficult to apply to day-to-day legal practice. None the less, the effort is made to take on important questions of moral responsibility because of the grave injustice of having a system that imposes significant criminal or civil liability without regard to such issues.

Among the most frequent points of contention are the insanity defence and the *mens rea* requirement in criminal law and the imposition of strict liability in tort law.

There is a general view that the imposition of either criminal or civil liability should be tied to circumstances where the person 'could have done otherwise'. However, to focus on that issue verges on the question of free will versus determinism ('in what sense could we have acted other than the way we did act?'), a notoriously intractable debate within metaphysics.

See moral luck; punishment; tort law

retribution An aspect of justice that requires the return of harm for harm. In considering punishment, retributive theorists argue for a punishment that 'fits the crime'. Retribution is often associated with the Latin term, *lex talionis* ('the law of retribution') and the biblical prescription (*Exodus* 21: 23–5) that punishment be 'an eye for an eye'.

Immanuel Kant (1724–1804) strongly advocated a retributive approach to punishment (e.g. in *The Metaphysics of Morals* (1797)), arguing that any other approach was a deviation from what justice required, and treated criminals with disrespect (by using them as 'means to an end' rather than as 'ends in themselves').

One problem with retributive theories of punishment is that they are difficult to transform into workable sentencing systems. While punishments should be 'proportionate' to the culpability of the act (or the culpability of the actor), how is such culpability to be measured across quite different types of crimes? Alternative objectives for punishment would include deterrence, rehabilitation, incapacitation, expression, and shaming.

See criminal law; deterrence; incapacitation; justice; Kant, Immanuel; punishment; rehabilitation

revealed preferences From economic analysis, the notion that a person's preferences among alternatives is implied ('revealed') by that person's choices (within the economic literature, much of the discussion of 'revealed preferences' goes back to Paul Samuelson's (1915–) work in the 1930s and 1940s). Even at this level of analysis, it is important to note that a number of different sets of preferences might explain a group of choices. The idea of revealed preferences is controversial among those who think that some values are incommensurable: i.e. that it is a false implication to say, for example, that because one is willing to take on a physically risky job for extra pay, or miss a meal with a friend when a good financial opportunity comes along, that these choices are a sufficient basis for determining the monetary price on one's value of health or friendship.

See preference

reverse discrimination *See* affirmative action

right answer thesis A view closely associated with the earlier work of Ronald Dworkin (1931–) (e.g. *Taking Rights Seriously* (1977) and *A Matter of Principle* (1985)), in which the claim is that all (or nearly all) legal questions have a unique right answer. 'Right answer' means an answer that was correct, and in existence, even before a judge decides the issue in a case.

While Dworkin's characterization of the argument varied over time, as did his justification for it (and the centrality of the claim to his legal theory), certain points remained relatively constant: e.g. an emphasis on the practice of participants in the legal process (the way both lawyers and judges speak—both before and after a case is decided—implying that there is a single right answer, already existing, to be found).

The notion is controversial because it is in conflict with a widely held view (one also supported by a number of important legal theorists, including H. L. A. Hart (1907–92)) that in difficult cases there is often no right answer.

See **hard cases; indeterminacy; legal gaps; objectivity**

rights 'Rights' operate as basic types of claims in both moral and legal discourse. The questions about rights include: (1) the connection or relationship between moral rights and legal rights; and (2) whether rights (in either or both areas) can be usefully analysed further, and, if so, in what way.

Most historians have concluded that there was no concept comparable to the modern idea of rights in ancient Roman law, and that this concept was not developed until the Middle Ages. According to these historians, when writers in ancient Rome discussed 'right' (*ius*), it meant something like 'the right thing to do'. In modern continental Europe, this meaning is sometimes characterized as 'objective right', while the usual Anglo-American understanding of legal or moral 'right' is labelled 'subjective right'.

Among those who have attempted to analyse rights further, Wesley Hohfeld (1879–1918) argued that the use of 'rights' could be clarified by distinguishing: (1) rights as claims, correlated with another party's duties, (2) liberties, (3) powers, and (4) immunities. Hohfeld was offering an analysis of the use of 'rights' within legal (and, particularly, judicial) discourse, but a similar form of analysis might be adapted to moral discourse as well.

In the discussion of the nature of rights, commentators often divide between those who find the essence of rights to be choice (the 'will theory' or 'choice theory' of rights) and those who find the essence of rights to be the protection of an interest through another party's duty (the 'interest theory' or 'benefit theory' of rights).

Ronald Dworkin (1931–) has analysed rights in terms of their effects—that they are particularly strong forms of reasons for action, reasons that trump other forms of reasons that might apply to a decision.

In particular, in considering legal or policy issues, a right takes precedence over utilitarian or majoritarian calculations that might otherwise justify a particular rule.

See animal rights; duty; Hohfeld, Wesley; interest theory (of rights); legal rights; Villey, Michel; will theory (of rights)

risk aversion It is frequently important in the context of economic analysis of choices and behaviour to consider the actors' attitudes towards risk. Those indifferent to risk are 'risk neutral'; those attracted to risk are 'risk seeking'; and those who dislike risk are 'risk averse'. Someone who is risk neutral would be indifferent between a certainty of being given £100 and a 50 per cent chance of being given £200; the risk-averse person might choose a certainty of £90 over the 50 per cent chance of £200; while the risk-seeker might, conversely, choose a 50 per cent chance of £200 even over a certain payment of £120.

As some commentators have pointed out, it may be more precise to say that these sorts of choices reflect differing preferences for outcomes rather than preferences for risks. For example, the person who chooses the certain £90 over the half-chance at £200, might on other occasions love the thrill of the gamble, but on this occasion be in desperate need of money for food. To put the same point a different way, the person who might strongly prefer the status quo to a 50/50 bet that could gain or lose £100 might simply have a 'declining marginal utility' for income: the pleasure this person would gain from an additional £100 is far less than the pain that would be felt from the loss of £100—and so a 50 per cent chance of the first does not counterbalance the 50 per cent chance of the second.

See law and economics; maximin principle; original position

Ross, Alf *See* Scandinavian legal realism

Rousseau, Jean-Jacques The French philosopher (1712–78) whose work on moral and political philosophy and educational theory made him both a prominent figure within the Enlightenment movement and a forerunner of (Romantic) criticism of the Enlightenment. His greatest importance for political and legal philosophy is arguably as the author of *The Social Contract* (1762), which presented an argument for political legitimacy in the social contract tradition (and contained the memorable phrase, 'Man is born free, and everywhere he is in chains'). The social contract tradition holds that government can only be legitimately grounded on a historical or ongoing agreement of free citizens. In *The Social Contract*, Rousseau also creates a metaphoric concept of collective self-government, 'the general will'. However, some commentators have found in the idea of a 'general will', a will of the 'social organism' potentially abstracted from the choices of actual individuals, the potential justification of tyrannical and totalitarian regimes.

See social contract

rule of law   A complex and contested ideal which can be traced back at least to Aristotle, under which citizens are to be 'ruled by law, not men'. There are various aspects to this ideal—and different commentators will vary in which they emphasize—but they tend to include that the standards of conduct are binding on all, including the most powerful; a rule's application should be consistent with its meaning; that rules should be promulgated; that they should be in clear language; and that compliance with rules must not be impossible.

Lon Fuller's (1902–78) (secular or procedural) natural law theory can be seen as an elaboration of the idea or ideal of the rule of law: when he writes of the 'internal morality of law', he means those moral ideals that require or are furthered by citizens being effectively guided by general rules. Other important advocates of a more formal procedural understanding of the rule of law have included Friedrich von Hayek (1899–1992), A. V. [Albert Venn] Dicey (1835–1922), and Joseph Raz (1939–   ). Some commentators have preferred a more substantive reading of the rule of law, one that entails either commitment to democracy or protection of certain individual rights (beyond those discussed in the formal/procedural idea of the rule of law).

See Fuller, Lon L.; Hayek, Friedrich A. von; internal morality of law

rule of recognition   Within H. L. A. Hart's (1907–92) legal theory, put forward in *The Concept of Law* (1961), the rule of recognition was a 'secondary rule' (in contrast to 'primary rules', which apply directly to subjects, 'secondary rules' are those regarding the identification, interpretation, and modification of 'primary rules') which 'will specify some feature or features possession of which by a suggested rule is taken as a conclusive affirmative indication that it is a [valid rule within the legal system]'.

The rule of recognition thus contains the criteria by which it can be determined which rules are part of the legal system and which are not. It is the final step in the normative chain of reasoning of why one ought (legally) to do what a particular legal rule states. As such, the rule of recognition plays the same role in Hart's system as the Basic Norm (*Grundnorm*) plays within Hans Kelsen's (1881–1973) legal theory; however, it is easy to overstate the similarities, given the quite different structures and purposes of the theories put forward by these two writers.

Hart argued (in *The Concept of Law*) that the 'effective acceptance' by officials of the criteria of the rule of recognition as standards of behaviour was one of two 'necessary and sufficient' conditions of the existence of a legal system (with the other condition being the general obedience to the system's valid rules by citizens).

At an abstract level, the existence of a rule of recognition is only an indication that there is a way of differentiating those rules (norms) that are part of the legal system and those that are not. At that level, though, the claim that every legal system has a rule of recognition is uncontroversial, and largely uninteresting. Even those writers (such as Ronald Dworkin (1931–   )) who see a freer interaction between law and extralegal (in particular, moral) standards do not entirely abandon the idea that one can distinguish, at any given time, whether a norm is or is not part of the current set of valid legal norms.

There is some controversy within the secondary literature as to whether the rule of recognition is best seen as a duty-imposing rule, a power-conferring rule, or some combination of the two. Also, some commentators who are otherwise sympathetic to Hart's project disagree with him that every legal system must have a rule of recognition, or that there can only be *one* such rule within a legal system.

See acceptance; Basic Norm; Hart, H. L. A.; legal positivism

rule-following considerations The name of an argument derived from central sections (generally, ss. 143–242, but particularly ss. 185–242) of Ludwig Wittgenstein's (1889–1951) *Philosophical Investigations* (3rd edn., 1958). The proper understanding of Wittgenstein's position is controversial, but a few matters seem relatively clear: (1) Wittgenstein spoke of 'rules' broadly, to cover most guided activities (most of his examples come from numerical series—e.g. 2, 4, 6, 8 . . . — and from the use of words); and (2) he rejected certain traditional explanations of how we are guided—e.g. metaphysical realism, or ideas in our head. A few commentators—most prominently, Saul Kripke (1940–   ) (*Wittgenstein on Rules and Private Language* (1982))—have interpreted Wittgenstein as proposing a sceptical conclusion about rule-following, but most commentators reject that reading.

The relevance of the rule-following considerations for legal theory is what this line of argument may tell us about the possibility of right answers, and *objective* right answers, for the interpretation and application of legal rules. The growing consensus appears to be that Wittgenstein's rule-following considerations offer no special or additional insight to the debates on legal interpretation, beyond perhaps a basis for challenging unconventional approaches to legal interpretation grounded on contrary philosophical theories of meaning. Those who argue for the relevance of the rule-following considerations often use Kripke's sceptical reading of Wittgenstein as a basis for arguing either for significant legal indeterminacy or for the importance of political or cultural agreement among legal interpreters as the grounds of determinacy or predictability in the law.

See rules; Wittgenstein, Ludwig

rule-scepticism A term used to describe the views of some of the writers within American legal realism and some later critical approaches. The 'scepticism' about rules concerns either the extent to which the following of (legal) rules is a good description of how judges actually decide cases, or the extent to which (legal) rules actually can determine the outcome of legal disputes. As to the first, descriptive point, the suspicion is that judges' decisions are in fact determined largely by conscious and unconscious biases. As to the second, more conceptual point, the argument is that the application of general rules to particular cases is often (some theorists might even say 'always') indeterminate.

Theorists who are labelled (or who label themselves) 'rule sceptics' tend to encourage an emphasis instead on 'what the courts actually decide', or on predictions of what the courts will actually decide.

See American legal realism; bad man

rules A rule is a standard meant to guide behaviour. Some commentators would distinguish rules from general normative considerations by the way those subject to a rule are meant to follow it without regard to the merit of the prescription (what is sometimes called the 'content-independent' validity of rules, or their 'peremptory' or 'exclusionary' force within practical reasoning).

While the terms 'rule', 'norm', 'principle', 'standard', and 'prescription' are frequently used interchangeably, some theorists seek to distinguish them in various ways in the course of making points about the nature of law or the nature of practical reasoning. In the course of such distinctions, rules are sometimes confined to standards that are conclusive when applicable, that have a canonical formulation, or that are relatively specific.

Because of the centrality of rules to most, and perhaps all, legal systems, a variety of discussions about the nature of rules, and the nature and variety of *legal* rules, appears within legal theory.

H. L. A. Hart (1907–92), in *The Concept of Law* (1961), emphasized the varieties of legal rules, using the examples of the distinction between primary and secondary rules (primary rules applying directly to citizens, secondary rules being rules about the creation, modification, interpretation, and application of primary rules), and between duty-imposing and power-conferring rules.

See norms; principles; rule-following considerations; rules, practice theory of

rules, practice theory of   The practice theory of rules is the label given to the theory put forward by H. L. A. Hart (1907–92) in *The Concept of Law* (1961) in the course of his criticism of John Austin's (1790–1859) command theory of law and the construction of an alternative approach to law.

Hart's analysis distinguished rules from habits, in that when someone (or some group) was acting according to a rule, the rule was cited as a reason for the behaviour, deviations from the standard required by the rule were criticized, and the rule was used as the basis for criticism.

When considered as a general theory of rules (as contrasted to simply being a part of the critique of John Austin's (1790–1859) command theory), the practice theory of rules has been sharply criticized by a number of theorists, including Joseph Raz (1939–   ) (in *Practical Reason and Norms* (1975)) and Ronald Dworkin (1931–   ) (in *Taking Rights Seriously* (1977)). Raz argued that the practice theory falls short by not being able to account for rules that are not practices, by being unable to distinguish between rules and widely accepted reasons (e.g. widely accepted strategies in a game), and by not accounting fully for the normative status of rules (that is, by focusing on whether people *think* that a standard creates a reason for action, it overlooks that certain standards may create reasons for action, whether anyone thinks so or not).

In the posthumously published (1994) postscript to *The Concept of Law*, Hart concedes that many of the criticisms of his practice theory of rules were justified.

See acceptance; Hart, H. L. A.; internal point of view; rules

S

Sacks, Albert M. Albert M. Sacks (1920–91) was the co-author, with Henry Hart (1904–69), of the casebook, *The Legal Process: Basic Problems in the Making and Application of Law* (tentative edn. 1958), the core text of the legal process school. He was a long-time member of the Harvard Law School faculty, and also served as its Dean from 1971 to 1981.

See **Henry M. Hart, Jr.; legal process**

satisficing A term within economic analysis that derived from the investigations of bounded rationality, and is usually associated with the work of Herbert A. Simon (1916–2001), who introduced the term in his article, 'Rational Choice and the Structure of the Environment' (*Psychological Review* (1956)). While neoclassical economics assumes that individuals are maximizing the satisfaction of their preferences, some theorists note that in real-world situations decisions are often made in a context of limited time and limited knowledge, and so individuals often seek not so much to maximize (or optimize), but to find an alternative that would at least be *satisfactory* on one or more criteria; this is 'satisficing'.

See **bounded rationality**

Savigny, Friedrich Carl von The German legal philosopher (1779–1861) who is generally considered the founder of the historical school in jurisprudence. His approach, strongly influenced by the German Romantic writers, emphasized the extent to which law, like language, expresses the culture, 'spirit', customs, and history of a people. His publications include *History of Roman Law in the Middle Ages* (1815–31) and *System of Modern Roman Law* (1840–49). Savigny's approach influenced many later theorists, including the English legal philosopher Sir Henry Maine (1822–88).

Savigny's historical approach to law was at times used (including by Savigny himself) as a justification for opposing codification. On a theoretical level, it contrasts sharply, with both natural law theory (which tended towards the view that one set of laws would be appropriate for all peoples at all times) and legal positivism (which focused more on laws consciously chosen by the sovereign or other officials, rather than the customary rules that develop on their own).

Savigny's importance also extended to an early explication of a will theory of rights.

See **historical jurisprudence; Maine, Henry; will theory (of rights)**

Scandinavian legal realism A theoretical movement that broadly paralleled, both in chronology and questioning tone, the American legal realist movement. Its leading theorists included Axel Hägerstrom (1868–1939), Alf Ross (1899–1979), Karl Olivecrona (1897–1980), and A. V. Lundstedt (1882–1955), with Hägerstrom being the acknowledged philosophical leader or inspiration for the others. The parallel with the American legal realists should not be overstated: the Scandinavian legal realists relied, in a way few if any of the American legal realists did, on an anti-metaphysical stance derived from the logical positivists.

Much of the original work of the Scandinavian legal realists can be summarized as an effort to translate legal concepts into the material of verifiable social sciences. Concepts such as 'right', 'validity', and 'obligation' were recharacterized in terms of psychology (e.g. perceptions of bindingness) or the inclinations or likelihood of certain behaviours. The legal concepts themselves were either discounted as 'mythical' or 'fictional', or discussed in near-anthropological terms, as in the 'magical' powers such terms seem to hold over citizens.

The Scandinavian legal realists were not uniform in their views: for example, Ross did not insist as some of the others did, that metaphysical-sounding terms should be excised from the legal vocabulary; Ross accepted such terms (e.g. 'rights') as useful shorthands. In turn, Olivecrona thought that Ross's work on rights was insufficiently sceptical, and did not reach to the 'real nature' of rights.

See **American legal realism; ontology**

scepticism Within the philosophical literature, scepticism generally refers to the denial that one can have knowledge within a particular area. Sceptical arguments of various forms have made regular appearances within legal theory. Those sceptical about morality have offered arguments about how this affects claims of legal truth. In recent decades, sceptical arguments have derived from a variety of sources: e.g. deconstruction, postmodernism, incommensurability, and (within one branch of critical legal studies) the 'fundamental contradiction'.

See critical legal studies; deconstruction; fundamental contradiction; incommensurability; postmodernism

Schmitt, Carl A German political theorist (1888–1985) who has been highly influential in much of Europe, though largely ignored in Britain and America. His significant efforts in support of the Nazi regime, his virulent anti-Semitism, and his unwillingness to repent for any of it later have made Schmitt's work unpalatable to many. Schmitt's political writings show a Hobbesian view of politics, as being about struggle and dealing with 'the enemy'. This view of politics, and of human nature, led to a critique of political liberalism, attacking it as an approach to governance that runs contrary to our combative nature and the inevitable enmity of peoples.

self-evident While many theorists use this term for its colloquial meaning of 'obvious', others, including some natural law theorists (e.g. John Finnis (1940–), and perhaps Thomas Aquinas (1224–74) as well), use the term to mean a correct matter that cannot be derived from more basic beliefs or axioms. For these theorists, a proposition's 'self-evidence' means *not* that it is something that no reasonable person could doubt, but rather merely that this proposition cannot be deduced from some other proposition (though it could be supported in other ways, e.g. by experience and observation, or by dialectical arguments that undermine contrary propositions).

semantic sting The name of an argument Ronald Dworkin (1931–) offered in *Law's Empire* (1986). Dworkin argued that many theories about the nature of law assert or assume that 'lawyers all follow certain linguistic criteria for judging propositions of law', but an approach grounded on that view would be unable to explain pervasive or theoretical disagreements about law among competent participants.

It is generally understood that the semantic sting argument was directed against the legal theory of H. L. A. Hart (1907–92), and legal positivist theories that derive from Hart's work. However, Hart and most other legal positivists have denied that such an argument would apply to their work, describing as inaccurate and uncharitable Dworkin's portrayal of legal positivism as merely semantic. The extent to which

Hart's position (or that of other legal positivists) depends on criterial semantics remains highly contested.

See **Hart, H. L. A.; interpretive theory of law; legal positivism**

semantics The study of the meaning of words and, more generally, the connection between words and the objects in the world the words signify. The relevance to legal theory is that issues of semantics sometimes arise in discussions about the proper approaches to judicial reasoning and statutory interpretation, and in debates about objectivity in law and legal determinacy.

semiotics In contemporary literary theory, semiotics is a general study of signs and symbolic systems, based generally on the works of Charles S. Peirce (1834–1914), Ferdinand de Saussure (1857–1913), and A. J. Greimas (1917–1992); semiotic theories tend to derive from, or overlap, structuralist approaches to understanding cultures and practices. Sporadic efforts have been made to apply semiotics to law; its most prominent advocates include Roberta Kevelson (1931–1998) and Bernard S. Jackson.

See **structuralism**

separability thesis A reference to a purported tenet or dogma of legal positivism, that law and morality are 'separate'. In John Austin's (1790–1859) lectures (*The Province of Jurisprudence Determined* (1832)), the claim was simply: 'The existence of law is one thing; its merit or demerit is another.' Austin's assertion can be viewed as stating simply that questions of the 'existence' or 'validity' of a legal rule, or the 'existence' of a legal system, are matters that can and should be determined separately from a moral (or political) evaluation of those rules and systems.

The same point is often phrased in terms of maintaining the distinction between 'what law is' and 'what law ought to be', though this begins to show possible points of ambiguity and controversy. When courts interpret ambiguous legal texts in line with the statute's purposes, or in a way meant to avoid an absurd or unjust result, this seems an example of the line between 'what law is' and 'what law ought to be' blurring, and similar comments could be made about common-law judicial lawmaking.

Sometimes the separability thesis is phrased in terms of there being no 'necessary' or 'conceptual' connection between law and morality. This way of phrasing the view recognizes the obvious point that there is a substantial overlap between law and morality—with much of criminal law, tort law, contract law, and other areas devoted almost entirely to discouraging morally bad behaviour or encouraging morally good behaviour. This way of phrasing the point also identifies a probable difference between legal positivism and some versions of natural law theory: that legal positivism denies that rules or systems of rules must meet some moral test before they qualify as 'legal'.

See **legal positivism; sources thesis**

signalling   An idea from game theory, developed by A. Michael Spence (1943–   ) (e.g. *Market Signaling* (1974)) and others, that now has broader application in economic analysis and other areas. Signalling refers to indirect ways of conveying information about products, opportunities, or people. Signalling is a way for people to indicate information about themselves through their actions: e.g. that they are trustworthy, competent, or rich. Wearing expensive clothing and presenting expensive gifts may be a way of signalling wealth, a signal a poor person would have trouble giving out for very long. Similarly, employers might prefer people who have obtained high educational degrees over those who have not, even if the degrees did not involve obtaining useful knowledge, because the degrees arguably serve as effective signals of the holder's ability and self-discipline. Signalling is usually behaviour that is difficult or costly in some way, being a credible indication in a way that mere assertion may fail to be ('talk is cheap').

See **game theory**

Skepticism   *See* Scepticism

slippery slope   A common form of reasoning within law (and law-school classrooms), according to which a position is rejected because though the particular position might be unobjectionable, it could lead to a position that is objectionable. The slippery slope argument usually works on the basis that if position X is accepted, there would be no principled way to avoid position Y (or, in the application of rules to facts—if X is considered an instantiation of the concept or an application of the rule, there would be no principled way to rule out Y as similarly within the category).

Smith, Adam   The Scottish economist and philosopher (1723–90) is best known for his work, *An Inquiry into the Nature and Causes of the*

Wealth of Nations (1776), which is considered the foundational text of modern economics. His arguments for the benefits of a free market, as against government regulation, for the promotion of the common good resonate strongly in the law and economics movement. His book of moral philosophy, *The Theory of Moral Sentiments* (1759), offers a theory of morality that is grounded in sympathy. This aspect of Smith's work has influenced legal philosophers who would build their view of social norms in a way quite different from theorists more influenced by Smith's *Wealth of Nations*.

Smith's famous metaphor of 'the invisible hand' (though expressly mentioned only twice in his works, once each in *The Wealth of Nations* and *The Theory of Moral Sentiments*) summarized the view that society benefits from the unintended consequences of self-interested actions. The idea that actions normally thought of as private vices might work to the public benefit can be traced at least to Bernard Mandeville (1670–1733), in his work, *The Fable of the Bees: or, Private Vices, Publick Benefits* (1714).

See **law and economics; social norms**

social choice theory Social choice theory concerns the way that individual decisions can (or cannot) be aggregated into social choices; in different terms, it is an analysis of certain formal characteristics of collective decision-making, including (but not limited to) voting. While aspects of social choice theory can be traced to the works of the Marquis de Condorcet (1743–94) and Jeremy Bentham (1748–1832), among others, modern social choice theory is thought to have been begun by Kenneth Arrow's (1921–   ) book, *Social Choice and Individual Values* (1951), and the best-known idea in social choice theory is Arrow's impossibility theorem, introduced in that text.

The impossibility theorem proves the paradoxical conclusion that it is impossible to create a group voting system that produces a consistent set of preferences from the preferences of the individual voters within the group. While social choice analyses of this type raise questions about the rationality or arbitrariness of collective decision-making, social choice theory should not be confused with the more sceptical view of institutional decision-making found in public choice theory (and based, there, not on logical proofs but on certain assumptions about human motivation).

Some commentators understand 'social choice theory' more broadly to include all questions about the rational action of individuals within groups—thus including many concepts usually associated with game theory (e.g. co-ordination problems, prisoner's dilemma, free rider problems, etc.).

See **Arrow's theorem; Condorcet jury theorem; Cordorcet's voting paradox; game theory; public choice theory**

social construction The notion that certain ideas, attributes or objects do not 'really exist' independently of our perceptions, beliefs, and values, but are rather the product of our collective beliefs and attitudes. 'Race' or 'racial identity' seems to be a clear example of a socially constructed category or attribute, as research seems to indicate that human genetics offers nothing 'real' that corresponds even roughly to the racial categories that we use. Social construction in this sense indicates the extent to which the way we view the world is contingent, and we might be able to reform it through laws, education, or communication (though these matters may not be subject to quick change or change by isolated individuals).

Some commentators' use of 'social construction' is somewhat different, deriving from or related to the idea of 'social facts' and 'institutional facts', that certain 'facts' are tied to human practices, but are 'facts' none the less.

See **critical race theory; critical legal studies; gender v. sex; institutional theories of law; race**

social contract An agreement among citizens of a community, or between the citizens and the government. Social contracts have been central to discussions of the limitations of government, and the circumstances of governmental legitimacy, for hundreds of years, prominently in the works of Thomas Hobbes (1588–1679), John Locke (1632–1704), Jean-Jacques Rousseau (1712–78), and John Rawls (1921–2002). Sometimes social contract theorists purport to describe an actual historical agreement that accompanied the founding of a society, but there is little evidence of there ever having been such agreements. More recent social contract theorists, such as Rawls, have presented the social contract in question expressly as a thought experiment.

The social contracts discussed usually refer to individuals giving up some or all of their natural rights in return for, or as part of, the establishment of a central government that will offer security, stability, and (in most but not all accounts) protection for their rights. With the prominent exception of Hobbes's theory, these accounts also involve certain constraints on the government established.

Social contract theories of government (and of justice) present society as a collective agreement for mutual advantage. This approach is usually grounded on a picture of human beings as rational maximizers of their own interests, which can be either a strength or a weakness of this approach, depending on one's perspective.

While social contract theories are meant to establish or justify the rights and duties of citizens, their basic argument can be challenged. Social contract theorists referring to actual past agreements need to show why current persons should be bound by those agreements. Those referring to hypothetical agreements have perhaps an even harder problem, in showing why anyone should be bound by such 'hypothetical consent' (especially 'hypothetical consent' by imaginary persons). These problems may indicate that the image of a 'social contract' may be misleading, in that talk of contract implies legitimation based on autonomy (the choice or will of an autonomous person); when in fact the arguments offered by most social contract theories tend, at bottom, to be about fairness or reasonableness (that these are substantially fair distribution of rights, or substantively fair trade-offs of liberty, security, and equality).

Social contract thinking is also a significant idea within moral philosophy; those who do not believe in standards of morality derived from divine revelation and are sceptical about deriving morality from certain basic claims about human nature, may be willing to think of morality in terms of certain principles agreed to by human beings as a matter of mutual self-restraint for everyone's long-term self-interest.

See **Hobbes, Thomas; Locke, John; Rawls, John; Rousseau, Jean-Jacques**

social norms Within legal philosophy, this term is usually used to define a particular project: explaining how altruism or morality could develop if the only or primary motivations for individual action are selfish. This is primarily a discussion within law and economics, where the dominant model assumes 'rational behaviour', where 'rational' means that one's efforts are directed towards satisfying one's own preferences. A parallel inquiry occurs within evolutionary psychology and sociobiology, where the selfishness is ascribed to evolutionary impulses. Some commentators (e.g. Robert Axelrod) have argued that co-operative social norms may have evolved as the (strategic) response to repeated prisoner's dilemma situations.

See **prisoner's dilemma; rationality; rational choice theory; Smith, Adam**

social thesis *See* sources thesis

socio-legal studies *See* law and society

sociobiology *See* evolutionary psychology

sociological jurisprudence The term 'sociological jurisprudence' was commonly used, especially in the early decades of the twentieth century, to refer to a wide collection of theories that tried to apply sociological methods and insights to the discussion of law. Such works include the broad social theorizing of Max Weber (1864–1920) and Emile Durkheim (1858–1917); and the more mundane, if critically insightful, arguments of Roscoe Pound (1870–1964). Pound's work focused on the objectives of legal rules, and the rules' efficacy in achieving those objectives, and was a powerful influence on the American legal realists.

One theorist often associated with 'sociological jurisprudence', Eugen Ehrlich (1862–1922), tried to show how social factors (e.g. poverty, social values) have as much influence on the outcome of disputes as the legal rules ('lawyer's law').

See American legal realism; anthropology of law; functionalism; law and society

sociology of law *See* law and society

sources thesis In Joseph Raz's *The Authority of Law* (1979), he discussed 'the social thesis' as the view that what is law is a matter of 'social fact', requiring no moral argument. Raz (1939–) stated that there are stronger and weaker versions of the social thesis, and he renamed the stronger version 'the sources thesis'. The sources thesis is Raz's interpretation of legal positivism, as well as, in his view, a true statement about law: 'the existence and content of every law is fully determined by social sources'. Social sources are to be contrasted with the use of moral argument to determine the content of laws.

The sources thesis can be seen as one brief characterization of the version of legal positivism known as 'exclusive legal positivism'. This approach interprets the separability thesis (regarding 'the separation of law and morals') as requiring no moral evaluation in the determination of the content of legal rules. As this view seems contrary to the usual understanding of many Western legal systems, which seem to have legal rules with embedded moral standards and judicial review of legal rules based on moral tests, the view requires some justification. Advocates of exclusive legal positivism usually construct the argument from positions regarding the nature of authority and the relation of law and authority.

See **legal positivism; separability thesis**

sovereign Both in conventional language and in much of legal and political theory, the sovereign is simply the head of state. That term has also been used in a more restrictive way in some legal and political theories. The concept of a sovereign, understood narrowly as someone who is obeyed but who obeys no one else (and is constrained by no laws—at least no laws not of divine origin), is central to John Austin's (1790–1859) theory of law. For Austin, law was basically the commands (orders backed by threats) of a sovereign.

Austin's notion of the sovereign seems to derive from that of Thomas Hobbes (1588–1679), who wrote of a social contract, under which citizens, more interested in their personal safety than in anything else, agreed to create a sovereign with absolute power in order to escape the worse fate of the State of Nature.

See **Austin, John; Bodin, Jean; Hobbes, Thomas**

Stammler, Rudolf An influential German legal philosopher, Rudolf Stammler (1856–1938) worked to create a legal theory within the structure of Kantian philosophy. In parallel to Immanuel Kant's (1724–1804) pre-experiential categories through which one is said to perceive, Stammler tried to determine what the categories or 'pure forms' were for law. The neo-Kantian exploration for what is common to all legal systems can be seen as similar to, if still distinct from, the inquiries made by traditional natural law theory. For Stammler, the potentially conflicting actions and purposes of a 'community of free-willing men' would find harmony in a society whose *form* was established by just law. Stammler's most influential work is arguably *Lehre von dem richtigen Rechte* (1902), published in English as *The Theory of Justice* (1925).

See **Kant, Immanuel; natural law theory**

stare decisis This phrase (thought to derive from the Latin maxim, *stare decisis et non quieta movere*—'stand by what has been decided and do not disturb the calm') is the shorthand term for the common-law treatment of precedent within judicial decision-making, though the reference of the phrase, like the underlying practice, probably varies from one common-law jurisdiction to another (and perhaps also in any one jurisdiction, over time).

Courts are bound by authoritative prior decisions, but the limits on when and how prior cases bind judges leaves room for the flexibility for which common-law decision-making is well known. Courts are bound by the decisions of courts higher in the hierarchy, and, on some occasions, by courts at the same level. Additionally, courts are bound only by a narrow aspect of the prior decision (usually some combination of the result and a constrained characterization of the rule or rationale underlying that result). Discussions of this aspect of *stare decisis* usually use the terms *ratio decidendi* (the principle of decision, which courts who are bound by the case must follow) and *obiter dictum* ('something said in passing'—matters not central to the decision of the case, which courts who are bound by the case need not follow).

See **common law; precedent**

Stephen, James Fitzjames Sir James Fitzjames Stephen, 1st Baronet (1829–94), is best known for his efforts to explain and reform the English criminal law—in works that included *General View of the Criminal Law of England* (1863) and *History of the Criminal Law of England* (1883). Within jurisprudence, he is probably better known for *Liberty, Equality, Fraternity* (1873), his reply to John Stuart Mill's (1806–73) *On Liberty* (1859).

Stephen rejected Mill's notion that the state should not be in the business of promoting morality. Additionally, he rejected the notion that liberty, as such, was valuable without regard to how the liberty was used. At the same time, Stephen was cautious or hesitant about most of the kind of enactments people have in mind when they talk about 'legislating morality'. He thought that privacy needed to be respected, that the compulsion of the criminal law should not be lightly used, the danger of error must be kept in mind, and that it is unwise to use the weapon of the criminal law against strong human desires (as occurs with legal rules requiring chastity), especially when no other person is clearly being harmed.

Stephen pointed out inconsistencies in Mill's general argument, in that Mill's 'harm principle' seemed to argue against *any pressure* being used against actions that do not harm other people, when Mill's own position seems only to exclude use of *criminal sanctions*; Mill seems not to object to the use of *social pressure* to try to create more virtuous, or at least less vicious, behaviour.

See Devlin, Patrick; harm principle; Mill, John Stuart; morality, legal enforcement of; perfectionism

strategic behaviour Often used in the context of talking about negotiation, and negotiation as part of an analysis within economic analysis or game theory, as referring (in a generally pejorative way) to parties' lying about their preferences and their intentions (including threats and false threats—'bluffs') in order to gain some advantage in the negotiation.

Sometimes the term is used with no particular pejorative force, to mean whatever 'strategy' people have chosen to deal with the choices they face.

See game theory

structuralism An approach to knowledge and understanding in a variety of fields (e.g. linguistics, anthropology, and political theory), which had its greatest influence in the 1950s to the 1970s, structuralism seeks the deep structure beneath surface variety. Its most important advocates include Claude Lévi-Strauss (1908–). There have been occasional attempts to apply structuralist methods and insights within legal theory, usually by theorists from one of the critical schools (critical legal studies, feminist legal theory, critical race theory, post-modernism): e.g. Duncan Kennedy's (1942–) discussion of a 'fundamental contradiction'.

See fundamental contradiction; semiotics

Suárez, Francisco A prominent Spanish philosopher (1548–1617) who wrote on a variety of topics. Within philosophy of law, his importance was as an innovator within the Thomistic natural-law tradition. He adopted a position that offered a compromise between a purely will-based approach ('voluntarism') and a reason-based approach. For Suárez, actions are *intrinsically* good or bad, but we are only obligated to pursue the good because God so commands us. Suárez's interpretation of the natural-law tradition strongly influenced later theorists, in particular Hugo Grotius (1583–1645).

See Grotius, Hugo; natural law theory; voluntarism

subjective Within legal doctrine, the '(purely) subjective', as the idiosyncratic perception of given individuals, is frequently contrasted with the 'objective' or 'reasonable person' test set down by many legal standards. Similarly, subjectivity in legal theory usually is raised only as part of an analysis of (or critique of) the idea of legal objectivity.

In some legal and political theories, the subjective is equated with 'values', which are considered to differ significantly from person to person, and not to be subject to demonstration (even if one thinks that there is one right moral or value system).

See objectivity

subjective rights *See* rights

sunk costs An idea from economics, indicating expenses that have already been spent or committed, and cannot be retrieved. The fact that costs are already 'sunk' in a particular situation could well affect the choices the parties make, and the strategies they use in making their choices.

Some commentators see 'sunk costs' as a kind of fallacy (with the comment, 'sunk costs are irrelevant' a common saying among economists), an irrational way of thinking, or an example of 'bounded rationality'. The argument is that whether one has invested in a particular option or path or not, the economically rational decision at any time considers the costs and benefits of the choices *at that moment*—and that will mean sometimes following earlier investments, and sometimes taking another path despite the earlier investments. Those who choose a path *simply* because of prior investments—and in the face of a greater benefit from choosing another path at this point—are simply being irrational (whether due to pride or some other reason).

This point is not to be confused with the simple (and quite rational) claim of 'opportunity costs': that in making any choice, one must take into account the alternatives or opportunities one would give up in taking one path rather than another. This is a point about choices now being made, rather than the (irrational) claim of 'sunk costs', that past choices should affect present decisions in a certain way.

See bounded rationality; opportunity costs; path dependence

T

tacit consent *See* consent

teleology The study of things according to the end-points or objectives towards which objects are moving. Teleological explanations were prominent in the work of Aristotle, and they are common in religious and metaphysical views of the world, but they are rare in modern secular philosophy. The relevance of this concept for legal philosophy is that teleological explanations are arguably common to the various approaches to morality and law that go under the rubric 'natural law theory'. Some natural law theories build moral systems from human nature, sometimes phrased in terms of the ideal towards which human beings naturally strive. Other natural law theories argue that law is best understood in terms of the political or moral ideal (justice or some related notion) towards which legal systems (or those who create or maintain legal systems) must be understood to be striving.

See **natural law theory**

textualism The belief that legal texts (always or usually) have objective meanings that are (largely or entirely) separable from their context and should be interpreted and applied in line with this meaning. This 'narrow' approach to interpretation is usually contrasted with 'broader' approaches, under which the text is to be construed in the light of the general purpose of the document or in the light of the document's specific drafting history (e.g. the legislative history of a statute or the negotiations prior to the signing of an agreement). Textualism has the greatest support in the context of statutory interpretation, where there are 'rule of law' arguments (e.g. due notice, predictability) in its favour. Textualism sometimes goes under the label 'formalism', which can create an unfortunate confusion between this theory of interpretation and (the usual referent of 'formalism') the cramped approaches to legal reasoning that the American legal realists attacked in the early decades of the twentieth century.

See **formalism**

therapeutic jurisprudence A term used by a small number of theorists to summarize the way in which legal rules and practices can, do, or should produce good or bad effects on the emotional and psychological states of those appearing before the courts, or those affected by the law in other ways. The term was initially used primarily in relation to mental health law, but has, on occasion, been applied more broadly.

tort law Tort law, or the law more generally regarding accidents (including worker's compensation, no-fault insurance, and other programmes) raises a variety of moral and political questions, e.g. regarding what responsibilities people have towards one another, and who should be responsible for the mishaps and injuries that occur.

One standard theme within recent discussions of the philosophical foundations of tort law is whether this area of law is better explained or better justified (explanation and justification are somewhat different, if overlapping, projects) in terms of corrective justice or in terms of economic efficiency. The argument between economic analysis and corrective justice sometimes echoes a different debate: whether tort law is, or should be, primarily about assigning responsibility and blame, or primarily about creating the right incentives for action (where the 'optimal' set of incentives will not always coincide with a moralist's view of who is culpable).

Other philosophical questions within tort law include whether exposure to risk, by itself, should be sufficient for liability; whether or when strict liability rather than negligence is the appropriate standard for liability; and whether standards of care should be analysed in terms of an objective or a subjective standard.

See causation; corrective justice; law and economics; responsibility

tragedy of the anti-commons This a variation of and response to 'the tragedy of the commons'. 'The tragedy of the commons' purports to indicate the problem of common ownership (that where individuals share access to common grazing land, there will be no incentive for individual restraint, leading to collective overgrazing; and similar effects will occur with many other collectively owned resources), and this argument has been used to support the need and importance of individual property rights. 'The tragedy of the anti-commons' (introduced by Michael Heller (1962–)) purports to describe a corollary problem: where the property rights are fragmented among too many individuals (or individuals who are too dispersed), are too many, or are too strong, with each rightholder having the right to exclude all others, innovation or efficient uses of resources might be impeded by the transaction costs involved in bringing the necessary rights together (whether it is in bringing together enough land, or gathering the necessary permissions and licences for some scientific development).

See **prisoner's dilemma; property law; tragedy of the commons**

tragedy of the commons Garrett Hardin (1915–2003), in an article in *Science* (1968), introduced the term 'the tragedy of the commons' to describe how public resources can be (are) overused, because private property rights are not present to exclude others or create incentives for more efficient use (the idea, without the useful label, had been discussed by other authors in some earlier analyses of resources not subject to private property rights). In game-theoretical terms, 'the tragedy of the commons' can be seen as a variation of the prisoner's dilemma, but with many players. If there is a common ('open access') grazing or fishing area, the long-term interests of the grazers and fishermen are modest restraint by all to maintain the future viability of the common area. However, each individual has an incentive *not* to co-operate, but rather to get as much benefit as possible from the commons, while hoping that others show restraint. With everyone having that incentive, no one shows restraint and the commons are soon overgrazed or overfished. 'The tragedy of the commons' is often presented as an argument for individual property rights (though, in principle, state ownership or state regulation could also avoid the 'tragedy' described).

Recent scholars have argued that there can sometimes be a mirror problem: how the granting of individual property rights can lead to so great a splintering of entitlements that no effective use of the resource becomes possible—what Michael Heller (1962–) has called 'the tragedy of the anti-commons'.

See **prisoner's dilemma; property law; tragedy of the anti-commons**

transaction costs A concept introduced (under slightly different terminology) by Ronald Coase (1910–)in his articles 'The Nature of the Firm' (1937) and 'The Problem of Social Cost' (1960), to cover the costs involved in real-world commercial transactions: the costs of finding a willing buyer or seller, the negotiation of the terms, the drawing up of the contract, and so on. The concept can be understood more broadly, to include, e.g., policing and enforcement costs. The existence of significant costs of transacting means that parties that in principle should be able to come to an agreement (because one party is willing to pay a price for a commodity above the price at which the other is willing to sell it) may fail to do so. Transaction costs play a significant role in Coase's own analysis: explaining why individuals form firms, and why the law might *sometimes* affect which activities occur.

See **Coase's theorem; liability rules**

transaction cost economics *See* **new institutional economics**

trashing A term Mark Kelman (1951–) offered for a form of critique frequently used by theorists within critical legal studies, in which a legal or policy argument taken seriously on its own terms is found to lead to absurd or silly results. The prevalence of this sort of critique was sometimes thought symptomatic of a weakness of critical legal studies: that it was much more interested in criticism than in offering constructive alternative positive ideas.

See **critical legal studies**

U

unconscionability An American contract law doctrine, with roots deep in the common law, which was first given more definite shape by the Uniform Commercial Code, precluding the enforcement of agreements, or terms within agreements, which are extremely unfair. The doctrine is usually held to require a showing of significant unfairness both in procedure (how the contract was entered—e.g. problems of fraud or duress) and in substance (the actual terms of the agreement). The doctrine has various roots or analogues: from the Roman Law doctrine of *laesio enormis*, allowing rescission of a contract for inadequacy of price (which has modern counterparts in French and German law) to the willingness of English Courts of Equity to grant relief on some occasions to parties who had entered contracts with one-sided terms.

The role of the doctrine within legal theory is that it is frequently a focus point of jurisprudential debates: e.g. Richard Epstein's (1943–) argument, grounded in law and economics, that the doctrine should rarely be applied (as fairness doctrines meant to protect the weak often work over the long term against their interests); and various analyses by adherents of critical legal studies and critical race theory regarding what the doctrine purportedly shows about the way the American legal system and American society deal with injustice.

See **contract law**

unconscious racism A concept of importance in critical race theory, developed by Charles R. Lawrence III (1943–) and others. The concept's importance may turn in part on the idiosyncrasies of American discrimination law. To prove unconstitutional race discrimination, the United States Supreme Court held in the case of *Washington* v. *Davis* (1976) that the plaintiff must show an 'invidious discriminatory purpose', and not merely a disproportionate impact on minorities. The idea of unconscious racism is to emphasize how much racism is embedded in our culture, and therefore transmitted at a less-than-conscious level. Therefore, racist ideas can be spoken without the speaker 'intending' to be racist—and even without the hearer perceiving the racism. Consequently, the American constitutional distinction between 'guilty and intentional' and 'unintended and therefore innocent' may be inappropriate when discussing racism.

See critical race theory; discrimination

utilitarianism An ethical theory grounded on maximizing the total amount of utility (a notion that approximates desirability or happiness). The view was developed by a number of different philosophers, most prominently Jeremy Bentham (1748–1832), James Mill (1773–1836), John Stuart Mill (1806–73), and Henry Sidgwick (1838–1900). Utilitarianism is often divided into act- and rule-utilitarianism. The former suggests that one should choose the action that maximizes total utility; the latter grounds the analysis on picking the rule (or principle or institution) that maximizes utility.

Utilitarianism, in some variation, appears in many different debates within the philosophy of law: for example, the nature of justice (e.g. John Stuart Mill believed that justice reduced to or could be explained in terms of utilitarianism); the nature of rights (e.g. Ronald Dworkin (1931–   ) has analysed rights in terms of 'trumps' of what a utilitarian analysis would otherwise justify); and punishment (e.g. some commentators have used utilitarian analysis in their discussions of the limits and objectives of punishment—as to the question of objectives, utilitarians would probably favour a focus on deterrence over retribution).

Utilitarianism has been subject to a number of criticisms: e.g. (1) that it is untenable, because the pleasures and pains of people cannot be effectively measured, compared, or summed; (2) that the doctrine is unworkable for difficult moral and political decisions, because one can rarely know to any useful level of certainty what the utility-consequences would be of the likely alternatives; (3) that individual or social utility is not, or should not be, the ultimate end of life; and (4) that utilitarianism would justify, at least in principle, grave injustices against a few if the overall utility were thereby improved.

Economic analysis—and its legal analogue, law and economics—can be seen to be grounded on a variation of utilitarianism, a variation that maintains on the one hand utilitarianism's view that one should maximize social effects and its refusal to judge the relative merits of people or their objectives; while trying to avoid, on the other hand, the criticisms to which utilitarianism has been subject. In the economists' discussion of 'Pareto efficiency', the focus is on individuals' subjective preferences, and the extent to which preferences are satisfied, and not on the more objective utilitarian reference to increased or decreased utility. Also, the objective of 'wealth maximization' used by some law and economics theorists avoids the problem of measuring 'utility', but arguably at a cost of being less morally attractive.

See Austin, John; Beccaria, Cesare Bonesana; Bentham, Jeremy; consequentialism; external preferences; justice; law and economics; Mill, John Stuart; Pareto efficiency; punishment; utility; wealth maximization; welfare economics

utility A term used in moral philosophy, political philosophy, and economics, intended to refer to some generic and basic unit of being valued, preferred, or desired. Utilitarianism is about maximizing total utility, where utility here is usually discussed in terms of pleasure and pain.

See utilitarianism; welfare economics

V

validity *See* legal validity

vagueness An imprecision of meaning, common on the borderline of a term's application. Within philosophy of language, it is controversial whether the experience of vagueness says something about the limits of meaning, the nature of truth (that there may be truth values other than 'true' and 'false') or the nature of knowledge, but the nature and cause of vagueness is probably not relevant to legal theory—only the fact (experience) of vagueness. The question for legal theory is whether the vagueness of terms (and categories) has implications for the determinacy of law.

Vagueness should not be confused with ambiguity. Ambiguity is a general term, referring to an (or any) uncertainty in meaning, including 'latent ambiguity', where an apparently clear phrase ('my cousin David') turns out to have multiple referents (I have two cousins named 'David'). By contrast, vagueness, in its narrowest philosophical sense, refers to terms *whose boundaries* are uncertain, but whose application at the core is usually quite certain.

See indeterminacy

veil of ignorance A characteristic central to the thought-experiment social contract John Rawls (1921–2002) uses in *A Theory of Justice* (1971) to develop principles of justice. The 'veil of ignorance' refers to the way that Rawls's imaginary negotiators are all ignorant of their place in society, their abilities and vulnerabilities, and their conception of the Good. The point of this 'veil of ignorance' is that it would make such a negotiator less likely to choose principles based simply on his or her self-interest.

See difference principle; justice as fairness; original position; Rawls, John

***Verstehen* approach** A notion from the hermeneutic tradition, grounded in the basic idea that understanding human texts and social practices is different in kind from the type of knowledge involved in the physical sciences. While aspects of the tradition can be traced back to Giambattista Vico (1668–1744) and Johann Gottfried von Herder

(1744–1803), the ideas were more fully developed by Wilhelm Dilthey (1833–1911) and Max Weber (1864–1920). One strand in this tradition views such understanding within the human (social) sciences as being an understanding 'from within', as the participants in the practice or the author of the text would understand (or would have understood) the practice or text in question. Social practices are to be seen in terms of the meaning and purposes of those actions.

The importance of this tradition in legal philosophy is its influence on recent writers in legal interpretation—a fairly natural application of the ideas—and, perhaps less expected, on the nature of law. In the latter category, H. L. A. Hart's (1907–92) form of legal positivism is grounded strongly on the 'internal aspect' of rules and law, which in turn is based on *Verstehen* views developed by Peter Winch (1926–97); and the institutional theories of law put forward by Neil MacCormick (1941–   ), Ota Weinberger (1919–   ), and others, also show the influence of this approach.

See **H. L. A. Hart; hermeneutics; institutional theories of law; internal point of view; Weber, Max; Winch, Peter**

Villey, Michel Michel Villey (1914–88) was a French legal historian whose influence on English-language legal theory has come primarily through his work on the history of rights. Villey argued that the modern view of rights (in continental European terms, 'subjective rights') was not developed until the work of William of Occam [sometimes spelled 'Ockham'] (*c.*1285–*c.*1349). This view has since been contested by other historians (e.g. Brian Tierney).

See **rights**

voluntariness As legal responsibility, civil or criminal, almost always depends on the assertion that the agent was acting 'voluntarily', how that concept is filled out is significant. Legal practice and legal theory tend to stay well clear of the grand metaphysical arguments about whether we have free will or whether all our actions are determined. However, discussions that approximate the free will debates do arise from time to time—e.g. in discussions of whether a criminal penalty should be reduced because the defendant had suffered cruelly in his or her childhood, or because he or she acted under an 'irresistible impulse'. Questions of voluntariness also arise when considering the doctrinal defences of duress or undue influence in contract law, the voluntariness (and thus admissibility) of confessions in criminal law, and in many other areas.

Voluntariness, in philosophical and policy discussions, often involves judgements of degree, that a decision can be more or less voluntary. Among the contexts where one might speak of 'voluntary to a (limited) degree (only)' are (1) situations where economic circumstances leave few good alternatives; (2) where one has only limited information about the alternatives and their consequences (thus, one speaks of '*informed* consent' to medical procedures when the consent is given only after full information); (3) where relevant and binding terms are difficult to discover (e.g. they are in fine print); and (4) where, because of what is sometimes called 'bounded rationality', one is less likely to have considered certain sorts of terms or certain sorts of consequences (e.g. one is less likely to pay attention to post-termination clauses when entering an employment agreement). In all these cases, one might say that a party's action or assent has 'not been fully voluntary', and that this lack of fully voluntary action might justify protective intervention (e.g. a refusal to enforce, or to enforce fully, some of the terms of an otherwise valid agreement, or the imposition of mandatory terms).

See **autonomy; bounded rationality; consent**

voluntarism Within philosophy or theology generally, voluntarism often refers to a position that gives priority to will. The term's most frequent appearance within legal theory is to describe one school within natural law theory, which equates the natural law with what God has willed or commanded.

One can go back to Plato's Socrates, who asks Euthyphro (in the dialogue *Euthyphro*), 'Is what is holy holy because the gods approve it, or do they approve it because it is holy?' Voluntarism is the position that something is good or morally required because—and only because—God has ordered that we do it (or bad/morally prohibited because of God's prohibition). Voluntarism of one type or another appears regularly in the history of natural law theory; the important seventeenth-century natural law theorist, Samuel Pufendorf (1632–94), was a prominent advocate of such a view. The opposite extreme, a reason-based approach, would equate virtue with reasonableness rather than tying it to the 'will' or orders of any entity. There is also a form of natural law theory that seems to take a compromise between a 'will' approach and a 'reason' approach: this form asserts that actions are intrinsically good or bad, but we are only obligated to pursue the good because God so commands us; this was Francisco Suárez's (1548–1617) view.

See **natural law theory; Pufendorf, Samuel; Suárez, Francisco**

W

Waismann, Friedrich Friedrich Waismann (1896–1959) was a philosopher of language, and a member of the Vienna Circle, the group that developed logical positivism (not to be confused with 'legal positivism'). Waismann's importance to legal theory is that H. L. A. Hart's (1907–92) notion of 'open texture' derives from Waismann's concept of the same name; however, Hart's and Waismann's notions are at best analogues.

Waismann's 'open texture' was introduced to respond to a particular problem of verification theory. If the meaning of terms is equated with certain statements about sense-data, definitions would be unable to respond to situations that were entirely unforeseen (e.g. cats suddenly growing to gigantic sizes).

Hart's concept of 'open texture' operates at a more mundane level of the 'unforeseen': how to apply legal concepts to borderline instances of the concepts (when a state excludes vehicles from the park, is a skateboard a 'vehicle'?) and how to apply legal rules to circumstances that had not been considered by the lawmakers who created the rules. Hart thought that in such circumstances, the judges applying the law should be thought to have discretion in deciding the matter.

See **Hart, H. L. A.; open texture; Wittgenstein, Ludwig**

wealth effect A term from economic analysis, sometimes used narrowly to summarize how the level of wealth can affect a person's level of spending and saving. It is also used more generally to summarize how greater wealth can affect aspects of economic analysis. For example, the argument that one can derive relative intensity of preference from willingness to pay (that A wants X more than B does, because A is willing to pay more for X than B is) must include cautions about the effect of wealth (a wealthy person may be willing to pay more for a loaf of bread than a poor and starving person, but it would be absurd to say that the wealthy person wants the bread more).

wealth maximization Some theorists in law and economics, especially early in that movement's history, advocated that government actors—whether judges deciding cases, or lawmakers enacting new legal rules—should choose that alternative which would maximize the total wealth held by all members of society. Equally controversially, some theorists in law and economics argued that wealth maximization explained why common-law rules developed the way that they did, that the judges in the formative periods of the development of the common law were consciously or unconsciously maximizing social wealth. Both the normative and the descriptive/historical claims for wealth maximization, at least in their strongest forms, are generally considered to have been disproved. Wealth maximization approximates the Kaldor-Hicks definition of efficiency, and is related to utilitarianism, but is different from the latter in important ways (for example, that many would find 'maximizing social utility' significantly more attractive as a goal than 'maximizing social wealth').

See **Kaldor-Hicks; law and economics; utilitarianism**

Weber, Max Though the highly influential German social theorist, Karl Emil Maximilian (Max) Weber (1864–1920), was trained in law and the history of law, his influence on law and legal theory has been largely indirect. His most important works include *The Protestant Ethic and the Spirit of Capitalism* (1904) and *Economy and Society* (unfinished, published 1922). Much of Weber's significance for legal philosophy has come from his important ideas about social theory methodology. Weber argued against a strictly scientific approach to human behaviour and social institutions, in favour of a *Verstehen* approach, under which the meaning of an activity for its participants is emphasized. Weber's notion of 'ideal types', using exaggerated versions of actual practices to help organize and summarize the complexity of data, has also been taken up by many theorists who wish to speak generally about law and legal practice.

In Weber's work on law, he distinguished substantively formal law (guided by a moral system or a political ideology) from a formally rational system, where the system is guided only by factors 'internal' to law, and where the rules and principles are comprehensive, fixed, and relatively abstract. Weber argued that the West's reliance on formally rational law was central to the development of capitalism there.

See *Verstehen* approach

Wechsler, Herbert A major figure in American legal life, Herbert Wechsler (1909–2000), helped to draft the Model Penal Code, represented the *New York Times* in the 1964 landmark first amendment Supreme Court case of *New York Times* v. *Sullivan*, and co-wrote with Henry M. Hart, Jr. (1904–69) what has been one of the most influential casebooks in American federal jurisdiction law. Within legal theory, Wechsler is best known for his 1959 *Harvard Law Review* article, 'Toward Neutral Principles in Constitutional Law'. The article, a key text within the legal process school, tried to find a basis for constraints on judicial action, while accepting the American legal realist critique that legal materials did not lead to unique right answers to difficult legal questions. Wechsler's position was that while the courts (including the United States Supreme Court, when interpreting the United States Constitution) might have discretion in interpreting legal documents, this discretion is constrained by the need for courts to decide cases on the basis of 'genuine principles of law', 'neutral' principles that transcended the immediate result. The article controversially criticized the Supreme Court's 1954 landmark desegregation decision of *Brown* v. *Board of Education*, not based on the result, but on the basis that the reasoning was insufficiently principled—that there was no 'neutral' principle for choosing 'between denying the association to those individuals who wish it or imposing it on those who would avoid it'.

See **Hart, Henry M., Jr.; legal process; neutral principles**

welfare economics An effort to evaluate actions and policies according to their effects on the welfare or well-being of the individuals affected. Here, 'welfare' or 'well-being' is meant to have much the same meaning as 'utility' has for utilitarian analysis. The relation with individual preferences is, in this analysis, sometimes more complicated—with 'welfare' or 'well-being' usually indicating a more objective measurement, while still responding to the individual tastes and values. This divergence can come because individuals have imperfect information about the effects of different choices, or even about their own preferences (e.g. that people can guess incorrectly about whether they will like a particular food or a particular job). If welfare depends in part on people's tastes and preferences, which might change with additional information (or over time), then it becomes a central problem for a welfare economics theory to decide whether to use actual (present) preferences or some future, hypothetical, or idealized preferences.

See **law and economics; utilitarianism; utility**

will theory (of rights) An approach to the nature of legal rights that focuses on the power of choice in the right-holder, and the control the right-holder has over the person bearing the correlative duty. H. L. A. Hart (1907–92), one of the most prominent advocates of the will theory (*Essays on Bentham* (1982)), referred to right-holders as 'small scale sovereigns'. Thus, the right-holder has the power to waive the duty in question, and also the power to enforce or not to enforce the right after the duty has been violated. (The will theory can be traced back at least to Carl Friedrich von Savigny (1779–1861). Some commentators trace the modern will theory back further, to Immanuel Kant's (1724–1804) work, in particular *The Metaphysics of Morals* (1797)).

While the will theory has the advantage of emphasizing what to some is an important and distinctive feature of (most) rights, it has the disadvantage of excluding from 'rights' (or 'rights in their fullest sense') inalienable rights and immunity rights (including many of the constitutionally based rights that some would consider the paradigm example of legal rights), as well as the attribution of rights to animals, inanimate objects, or human beings who are physically or legally incapable of meaningful choice.

The usual competing theory of the nature of rights is the 'interest theory', which equates rights with being the beneficiary of a legal duty imposed on another.

See **animal rights; Austin, John; interest theory; Kant, Immanuel; legal rights; rights; Savigny, Friedrich Carl von**

Winch, Peter An American philosopher (1926–97), whose best-known work, *The Idea of a Social Science and its Relation to Philosophy* (1958), attempted to apply some of Ludwig Wittgenstein's ideas about language and rule-following to the social sciences. Winch's importance for legal philosophy comes from two sources: (1) the *Verstehen* approach idea put forward in *The Idea of a Social Science*, which seemed to argue that it was improper to judge morally the practices of alien societies, a view that has had influence in fields as diverse as anthropology and literary theory, but also has applications to some discussions within legal theory; and (2) the influence he had on H. L. A. Hart's (1907–92) understanding of rules and rule-following, concepts key to Hart's *The Concept of Law* (1961). Winch, along with Friedrich Waismann (1896–1959), was the intermediary through whom Wittgenstein's ideas were initially transmitted to Hart and many other legal theorists of that generation.

See Hart, H. L. A.; *Verstehen* approach; Waismann, Friedrich; Wittgenstein, Ludwig

Wittgenstein, Ludwig A thinker (1889–1951) whose incisive, but sometimes cryptic, reflections on language, meaning, mathematics, and certainty have created a substantial following and much debate within philosophy. Wittgenstein's impact on legal theory has been through attempts, largely unsuccessful, to use his work to justify particular positions in debates about legal interpretation and legal determinacy.

In Wittgenstein's *Philosophical Investigations* (1953), he offered a series of remarks on 'rule following': on learning and application in the context of simple mathematical series, simple colour words, and the like. Most commentators have read these remarks as an effort to show that meaning is neither 'in our heads' nor dependent on Platonic (metaphysically realist) entities. Saul Kripke (1940–   ), however, used the rule-following remarks as the starting point for a sceptical theory of meaning (*Wittgenstein on Rules and Private Language* (1982)). Both Kripke's sceptical version of Wittgenstein, and the more conventional anti-sceptical reading have been offered as justifications for particular approaches to legal interpretation. A third response, at least as persuasive, is that Wittgenstein's remarks have no direct relevance to legal interpretation.

There are also more precise points of influence: e.g. H. L. A. Hart's (1907–92) concept of 'open texture' derives from an concept of the same name within Friedrich Waismann's (1896–1959) philosophy of language, and Waismann's concept in turn was an attempted elaboration of some of Wittgenstein's ideas.

The influence can also occur at a more general level. For example, Wittgenstein is sometimes listed (along with other theorists) as the inspiration for a more 'pragmatic' or 'contextual' approach to legal interpretation and understanding.

See **open texture**; **rule-following considerations**; Waismann, Friedrich; Winch, Peter

Wollheim's paradox A paradox, suggested by Richard Arthur Wollheim (1923–2003) in a 1962 article ('A Paradox in the Theory of Democracy'), that supporters of majority rule would want the outcome supported by the majority even if it is contrary to the outcome they personally preferred (prior to learning of the majority's will).

Wright, Georg Henrik von A Finnish philosopher and logician (1916–2003), who had been a student of Ludwig Wittgenstein (1889–1951), and his successor as Professor of Philosophy at the University of Cambridge, before returning to teach at the University of Helsinki. He was best known for his work on logic, causation, induction, and ethics. Von Wright's work on deontic logic, the logic of norms (e.g. *Norm and Action: A Logical Inquiry* (1963)), which remains controversial, has obvious implications for thinking about the nature of law, and discussions of inference and truth within law.

Von Wright distinguished between analysis of norms and that of norm propositions, where the former is prescriptive, and the latter is a description of which norms 'exist' within an established normative system (such as law). Von Wright was sceptical of the application of 'truth' and 'falsity' to norms, but allowed such application to norm propositions. On the other hand, while one could claim that norms are 'gapless' (for any activity, one is either permitted, prohibited, or required to do it) and without contradiction, neither is necessarily the case for law, as a collection of normative propositions.

Von Wright also suggested a distinction between norms understood as 'what ought to be the case' and norms understood in terms of 'what ought to be done', arguing that one's understanding of the logic of obligation and practical reasoning may vary depending on which conception one uses.

See **deontic logic**

Z

zero sum game A term from game theory indicating a game or situation where the participants' collective losses and gains add up to zero. The term is often used more loosely to indicate a situation (or an approach to a situation) where one party can win only if another party loses (as contrasted to a co-operative situation where all parties could end up gaining).